A Rough Sort of Beauty

A Rough
Sort of
Beauty

*Reflections on the
Natural Heritage
of Arkansas*

EDITED BY
DANA STEWARD

The University of
Arkansas Press
Fayetteville ∿ 2002

06   05   04   03   02   5   4   3   2   1

Designed by Ellen Beeler

⊚ The paper used in this publication meets the minimum requirements of
the American National Standard for Permanence of Paper for Printed
Library Materials Z39.48-1984.

Library of Congress Cataloging-in-Publication Data

A rough sort of beauty : reflections on the natural heritage of Arkansas /
edited by Dana Steward.
       p. cm.
     ISBN 1-55728-729-5 (pbk. : alk. paper)
     1. Natural history—Arkansas. 2. Hunting—Arkansas. 3. Fishing—
Arkansas. I. Steward, Dana, 1943–
     QH105.A7 R38 2002
     508.767—dc21   2002004370

To Bill

How green is our valley

There have already been too many compromises. . . . We happen to live on a small planet with limited resources. As its custodians, if we don't lead the way in taking care of it with both love and wisdom, then who will?

—ALICE ANDREWS

Congressional Wilderness
Hearing Testimony
1984

Contents

❧ PART TWO

Kentucky Wonders: Stories of Arkansas People

ᔛ PART THREE

At the River: Life in the Modern Age

❧ PART FOUR

Disturbance: Creatures of the Land

❧ PART FIVE

Should've Built the Wall: The Varied Voices of the Conservation Movement

Epilogue

Preface

ERIN DALTON

It strikes me that when people try to describe Arkansas, they usually describe Arkansans. Admittedly, many of their descriptions are wrong. For instance, we tend to wear shoes here as much as people in any other state, and most of us do not marry our cousins, kissing or otherwise. Arkansas's people have long borne these misconceptions and, in some cases, taken them up with pride.

Actually, I am glad that Arkansas is known by its people because the people are a large part of what shapes the place. However, Arkansas's people are shaped by Arkansas in return: its trees, its lakes, its hills, its mountains, and a myriad of other natural wonders, along with its chiggers, its heat, its relative isolation. Arkansas people grow up in nature. And yes, it is true, we sometimes even take off our shoes to feel the grass beneath our feet. It is a wonderful feeling—the soft, warm summer grass on your soles. Every child knows that feeling; Arkansans just do not let themselves forget it.

As illustrated by that grass, Arkansans feel countless links with nature. It is impossible to get away from it in this state, and, really, there is not much reason to try. As we come of age here, nature teaches us many lessons. We learn lessons about life, love, nature, and when comes the time, we learn about death. For many children, coming of age in Arkansas means learning to carry a gun or perhaps a fishing pole. This is a skill and a love they will probably keep for the rest of their lives, even if they do not enjoy hunting or fishing. You see, these sports are not just about hunting an animal or catching a fish; in fact, this is the least of their definition. They are more about the people who surround us and the stories that are told. They are about learning our past and underpinning our future.

Nature is a parent in every Arkansan's life. It nurtures and teaches throughout life, and it provides beauty, shelter, and comfort. But like every parent, there comes a time in life when nature too needs to be nurtured and defended. And so Arkansans learn to defend nature, to help her out, and to save her ways. They come to recognize they must strive to keep that which makes them hold this state so dear.

Not everyone agrees on the best way to do that. Growing, learning, and fighting in Arkansas: many people have done so, and people will continue this tradition. There is no blueprint. These stages of life—from being nurtured to becoming a protector—are not set and marked, but glide gently into one another so that a person does not even notice they have passed until they are gone. But, as we look back at the close of our lives, or the close of a century, we can remember. Remember the way the state was and the way it has changed. For the good or for the bad, it has changed.

Arkansans will always reflect on the times they have had in nature. Within these pages are the stories of many of the people who love this state so dearly. I hope there will always be more stories that can be added.

Literature and the Natural World Class
Hendrix College, June 2001

Introduction

DANA STEWARD

It began with no more than my husband's love of new toys—tents and stoves and sleeping bags—and my casual interest in wildflowers, stirred a bit by a midlife restlessness, but our quest for the natural Arkansas has become a passion that appears to be incapable of being sated.

Some primal need propels us up into rock-strewn box canyons, over chattering waterfalls, and down pastoral valleys, so that the more we go to the woods and the rivers of our Arkansas homeland, the more we are called to go.

Sometimes we walk with fellow nature enthusiasts, ringing a showy lady's-slipper with our sunburned faces or dangling tired toes in a communal waterfall; more often, undaunted by the temperature or weather conditions, we go alone.

But never really alone, because whether we are walking an abandoned narrow gauge railway in the Flatside Wilderness or floating a protected stretch of the lower Arkansas River or following a gouged earthen wagon track on Crowley's Ridge, we share our solitude with ghosts—the generations past that walked or paddled by, leaving traces of their presence we are gradually learning to read.

In 1990 we walked at the invitation of Arkansas Game and Fish bear biologist Joe Clark. Who wanted, he asked, to come out on a drizzly cold Saturday morning in early spring in the Ozarks and hike three miles or more over hardscrabble mountainous terrain to help pull a two-hundred-pound bear from a den in order to weigh her, check her teeth, give her some shots, and count her cubs? More than a dozen persons patiently waited for him in the parking lot at Cass when he pulled off the Pig Trail. They were rewarded by getting to help with the work-up of a fine mama black bear and two cubs and by knowing that they had been a part of the restoration of black bear to northwestern Arkansas. The project was to become so popular and so successful that Clark, and future biologists who replaced him, were forced to limit participation. Now a viable population of black bears roam the Ozark hills again.

Since the harsh years of the Civil War and Reconstruction, the state of Arkansas has struggled with its identity, especially its economic identity. Its early motto around 1900 was the "Bear State" because the land was richly populated with bear and other game: deer, elk, mountain lion, bison, wolf. Unfortunately, elk and bison were gone way before 1900, and the Bear State appellation was no longer appropriate by the 1920s when, according to Sharon Bass writing in the Ozark National Forest history *For the Trees*, "The woods had taken on a peculiar silence. Few deer could be seen. Wild turkey and bear had become the stuff of mountain dreams and campfire stories. Legend became the final habitat of the wolf." Hunting for sport, for food, for oil, for clothing, the nineteenth-century frontiersman gave little thought to some future depletion of game; the assumed abundance and his own necessity would have made such a warning inconceivable.

The same may be said of virtually every one of Arkansas's various natural resources. As *Arkansas Democrat-Gazette* columnist Richard Allin points out in "Should've Built the Wall," schoolchildren were being taught as late as the 1950s that Arkansas was uniquely blessed with resources, so much so that its citizenry could actually build a wall around the state and survive quite nicely. After all, the state had diamonds, oil, bauxite, timber, rich farmland and—most precious of all gifts—water. The complex geography, while it often divided the state, offered a smorgasbord of choices: "scenic mountain tops, deep caverns, primordial swamps, everflowing springs, and rich black earth." Perhaps this abundance is the reason that for a time between World Wars I and II, Arkansas christened itself the "Wonder State," though really one can only wonder why. After all, we had already seen a first wave of agricultural land depletion, mineral depletion, old-growth forest depletion, with little on the horizon to replace these resources. Perhaps our citizens had simply begun to wonder when the destruction would stop.

We had been warned, of course. An *Arkansas Gazette* article in 1827 reports: "Very little digging has been done in this country yet; the time is to come when it will be penetrated with great interest. At present, the people of Arkansas are somewhat extravagant, and not very industrious." How unfair it would be, though, to project our contemporary sensibilities about the state's resources on our forefathers.

Imagine the settlers in places like Dwight Mission near Dardanelle in the 1820s, when they cut their first saw log from a forest so dense "no man could see through it" to clear land for their homes and school, worrying about the loss of virgin hardwoods. Consequently, by the time the National Forest Service was delegated the responsibility of maintaining the remaining forests in the first years of this century just past, most of the finest old-growth trees were gone. Bass says that even in the face of the clearly diminishing forests, rangers still had greatest difficulty in persuading the locals by both education and in some cases physical force that they should not burn the forests. In fact, earliest efforts to protect the forests were often opposed even by the Arkansas General Assembly, which appeared to pull designated lands out of Forest Service management almost as quickly as they were set aside. According to Ken Smith in his book *Sawmill,* it wasn't until private timber men like the Dierks brothers in south Arkansas began to believe in reforestation or second-growth forests in the '30s that a tenuous shift toward conservation appeared.

Picture the eastern Arkansas farmer in 1850 inch by inch pushing back the tangles of wilderness to pierce the rich soil with his plow, only to end up running for the high ground of Crowley's Ridge when the inevitable seasonal floods came. This is land wonderfully described by Gifford Pinchot, first head of the Forest Service, when he visited at the end of the nineteenth century: "For miles on end Fernow and I rode our horses through the great flatwoods of superb Oak timber —miles of the richest alluvial soil, where there wasn't a stone to throw at a dog, and the cotton in the little clearings grew higher than I could reach from the saddle." Imagine how the farmer would have shaken his head in disbelief at the thought that his ditches to control flooding and his clearing for more tillable land would eventually choke the rivers, and that runoff from his constant straight-row plowing would silt them even more until much of the land itself no longer supported the cotton. The battle over flood control, the question of balance between tillable land and swamps and bottoms preserved, was not yet even a gleam in a conservationist's eye, but, it was coming.

Read *A Documentary History of Arkansas* and try to fault the optimism of south Arkansas residents as they heard then-governor Charles Hillman Brough announce the Arkansas-Louisiana Road:

> The entire project will probably be completed by January 1, 1920. . . . It is difficult to realize the magnitude of this highway without appreciating the wilderness of the country. The greater part of the road is being cut through virgin timber, a wide pathway tearing apart . . . the jungle, which a scant fifteen years ago lay under ten to fifteen feet of water at springtime.

Consider the citizens of Ponca and Rush in the early 1900s, pocketing hard-earned coins for snaking thousands and thousands of cedar logs down the Buffalo on the way to pencil manufacturers or by venturing into the darkness of the zinc and lead mines that came—and then were gone.

Finally, even as late as the 1940s, listen to the squeals of delight that our worn-faced grandmother would have made when electric power lit up the barn and fired the pump as the Rural Electric finally came over her hill or the first bit of pea gravel went down on the dusty lane. Watch her wary eyes, darting into the deep woods, as her children play. How she would have hooted at the idea of light degradation or the concept of endangered species.

Over the past century, the environmental sensibilities of Arkansans have been interwoven and held hostage to some very basic economic needs. Forests that were being cut provided more jobs at that moment than forests preserved; wildlife existed at the pleasure of and for the benefit of man; additional cropland meant economic growth for the day, although it might not be sustainable with adequate water in the future. And in many instances, it was quite possible for our forefathers to plead ignorance. When an early twentieth-century east Arkansas businessman brags in 1912, "There is no end to the future. The land we have wrested from the wilderness is black and rich and will produce anything. And there are many wetlands yet to clear, which we grant will be just as productive," this boosterism, as dramatically ironic as it appears to us now, was not unwarranted. Arkansas was indeed still so environmentally rich at that time that the idea of boundless resources could go unchallenged.

Such an attitude lent itself after World War II to a new name. We designated ourselves as the "Land of Opportunity" and prostituted many of our resources—land, water, and even our people—to cheap industrial growth. The good news in all this is that we were not successful. The authors of *Arkansas and the Land* write that "one of the reasons for the state's lack of clear identity is its inherent diversity, a diversity that is not apparent within a given area, but is seen most clearly in comparisons between the regions." The lack of a single identity in who we were and what we had to offer (exacerbated by the dramatic physical and cultural differences within the regions of the state from the Delta of the east, which isn't really a delta, to the mountains of northwest Arkansas, which are really a plateau) no doubt hampered our growth. It also—if only by lack of opportunity—protected our dwindling natural resources.

By the mid mark of the twentieth century, the situation had begun to change. The second half of the 1900s was marked by fierce environmental battles statewide, unwittingly foretold by the new informal characterization of Arkansas in the '70s as "Arkansas, the Natural State."

In 1971 the Arkansas General Assembly passed its first land reclamation acts, in effect saying to industry, "Put it back the way you found it." For many years the Soil Conservation Service had defended the land within agriculture mandates, and now a new agency, Arkansas Department of Pollution Control and Ecology, would assume responsibility for policing water and air, especially as those resources were affected by industrial development. Standards were toughened for the drilling of gas and oil. For more than a decade, these victories, along with the influx of retirees and tourists attracted in part for the state's beauty and a new period of prosperity in the state and nation, promoted an atmosphere favorable to the concerns of conservationists.

At the same time, far-reaching opportunities for development of our natural resources flowed from the new dams on the White and the Ouachita Rivers, along with hydroelectric power. The McClellan-Kerr Navigation System on the Arkansas created a new economic potential for the Arkansas River. However, not everyone was happy with the growth.

In northeast Arkansas, the land was cleared until almost no forests remain. The drive for ditching would culminate with a fierce battle to save the Cache River from channelization, a drive conservationists won. A major shift in attitude during this period is marked by language used in an *Arkansas Gazette* editorial in 1971 against channelization: "Sometimes 'progress' can be made by leaving things as they are, letting nature take its own course."

In northwest Arkansas, big dams and a fledgling poultry industry met with mixed emotion. The dams brought controversy between local landowners and the Army Corps of Engineers over property rights to the extensive acres of land condemned for the lakes. One of the fiercest was waged at Beaver Lake over land condemnation and the submersion of historic Monte Ne, Coin Harvey's monument to the Gold Standard. On the whole, though, the lakes were well received by businesses and towns in the area because of the economic boost they provided in tourism and real estate development as much as, if not more than, for the flood control, electric power, and recreation.

No doubt, the best-known conservation battle of the century in Arkansas was waged over the proposed damming of the scenic Buffalo River, beginning in the early sixties. It took more than a decade, but Neil Compton, inspired by his lifelong love affair with the area and the powerful rhetoric of conservationist Harold Alexander, along with his dismay at earlier losses of historic natural properties, marshaled an eclectic group of volunteers to form the Ozark Society and provided leadership to stave off the building of more dams. Proposed dams at Lone Rock and Gilbert would have created new lakes but left a dying river, the pristine Buffalo. In a dramatic finale to that battle, then-governor Orval Faubus tipped the scales for the conservationists by refusing to give his support to the dams, and the avenue was opened up for the Buffalo to become the first National River in 1972. For a brief time Arkansas provided the conservation model for the nation.

That did not prevent a dramatic exchange between certain property owners and conservationists over the rights of passage on the Mulberry River in 1980. Only after numerous violent confrontations between the parties and a lawsuit that ended in the Arkansas Supreme

Court were the rights of the public to float the Mulberry (and consequently many other freeflowing streams) upheld. In doing so, the
court extended the definition of "navigable" stream to include recre-
ational boating, a decision that would have far-reaching effects for
stream preservation in the state.

Imbued with that victory, conservationists continued to fight the
forest industry and the U.S. Forest Service in earnest for the public
lands on the Ozark and the Ouachita National Forests. Clear cutting,
chemical spraying, and forest management and planning all caught
the attention of the advocacy groups such as the Ozark Society and
the Arkansas Wildlife Federation and the Arkansas Conservation
Coalition, to be followed in time by other grassroots efforts like the
Ouachita Watch League and the Newton County Wildlife Association
and the Sierra Club. The "stink" over chicken and hog farming, and
the resulting water pollution from animal waste, continued to ripen.

Issues concerning the environment versus the economy became
increasingly politicized. One especially hot issue, beginning in 1977,
centered around a proposal initiated by the Congress to create new
wilderness areas around the nation—a fight that in Arkansas stale-
mated in the designation of nine additional wilderness areas on federal lands throughout the state. The word *stalemate* being a conscious
choice here because most foresters and industry and even school
administrators fearing loss of income felt far too much land was set
aside, while conservationists, although celebrating a major victory,
still rue the choice to leave some proposed areas undesignated.
Regardless of positions taken, however, that debate provided some of
the finest rhetoric citizens and statesmen in Arkansas have ever produced at a volatile Senate subcommittee hearing in Little Rock,
chaired by Senator Dale Bumpers, in 1984. Waves of well-known
churchmen, suburban housewives, scientists, Boy Scouts, public
school administrators, and others stepped to the microphone to speak
for their disparate visions of Arkansas, the "Natural State."

Although the wilderness testimony and the groundswell of public
support for a natural Arkansas clearly flagged the changing attitudes
about our perception of nature and the balance of economic growth
and preservation, the last decade of the millennium brought an
onslaught of new issues and a sea change in political leadership in

Arkansas. Timber cuts and roadless designation in the national forests, threats to the lower White River and Arkansas River area because of the controversial Corps of Engineers' project Montgomery Point Dam, continued gravel mining on Crooked Creek and other streams in north Arkansas, the dissolution of the Natural and Scenic Rivers Commission, and gubernatorial support for a new dam on Bear Creek threatening the Buffalo River watershed brought all the players back on to the field.

Even looking back over time, none of these issues has been more seriously debated than the question of additional takings of water resource from the White River basin and adjoining wetlands for agricultural development. An Arkansas Geological Commission report on Water Resources of Arkansas, released in 1997, does not overstate the situation when (after acknowledging that Arkansas has "an abundance of water compared to many other states") it sums up: "Because of water's significance, any change or trend showing a decline in either the quantity or quality of the state's water resources is of major importance. The increasing demand for ground water in eastern and southern Arkansas is a concern for many."

The fact is, those changes or trends do reflect quantity and quality declines. To the degree, in fact, that we are finally being forced to answer some hard questions. Do we drain the meager 8 percent of the wetlands left in what was once the largest wetlands west of the Mississippi? Do we allow the trees remaining to be cut, the fields planted, and the aquifers to drop lower, so that even our drinking water is threatened? These are not new questions, but they become increasingly urgent ones demanding answers.

Back in 1910, in the preface to a rather obscure book entitled *Geological Survey of Arkansas: Coal Mining in Arkansas*, then-state-geologist A. H. Purdue writes:

> In as much as some of our essential natural products are limited, the State should stand guardian over them for posterity. While the people of the present should not be deprived of their use, it is but a duty to the public to prevent waste of these precious heritages. To justify ourselves in the wasteful use of the gifts of nature upon the belief that the ingenuity of man will always sup-

ply the demands of our increasingly complex civilization, is rank egotism. It is thoughtless vandalism.

Certainly, not everyone will agree on the definition of terms like *wasteful* or just what constitutes *vandalism*. It is unlikely that conservationists, who themselves do not speak with one voice, and those looking for any answer depending on short-term economic development will ever agree. We have brought back the black bear; and although we cannot replace virgin timber, we are capable of reforestation; so far, however, there seems to be no substitute for water.

This brings me finally to the end of my historical "nature walk." Just as in the past, the manner in which these environmental issues get resolved will depend a great deal on whose voices are heard in the debate. The basic philosophy of this book is that not every spokesperson for a natural state writes in the voice of a political savant or a wild-eyed tree hugger. Indeed, most of the voices in this collection validate something much deeper than political philosophy. They express a relationship, the relationship Erin Dalton refers to in her Preface to this book: a love of the land and the water and the air that has been so completely a part of their lives they scarcely sense it is there until it is gone. In honest, winsome tones, they claim, "There was a river by my house," "There was the sweet scent of wisteria," "There is a dark and musty bayou that I love." And ironically they write not just of the beauty but of the thorns and the dust. Of course, they don't express their thoughts in the same manner: some are angry in tone, bitter about natural resources which have been destroyed. Some are charming or reflective, willing to take a longer view. Some humorous, others matter-of-fact. Together, their voices become pieces of a complex puzzle, whose picture of Arkansas and its future as a natural state, though palpable, even now is none too clear.

No selection in the anthology is more heartfelt than the essay by outdoor writer Keith Sutton. Keith's favorite place on earth is the White River Refuge in east Arkansas; he also lists it as the most endangered, and his description of the new dam on White River will make you cry. Kirk Wasson is an electronics expert for a power company, a formidable leader in the fight for land set aside as wilderness. However, his pieces here are colloquial looks at the meaning of the outdoors for him. Jim Allen is a retired insurance man who makes us laugh at the arrogance of the wily turkey, suggesting that perhaps human nature isn't so "human" after all. Young Watkins Fulk-Gray takes us backpacking. Francie Jeffery reminds us that sometimes what we are willing to do tells us a lot about who we are.

I have shared the work of the book with my students in my Literature and the Natural World class at Hendrix College, and I am very proud of their contribution. They helped plan it, and they accepted the huge task of reading submissions and helping choose the pieces. In addition, they too wrote for the book, recognizing that their own relationships with nature probably carried even more weight here than the historical academic readings by Thoreau.

These voices and so many more.

However, none other resonates as well with me as that of a woman I never had a chance to meet named Maxine Clark. It was upon encountering Maxine's wildflower columns that I decided to pursue this project. Maxine Clark co-edited the *Ozark Society Bulletin* during the years of struggle for the Buffalo National River designation. She was an ardent conservationist and a wildflower authority, who chose to strike her own blow for nature by taking us there, opening our eyes to how breathtakingly lovely Arkansas is, down to the tiniest lichen clinging under a mossy spring, and then chiding us to keep it that way.

Presently, through the faith and the hard work and sacrifice of a host of people like these writers, Arkansas can and does call itself the Natural State. Whether that remains to be so rests on all of us collectively, but also on each of us. Noted writer and editor of nature literature Robert Finch has written: "Nature writers story the landscape. . . . By storying the place where we live, it gives us back a sense of who we are and where we are. Through stories, we literally identify with the land. We love what we come to call home. Nature writers teach us to recognize home." I hope these stories and poems will cause you to treasure your own nature story, your own poem, your own home.

PART ONE

Coming Home

Heritage Stories of Place

When I was just a little boy, my daddy took me out into the hollers and bluffs of the Ozark hills. He tried to instill in me some appreciation for the land, as his father had done for him. He gave me my first .22 rifle—I still have it at home—but he also showed me the fern beds, the shagbark hickory, and the wild orchids, too.

This is part of the heritage that I hope to pass on to my son.

—JOHN LEFLAR
Congressional Wilderness
Hearing Testimony
1984

Coming Home

DIANE REEVES

"Coming Home" first appeared in Diane Reeves's second book, A Scoundrel Breeze, *published by August House Publishing in 1983. She is currently marketing a fiction novel and learning how to be a military wife.*

The California woman smiled,
Glancing at my shoes;
"So, you're from Arkansas?"
The years since I'd left home
Tumbled like fat puppies
In my afternoon mind and
I remembered . . .
Redbuds blushing in April rain;
Wooden porch steps worn smooth
By heavy work shoes and
Children's bottoms; shelling peas
Into a washtub; cane-bottomed chairs
In sycamore shade; purple fingers;
Beech trees and butterbeans;
Osage arrowheads in the corn patch;
Tent revivals and cardboard fans
With "Jesus in Gethsemane" on the back;
Frosty dippers of buttermilk from
Stone crocks in the springhouse;
Porch-swing kisses from colt-awkward

Country boys in clean overalls,
Silken-eyed with smiles like summer honey—
Slow and achingly sweet;
Autumn creek mist ghosting through
Red oak woods; fiddle music and
Whippoorwills; screech owls in the
Box elder by the barn; dusty August roads,
Nickel Nehis and Hershey bars eaten
Slowly, one square at a time;
Blacksnake in the chicken house;
Rattler in cool hollows;
Barefoot in blackberry patches; plump
"Pings" in a tin bucket; fried chicken
And ripe tomatoes; cornstalk whispers
Beneath a melting moon; the light, sharp
Tracks of a summer buck among tangled
Pea vines; pallets on screened porches;
Bobcat screams from the dark creek bottoms;
Ghost stories, half-believed; moon-shadowed
Branches; katydids and heat lightning;
Sweet cider and sassafras tea; chigger
Bites and brier scratches; fawn-shy children
And solemn men with sun-wrinkled smiles;
A country woman's hands, work-thickened,
Gently strong, never stilled;
My hands. My people. My Arkansas.
"Yes, Arkansas," I mumbled. And, on the
Plane home, I kicked off my shoes.

Land of the Big Sky: Grand Prairie

JIM SPENCER

Jim Spencer is writer and assistant editor of
Arkansas Wildlife *magazine, published by the*
Arkansas Game and Fish Commission, where this
article about his native Grand Prairie was pub-
lished in November of 2000.

Draw a line from DeValls Bluff to Lonoke to Humnoke to Humphrey to Gillett to St. Charles to Roe and then back to DeValls Bluff. You've just enclosed what was once a vast tallgrass prairie that defied the ocean of dense hardwood forest originally covering most of Arkansas. This expanse of open ground encompassed one thousand square miles. They didn't call it the Grand Prairie for nothing.

Early settlers bypassed the Grand Prairie during the early days of western expansion. The first pioneers who broke onto the prairie after struggling across the malaria-ridden swamps and slow-moving rivers of eastern Arkansas didn't think it was fertile. If it wouldn't grow trees, they thought, it wouldn't grow corn or cotton, either. So they pushed across its vast sweep of waving grasses that often reached to the hat brim of a man on horseback, perhaps stopping long enough where the grass was shorter to shoot a bison or a few deer to replenish their food supplies. Then they pushed on westward into the forest, leaving the prairie and its wide-open spaces behind—and thereby made a serious mistake in judgment.

Those early settlers missed some important clues. Just because the prairie didn't grow trees didn't mean it wasn't moist and fertile; the abundance of wildlife and the diversity of prairie vegetation and wildflowers should have told them that much.

This was a prairie, not a desert. Bison, elk, and white-tailed deer lived here in numbers beyond counting, leaving their droppings and their bones to further enrich the soil. Prairie chickens were as common as red-winged blackbirds. In winter, waterfowl blackened the skies.

The grasses and forbs were beyond counting. Dominated by big and little bluestem, Indian grass, switchgrass, and sloughgrass, the Grand Prairie also was home to a host of lesser plants that added variety and color to the sunny landscape. Their names are so pleasing it's impossible to resist stringing them out here: prairie dropseed, sideoats grama, rattlesnake-master, leadplant, Indian paintbrush, blazing-star, wild indigo, oxeye daisy, compassplant, yellow star-grass, blue-eyed grass, puccoon, pestemon, purple coneflower, fringed gentian, bottle gentian, wood betony, lupine, New Jersey tea, turk's-cap, partridge pea, butterfly milkweed.

Like most natural prairies, east Arkansas's Grand Prairie was the product of mysterious natural forces that included a fire ecology, both natural and man-caused. Unlike most natural prairies, the Grand Prairie had abundant rainfall—more than forty inches annually, enough to support a forest. As proof of that, the early prairie was dotted with numerous islands of hardwood timber—locust, willow oak, water oak, sugarberry, persimmon, hickory, elm, hornbeam, maple, willow, sycamore, cottonwood and other species—growing in wetter places where the periodic fires couldn't penetrate.

Unlike many prairies on deep glacial soil—prairies that exist at least partly because rainfall is too scarce to support forest—the Grand Prairie's rich surface loam is underlain by a heavy claypan subsoil virtually impervious to water. This set the stage for the agricultural development that brought the region national recognition as a producer of rice and soybeans.

But that era of the prairie's history didn't get into full swing until three decades after the Grand Prairie was finally settled by a band of immigrants from Stuttgart, Germany, who in the late 1880s established a community in the north end of what is now Arkansas County. They named it after their German home town.

This new-world Stuttgart was not quite seventy years old—just about my grandfather's age—when my mom and dad moved there in October 1954. I was seven at the time, and I fell in love with the town within a week. It took me a little longer to fall in love with the place because I had to add a few years to my tender total before I was allowed free run in the wide-open countryside surrounding the town.

Most of the original prairie was converted to rice and soybean fields by the time I got there. I missed seeing it by a scant two or three decades. But I remember stories told by the geezers on Main Street and in the City Cafe and under the big willow oaks on the courthouse lawn. I listened wide-eyed as they told of the vast, undulating seas of grass they knew when they were young, grass so tall and far-reaching that cows would get lost in it for weeks. I listened as they told of the abundant prairie chickens they hunted for the dinner table, hard-flying birds that often traveled twenty miles or more between roosting and feeding grounds and gathered together in huge flocks on communal booming grounds each spring for their complex mating ritual. I listened as they told of the packs of red wolves—true wolves, these, not coyotes—that roamed the prairies and filled the night sky with wild song, and that had only been wiped out a scant few years before I arrived on the scene. I was barely too late to hear them.

I'm the geezer now, but to this day, I remember those stories. And to this day, I feel cheated when I remember because I wasn't there early enough to see it.

Bison were gone from the Grand Prairie by the time the old men I listened to were born to it, but buffalo bones were still so plentiful in places they were a hindrance to plowing and a hazard to the horses' hooves and fetlocks. Even today, I can show you several old buffalo wallows, places where great herds of shaggy beasts rolled in the mud and carried away tons of it on their backs, leaving craters several feet deep in the prairie loam. There are still bone chips in these places. *Bison* bone chips. Imagine that.

By the time I became a resident of the Grand Prairie, the prairie chickens were as gone as the buffalo, but much more recently. The chickens disappeared sometime between World War I and World War II, partly from over-hunting but mostly from wholesale habitat destruction, as the vast native prairie was broken and tamed and put into row crops and rice.

Although the big expanses of prairie were long gone by the 1950s, there were still quite a few prairie remnants scattered here and there. As luck would have it, a few were within bicycle range of town. While most of my classmates played baseball and football and spent off-season Saturdays watching cowboy matinees at the Majestic Theater, I had other priorities. I spent hundreds of hours of my childhood outside town, prowling these shaggy, unbroken patches of virgin prairie in an endless search for high adventure. I found it, too, in the riot of unusual flowers that erupted in spring, in the bright yellow chests of the sparrow-sized dickcissels that nested here in summer, in the eight-foot-high forests of big bluestem that towered overhead in fall, in the sound of the wind as it whistled through these same bluestem stalks in winter.

When I was a little older, I prowled these prairie remnants with gun in hand, hunting rabbits and doves and ducks, pretending these small critters were great, shaggy bison and I was a buffalo hunter. I still remember those as some of the best days of my youth—some of the best days of my life, really.

A pitiful few of those prairie remnants still exist. One is the forty-acre Roth Prairie a few miles south of Stuttgart, which was one of my childhood haunts. It's now protected as a Natural Area by the Natural Heritage Commission, and it will be there for some young Huck Finn of the future to lose himself in, the way I did in the 1950s. But the vast majority of the original prairie habitat is gone, as gone as the bison and prairie chickens that used to call it home.

But the Grand Prairie itself, that wide-open, big-sky land that still defies the forest, is still there. It called to me when I was a boy, and nearly half a century later, it calls to me still. I was then, still am, a dyed-in-the-wool, no-holds-barred outdoor type, and the Grand Prairie isn't a bad place to be if you're so afflicted. The first time I ever saw a wild duck was in a flooded rice field less than six blocks from our modest house on 19th Street. The first time I ever went fishing without the steadying, restricting influence of adults was in an irrigation canal that bordered that same rice field. The first rabbit, quail, dove, and duck I ever shot all fell within bicycle-riding range of that same house.

As I got a little older and extended my range with the aid of the internal combustion engine, I quickly learned that we European and African invaders weren't the first human hunters to utilize the abundant wildlife of the Grand Prairie. Those earliest German immigrants settled a landscape already littered with the signs of thousands of years of human occupancy by American Indians. Burial, ceremonial, and campside mounds were everywhere, and most were left alone until the mechanical revolution that followed World War II spread to agriculture and made large-scale farming possible. Most of those mounds are gone now, dirt-panned to level ground and used to fill in low spots in fields during the 1950s and 1960s. But here and there some remain, mute reminders that we weren't the first to live here.

Less conspicuous but far more common were the stone artifacts turned up by plowing. The Three Rivers area south of the Grand Prairie, around Tichnor and Arkansas Post, was a common-ground trading area for Indians from the entire middle third of the country. The trading parties followed the White, the Arkansas, and the Mississippi to this region each year to trade goods with other tribes. Eastern woodland Indians swapped wares with Western plains Indians in this neutral zone, and Gulf Coast tribes traded with Great Lake tribes. After completing their trades, many trading parties headed to the Grand Prairie to make meat before starting the long trek home.

They left their stone and fired-clay calling cards in abundance: arrowheads, scraping tools, metates, beads, game pieces, spear points, knives, pottery. One September afternoon, walking the bank of a channelized creek on ground normally covered by the waters of an irrigation reservoir, two friends and I stumbled over a cache of stone scraping tools made of creamy white flint. The tools, laid bare by wave action as the farmer pulled water out of the reservoir to water his crops, littered the ground like huge snowflakes. We picked up more than a hundred in that one spot. An anthropologist later told me the stone probably came from eastern Kansas, and the workmanship identified the tools as having been made six thousand to eight thousand years ago.

Although finds like that always have been rare, the Grand Prairie is still a rich hunting ground for Indian artifacts. Even after more than a century of being picked over by barefoot boys walking turnrows after a spring rain, there are still places where a sharp-eyed arrowhead hunter can pick up a pocket full of points and flint chips in a few hours.

No doubt, the Indians who left those white-flint scraping tools along the bank of that little creek thousands of years ago would have a hard time recognizing the Grand Prairie if they saw it today. Or would they?

Many things have changed, but maybe the important ones remain. The long sweeps of waving bluestem are gone, but the big sky is still there, and wildlife is still abundant. Ducks and geese still darken the skies, and while the bison and elk are history, white-tailed deer have returned. If you position yourself properly, get your mind right, and use a little imagination, it's not hard to see the prairie as it was then, big land and big sky, bounded by far horizons.

I'm stumbling here, trying to put into words something I feel deeply but am not talented enough to express. Let me bow to my betters and steal the words of my departed friend John Madson, another prairie rat (prairie dog?) who grew up prowling the tallgrass prairie remnants of Iowa twenty years before I started prowling the ones in Arkansas. This is from his eloquent book, *Where the Sky Began:*

> There are only a few tall prairies left today, but they are worth seeking—worth going to and being in. They are the last lingering scraps of the old time, fragments of original wealth and beauty, cloaked with plants that you may never have seen before and may never see again. If you are a man, stand in such a place and imagine that you hold your land warrant as a veteran of the War with Mexico, looking out over fields of lofty grasses on your own place at last, your own free-and-clear quarter-section share of the richest loam in the world. If you are a woman, watch your children at play in wild gardens of strange flowers, and imagine your nearest neighbor twenty miles away.
>
> If you are a child, lie in a patch of blazing-star and dream of Indians.

That's what I was trying to say.

Sea of Grass

HOWARD NOBLES

*When he isn't writing poems about places in
Arkansas, Howard Nobles continues a thirty-one-
year education career. He has been a teacher,
supervisor, and administrator in the Benton
School District where he now serves as assistant
principal of Benton Middle School.*

I plow the sea
of grass
Leaving cut blades
in my wake
As well as robins
that fly down
To plunder the
evicted crickets.

The smell of the
rolling sea
Penetrates the air
of summer,
And the soft spray
leaves debris
On my shoes
and ankles.

Out on the sea
of grass
I leave cut blades
in my wake
While beneath the
waves
The sea
gathers to rise again.

Boston Mountains: My Roots Are in Cass

BARBARA PRYOR

This essay first appeared in Somewhere Apart, *an anthology of collected answers from celebrated Arkansans to the question, "What is your favorite place in Arkansas?" Barbara Pryor, a Fayetteville native, has been a part of the Arkansas political and cultural scene all her adult life, working with her husband, former Arkansas Governor and United States Senator David Pryor, and generously supporting the work of Arkansas artists.*

My favorite place in Arkansas? No way. There are so many of them, and they are all so diverse and special. I hardly know where to start.

David and I have traveled this magnificent state for over three decades. I recall some special thing about every county and court-house, every pie supper, fish fry, bar-b-que, political rally, and graduation. I recall the Delta at sunset in the reddest light, the pine forests, the wolf and fox hounds.

I especially remember the days and nights going to and from, the shortcuts and byroads, the bridges, rivers, and streams that bind the state together—and always the people who weave a magic quilt of oneness that defines the character and soul of the state.

I'm a child of the hills. My roots are in Cass, in the Boston Mountains, where my great-grandmother (whom I call Grandmother) grew up on the Mulberry River. It's where her daughter and then her granddaughter—my mother, who never knew her mother—were also born. This has to be my favorite place of all.

My family were Turners, descended from Eli Turner of Turner Bend on Highway 23. He was reported to have fathered twenty-five offspring.

Bears used to roam within a few feet of the house and the pig trails. Legend has it that Jesse and Frank James rode those same trails, looking for who knows what kind of mischief. They are supposed to have spent the night at my grandmother's house.

For over 150 years, people have eked out a living among the rocks and hills that surround the Mulberry River. I left there—but not for good—at about the time my great-grandmother died. My memories of Cass will never leave me.

In spring the sky is as blue as a bird's wing. The new leaves meeting over the road are the palest green you ever saw—they're almost edible. Later, wild dogwood and redbud trees burst forth in the whitest and pinkest splendor. In the summer the ground becomes a hardwood jungle. Fall is a time when the trees seem to be on fire with the strongest, earthiest colors. And in winter single trees stand bare against the light, as if made of the finest lace.

At night, all things grow country dark.

In my earliest memory I'm standing in my grandmother's yard, looking up at her flowers that were taller than I. And since she had a green thumb, everything she touched promptly grew—including children.

She cooked on a wood stove, and the main meal was at noon. There was a table full of vegetables, biscuits, chicken, ham, deer, and a peach cobbler made from peaches that came off one of her own trees. Supper was usually some kind of cornbread and cold milk, or ham wrapped in a biscuit. We ate on benches at a long table.

Grandmother grew her own tobacco and smoked it in a corncob pipe. I clearly remember the richness of the smells and the mix of wood smoke and tobacco.

The house was a log cabin with a screened-in porch running across the front. On one end was a grape arbor. This was my safe place.

There were three rooms in the house. The living room had iron beds and feather mattresses in each corner, a fireplace, rocking chairs, and coal-oil lamps. At night we were tucked in our beds, where we could listen to Grandmother and Mother talk and tell stories about the family. I recall their soft voices, and the laughter, and sometimes the tears.

They spoke of Grandmother's first husband, a young medical student who had smallpox and died. And they told stories of the Yankees who came and burned the barns and stole livestock.

Grandmother loved to tell the story of the day my mother came to live with her. She stood on the rock steps of her porch and watched a man carrying a child and leading another one by the hand. They walked through the middle of a huge field of corn that grew in front of her house.

The man was Grandmother's daughter's husband and not long a widower. He was bringing her two grandchildren for her to raise. He left them there on the porch, and when he had gone on his way, she gave the little girl her own name—Rosa Lee. That was my mother.

When I was a child, my mother would put my brother and me on a bus and tell the driver to take us to Turner Bend. The road was gravel then. We would spend the night at Uncle Champ's store and sleep on a pallet in the loft over the store.

The next morning he would drive us seven miles down the road where Uncle Jake would be waiting with a flatbed wagon and a team of mules. We would ford the creek and go to Grandmother's house.

Grandmother collected bits of broken china and colored glass bottles and saved them for me. I would spend hours in the arbor's soft dirt, in the slanted light of the afternoon, endlessly arranging and rearranging the remnants.

We learned to swim in the cold green water of the Mulberry River. There was a large hollow rock where my mother would bathe my little brother. Sometimes we stayed in the creek all day long, and Mother would make coffee in a skillet, and we would drink it out of tin cups.

Years later, I took the same bus with my own young son and went to my great-grandmother's funeral in Ozark. She lived to be one hundred, and when she died she had some gray in her hair. But it was mostly still black as night—like my mother's when she died, and now like my son Mark's.

These days, when I turn off the interstate and onto Highway 23, no matter how tired I may be, I take a deep long breath of that sweet clear mountain air, and I drink the fresh cool water and feel restored. I know then that I'm home.

All this brings me to Eudora Welty, one of my favorite writers, who remembered the hills of West Virginia in her book *One Writer's Beginning*. Here's how she recalled the feel of the landscape, so similar to my own:

> It took the mountain top, it seems to me now, to give me the sensation of independence. It was as if I'd discovered something I had never tasted before in my short life. Or rediscovered it—for I associated it with the taste of the water that came out of the well, accompanied with the ring of that long metal sleeve against the sides of the living mountain, as from deep down it was wound up to view brimming and streaming long drops behind it like bright stars on a ribbon. It thrilled me to drink from the common dipper. The coldness, the far, unseen, unheard springs of what was in my mouth now, the iron strength of its flavor that drew my cheeks in, fern-laced smell, all said *mountain mountain mountain* as I swallowed. Every swallow was making me a part of being here, sealing me in place, with my bare feet planted on the mountain and sprinkled with my rapturous spills. What I felt I'd come here to do was something on my own.

Arkansas Waterfalls Pour Refreshment

JOE DAVID RICE

Front Porch *magazine featured Joe David Rice's musings about Arkansas waterfalls in spring 2000. Joe David's "weekday" position is director of tourism for the Arkansas Department of Parks and Tourism.*

Ask a dozen Arkansans for their favorite springtime topic, and you'll get a dozen answers. I know because I tried it.

My wife mentioned wildflowers, my mother thoroughbreds, and my father countered with white bass. Back in the office (and it's midwinter while I'm writing this), the list quickly lengthens with the likes of jonquils, hiking, strawberries, turkey hunting, and picnics in the country. And most people were more than eager to argue the merits of their choice. Cabin fever, I reckon.

As for me, come spring and I'll make a beeline for an Arkansas waterfall. I'm still not sure why I feel compelled to perform these seasonal migrations, but I'll do it as sure as the tarantulas cross our highways in October or the geese move down in November. My own suspicion is that it has something to do with the fact that a waterfall is one of those rare elements that really and truly stimulates each and every one of our senses.

There's no question that waterfalls are visually appealing. After all, we've sold thousands and thousands of posters of Petit Jean State Park's Cedar Falls. As pretty as that poster is, it cannot compare to seeing the falls in person and watching the water cascade over the rocky edge, through a rainbow, and into the canyon below. And my mind has forever frozen the image of Hemmed-In-Hollow Falls plummeting two hundred feet toward its base, the trail of water slowly moving in the wind from one side of the gorge to the other.

The ears are not left out in all this either. They're intrigued by the melodies of the small, unnamed cascades hidden along the hillsides but intimidated by the roar and thunder of Richland Falls. The other senses are affected as well. Waterfalls have a nice, distinctive smell—sort of a clean, fresh essence that detergent manufacturers would do well to copy. And if you get close enough to get drenched from the spray of waterfalls, you can actually taste them—again, a pleasant experience. But maybe the best way to really experience an Arkansas waterfall is by way of that fifth sense—the sense of touch. At Haw Creek Falls, you can perch right on the bedrock and let the water flow over your hands as it dives into the channel below. You can swim in the big pool below Falling Water Falls and allow the ten-foot shower to massage your head and shoulders. At Little Missouri Falls, you can use the turbulent water to put some life back into your feet.

By reaching out and touching these lively waters, you'll develop an appreciation for the power of moving water. At King's River Falls, you may be able to visualize the site of the mill that was powered by the stream back in the old days. And today at Cossatot Falls, stick your arm in one of the drops and you'll come away convinced that a shoulder separation could be a distinct possibility. The concept that water can literally move mountains and change the face of Arkansas landscape doesn't sound so far-fetched anymore.

So, yes, I'm partial to waterfalls. This spring if I'm not at one already named, you can find me at Eden Falls, Twin Falls, Bailey Falls, or perhaps one so remote that it has no name—at least officially. And my case of cabin fever will be cured.

Prologue: The Cadron

LIL JUNAS

While working as a photographer/photo editor for the Log Cabin Democrat *in Conway, Lil Junas completed her book from which this "Prologue" was taken.* Cadron Creek: A Photographic Narrative *was published by the Ozark Society Foundation in 1979. Lil, who is now an associate professor of communication at Wartburg College in Waverly, Iowa, just released her new book,* My Slovakia: An American's View.

The morning was cool and fresh with the fragrance of spring blossoms and new plant growth. Beyond the tiny leaf buds on the trees, the sky was cloudless. Anxious to get moving, I put my camera box and bucket of food and film in the canoe. My partner tossed in a few cushions. We were off—my first encounter with Cadron Creek. Only the water dripping from each paddle stroke broke the silence as we glided through the calm green water.

Soon, however, gurgling water alerted us to the rapids beyond our view. We approached the curve slowly and aimed the bow at the "V" atop the waves. Our canoe took them with ease, and our excited shouts rang out with every wave we crashed. The creek was about thirty feet wide at this spot on the North Fork, and the water was deep enough to carry our canoe swiftly over the rocks.

For the next few minutes we paddled steadily through a long pool, with wildflowers and birds greeting us along the way. Emerald mosses and patches of orange and yellow crustose lichens gave an elegant touch to the bluffs. Streamlets coming from crevices in the layered sandstone formations enticed us to explore further. We climbed on a pinnacle and beheld the panorama of the creek behind us and the valley and hills we were about to traverse. As we rested on the summit, the horizon in the east slowly exposed the sun which painted the tips of trees and bluffs in pastels. I was eager to see what lay ahead, so we returned quickly to the creek.

As we continued downstream, we passed a young couple sitting on a large flat rock near the water's edge and two older women in wide-brim sunbonnets fishing from folding chairs on a sandy bank. "Catching anything?" I asked. "Oh, a few," answered one, lifting a string of bass from the water. A hawk, silhouetted against the sky, escorted us about a half mile downstream, sailing back and forth across the creek, occasionally lighting on a high branch.

Another time, while hiking along the upper stretches of the East Fork of the Cadron, my reverence for the creek environment had renewed my bond with the outdoors. The intimate beauty had grown incredibly as I walked farther up the creek. It was comforting to experience the environment of the early settlers, an unspoiled habitat of small wild animals and birds, with no evidence of commercial or industrial development. A feeling of freedom—a feeling of owning a share of the sounds of the creek's current and sights of the faunal spectrum—grew in me.

My acquaintance with the stately tupelo gum trees had hardly prepared me for the mysterious, bayou-like setting further upstream where the gnarled gums dominated the creek, dividing its current into a maze of channels. Blossoming wild plum trees perched atop the bluffs like bursts of fluffy clouds. The shocking pink of redbuds accented the greens and grays of the brush. The saxifrages and May apples already were responding to the call of spring.

The following winter I retraced my route along the East Cadron. The varied hues of the blooming flowers and trees were gone, but the silver cascade of ice on the bluffs and the ringlets of ice beads dressing the willow bushes and tupelos were a sight worth the journey. That day I met a young fellow returning home from hunting. A squirrel hung from his belt. The only other creatures I saw were a chipmunk scampering around the rocks and a lizard circling a tree trunk.

Robert L. Gatewood in *Faulkner County, Arkansas, 1778–1964* refers to the largest stream in the county as "The Great Cadron Creek." For the farmers who live along the creek and for others who come to enjoy its resources, the Cadron is still "The Great Cadron Creek"—the pride of central Arkansas. Meandering through hills and bluffs, marshes and lowlands, the Cadron makes a twisting descent in its quest for the Arkansas River. Along its capricious route, young and old alike have been enticed by its kaleidoscopic grandeur, its diverse moods. Years of human experience compose the story of Cadron Creek.

The Buffalo

SUSAN MORRISON

Nationally acclaimed artist Susan Morrison has spent her life and her career in the artistic expression of Nature. Her business, Morrison*Woodward Gallery in Eureka Springs, published a documentary celebration called Arkansas Wilderness *in 1983, which included this poem.*

Giant Bluffs
Rise like Medieval Castles
above this Ancient River

Sending us back to a time
when all our land was wild

Leaves rustle with stories
from a past known only to the land

Legends whispered
from one forest glen to another
Of brave deeds
Performed by magnificent antlered stags
for doe-eyed mates

Nature's memories
held safe captive

By these towers of time . . .
By this Wilderness

The Plantation

CRYSTAL WILSON

*Crystal Wilson wrote this piece as background for
an award-winning short story, "Mama," published
in 1996. It first appeared in* Hearts and Bones, *a
University of Arkansas at Little Rock expository
writing class anthology. Crystal was a program
manager for the Centers for Mental Healthcare
Research when she died in January 2002.*

The Delta is a place of many contrasts. From lush and
green to gray and barren. The land always mirrors the passing sea-
sons. In late winter plows cut deeply into the crusty gray topsoil to
reveal the rich dampness beneath. The early spring months burst forth
with tender young stalks of cotton, soybean, and rice that carpet the
dark soil with vibrant green. The summer months are marked by the
deepening color of the fields and occasionally the need for sparkling
cool water. Fall roars on to the scene with a bounty of gold, white, and
pale yellow. The people who inhabit the Delta are a reflection of the
land. They are hardy and resilient out of necessity. They revel in a
good year, bragging about their harvest, and in lean years, vow to
make it better the next spring.

Summers are hot and dry with clear vibrant blue skies. Rows of
verdant green cotton and soybean plants fuse with shimmering rice
paddies to create a patchwork quilt across the landscape. Billowing
clouds of fine, rich loam mark the passage of huge tractors. The bright
flash of red, blue, and white pick-up trucks, beating a path up and

down the turn roads, serve as a constant reminder that the land and nature are faithless things. It is a never-ending quest, from first planting until harvest, to keep weeds at bay, to quench the thirst of the slowly wilting stalks, and to kill the tiny insects that feed on the tender shoots and bolls. You curse the lack of rain. You curse the tiny insects. You keep the hoes sharp. You move the heavy equipment around like a general. You come home at the end of a day, when it is too dark to see, and collapse. Bone tired, hungry, grimy from the fine grains of sand that are a part of the very thing you love the most—the land. Living on a large plantation, being close to the fickle soil, can rob a person of their sanity. I know because I have lived there.

When the season is good and you prosper, the work does not seem so pointless. A new pick-up, or tractor, a color television, a window-unit air conditioner, and a riding lawnmower are your rewards for a bountiful harvest. Your children receive the bicycles they wanted. You purchase a new washer and dryer for the wife. You recount to cronies how many bales per row your cotton crop yielded this year. Even the family garden produced well, and the freezer is full. There is a side of beef and one of pork tucked away for the long winter months ahead.

Everywhere you look, down to the poorest hands, people have made their extravagant purchases. The children all have new shoes and clothing. There is a new metal chimney in one house. They will, for once, be warm this winter. Another family is getting a telephone. You saw the telephone truck parked in their yard yesterday. Mama said she hoped they understood about a party line. And there are the crap games you aren't supposed to know about but you do because you have heard the quiet, late-night knock on the backdoor and the guttural, "I lost it all, Mr. Joseph, and I need to feeds da kids. Could I borrey five dollars? I'se got ta feed da kids." You knew there was a quiet exchange, and the man left your back porch with money in hand.

On long summer days there could be found an abundance of kids playing in any yard up and down the main gravel road. The road ran straight for as far as you could see. In late August it looked like a living thing with the heat rising up in clear, wavy flames. The rocks could get so hot they would blister the bottoms of your feet if you were silly enough to cross the road barefoot. Along this narrow straight stretch of rocks and dust were the farm owners or renters. It seemed as if the ancient old practice of having enough children to help you till the soil had not died out even in this modern age. There had to be a connection between the fertile soil and the large families that lived along the gravel road. There were five in my family, six boys at the next house, two boys and two girls at the next house, and on and on—just like the road.

The plantation owners lived on the highway, a blacktopped wonder that snaked over the countryside passing by the most prominent landowners' driveways.

In the Delta there was a strong class system. There were the plantation owners, the farmers, the riding bosses, and the field hands. The plantations were huge in terms of acreage, and their owners were the elite in the Delta's social structure. The farms were not quite as large as a plantation; therefore, the owners were not as prosperous, even in the good years, as the plantation owners. I belonged to the class of riding bosses. We did not own the soil, we just worked it for the plantation owner. The only problem was there were not too many of us. So having a place in the tight little society that ruled our area was difficult for me and my sisters.

The field hands were divided into two groups. There were those who worked in the shop and drove the equipment and those that picked and chopped cotton as well as chopping the soybean fields. I was, by benefit of my father's employment, too good for these kids. But during long, hot summer days, that really did not matter, and it really did not matter to me. So, it was within this group that I made my very first friend. Goodie was a timid, tiny girl with dark blonde hair and big blue eyes. She and her family moved into one of the houses in our row in the early spring. Her daddy drove a tractor on the farm, and her mama stayed home with all the kids. I remember them as being very poor but very proud. They kept their home and yard clean, their garden rivaled Mama's in size and productivity, and their clothes, although worn, were always clean.

Eventually, as spring grew into summer, Goodie, Lissa, and I became great friends, and our yard was most always full of kids playing with the water hose. Mama never had to worry about watering the yard. She only had to be sure there were ample chemicals in the tank that "softened" our water after a day of play with the hose. We also used to play hide-'n'-seek in the cotton fields, and we swam in the irrigation ditch that was close to the house, once.

The ditch was eight feet across, six feet deep, and ran parallel to one side of the rice field in front of our house. A powerful pump sucked water up through a pipe sunk many feet down into the hidden lake of water beneath the earth's surface. A long pipe extended from the pump that spewed the water out like a giant water hose. The water flow was measured in cubic feet per second and was powerful enough to knock a man off his feet and keep him down. On the fringes of the main flow, if you stuck your hand into the spray, it felt like thousands of needles striking your flesh at once.

Swimming in the irrigation ditch was a risky adventure because none of us could swim and water moccasins liked the cool muddy water, too. One day I, my sister Lissa, Goodie, John, and Marthie decided we would take a swim in the irrigation ditch in front of our row of houses. It was early in the day, but the dew had already been dried away by the incessant heat of early July. The sky was a cloudless, pale blue and the sun was an undulating orange ball. We left the swing set on the east side of our house and quietly scampered across the narrow dirt road that served as a driveway for other houses on our row and carefully slid over the mound of dirt at the top of the ditch just to the other side. From this position we could see the house, but Mama could not see us. It put us just at the edge of the water, sitting in the cool mud.

When the yard suddenly became quiet, Mama stepped out of the house onto the front porch and called our names. First mine, then Lissa, then the names of the other children we were playing with. We did not answer her call. We watched from our hiding place as she stood on the porch for a few more minutes and then went back inside the house. As we sat there in the mud, Lissa asked, "Do you think we should have answered her?"

"Naw, don't you want to swim?" I asked.

Being the oldest child, all of nine or ten years old, I was the leader. Lissa was almost seven and the others were between our ages. The five of us discussed what we should do. Then Mama stepped out on the porch again. This time after calling our names she issued a warning—

"I am going to call your Daddy if you don't answer me this minute!" Well, we did not answer, and being somewhat fatalistic Lissa said, "We better go on in 'cause we're in trouble now."

After some debate about who was going to slide into the water first, I rolled over onto my stomach and inched my feet first into the cold, clear water. At first it took my breath away because it was so cool. I panicked when I realized my feet would not touch the bottom. As I struggled to gain a strong hold, I discovered my toes would sink into the mud on the sides of the ditch, offering a sense of buoyancy that would keep me from sinking below the surface. After trying this out for several minutes by moving up and down the side of the ditch, I told everyone how to do it so they would not sink. One by one they followed my lead and slid belly first into the cool water squealing and gasping at the shock. It took each of them a few minutes to become accustomed to the surprising temperature change, but after a little more instruction on how to move about we began to play. We played for quite some time, disturbing crawdads, mudpuppies, and bullfrogs as we went. Fortunately, we did not encounter any snakes. While we were oblivious to her third call, Mama heard us all playing in the water, and she informed Daddy of our whereabouts when he came home for lunch. Wrapped up in our game, we did not know lunch time had come and gone. Growing tired from all our hard play, we crept out of the ditch in front of the third house down the row and jubilantly ran across the road to sit on the porch and dry out, forgetting all about the warning Mama had issued.

We had only been sitting on the porch for a few minutes when this very angry deep male voice boomed across the porch saying, "Crystal, you and your sister had better start running for home. I mean now!" Lissa and I jerked to attention and screamed in fright. Mama had told Daddy! He was standing at the end of the porch and had his belt off! We dove off the porch and headed for home as fast as our feet would carry us. I was faster than Lissa so Daddy caught up to her first. I could hear her yelps of pain and the crack of the belt as Daddy laid it across her butt and the backs of her bare legs again and again. I was running so hard and so fast that I reached the edge of our yard before he caught up to me. I did not hear his footfalls because of the roar of blood in my ears from fear. The surprising sting of the belt as it connected with the backs of my legs caused me to lose my footing, and I fell, rolling over and over on the grass. The fall cleared my hearing, and reality dawned on me as I heard Lissa crying in pain and saw her, from where I lay on the ground, shuffling slowly up the dry dirt road, that my time for punishment had only just begun. The belt connected again with the bare flesh of my upper legs, and I howled in pain. I tried to get up, but he just kept on swinging his belt. With each stinging report of the leather I howled louder until Mama came barreling around the side of the house yelling for Daddy to stop.

I recall going to bed without any supper after that foolhardy escapade into the ditch. However, Mama quietly came to our room, after Daddy had gone to sleep in his chair watching television, with a cheeseburger and a piece of chocolate pie for my sister and me. She sat on the side of our bed while we ate, offering the kinds of comfort only a mother can give and an explanation for Daddy's harsh punishment. She explained to us what could have happened to all of us if we had been bitten by a snake or if one of us had drowned. She said it was the fear of these things that had driven Daddy to spank us so soundly. With eyes as big as the plates our food rested on, my sister and I solemnly promised we would never do that again. Since that day I have had a terrible fear of snakes.

Southwest Arkansas Images

ANN BITTICK

Ann Bittick is a writer, visual artist, teller of tales,
and adjunct instructor of basic composition at the
University of Arkansas Community College at
Hope. She turned her thoughts to "trees" in the
summer of 2001.

Profiles, faces, figures appear in lines of historic and current measure in the village of dear old Washington, Arkansas, and the surrounding area. And in this "once-upon-a-time" setting there is a wealth of connection to the most ancient moments in the earth's story. Environmental influences in the molding, enveloping, modifying, and shaping of the human story have been extended in a multiplicity far too rich to ignore. Links to the past are more than academic; the mystery of the unknown claims so very much.

The *Texarkana Gazette* printed an Associated Press article about Nancy Arbuckle's finding of pre-dinosaur-age fossils (the Paleozoic Era) in a seventeen-mile radius around her home in Columbia County, which borders my home county, Hempstead, in southwest Arkansas. The Paleozoic Era ran from 544 to 245 million years ago, and was a time when the earth's land forms were splitting and colliding as the continents began to take the shapes we now draw on our globes. The Paleolithic ("long ago"), Pleistocene, and Neolithic Eras preceded the Tertiary period (65 million years ago), which hosted the rise of mammals. Mastodons lived where the Red River now washes through the sand and clay a few miles west of my house.

Most of us have read that during the all-covering Ice Ages humans and other creatures walked across from what was to be named Asia to what we now call the Americas. Southwest Arkansas, as part of the Gulf Coastal Plain, has been inhabited by humans since circa 10,000 B.C. The study of our environmental images begins with scenes unrecorded from these eras and with some basic understanding of cause and effect. The human perspective is outlined, marked, and measured by dates, time spans, classifications, geographic parameters, and illustrative dimensions of the known and the unknown.

Today only a very low percentage of Americans have taken a walk in the woods—and many never shall. But one strong human characteristic is the notion that the blend of fact and fiction opens special doors to understanding. And walking up to an old tree in this part of the country is to encounter the mysteried, uniquely shaped, long-forsaken rhythms, and the storied silences that have lived here for so very long.

The human story of "creation" allows the secret saving of chapters of birth and rebirth. Anthropologists can categorize and date arrowheads made by the people living here thousands of years ago. And I blend that fact with the question: which kinds of trees offered shade and cover to those we have named "Caddo Indians" who lived here in the West Gulf Coastal Plain? As a child I found near Seven Springs—a few miles east of my present home—a large number of arrowheads, and a few years ago I asked some of the Henderson State University anthropologists to date my collection. When I say good morning to any one of the ancient trees of dear old Washington, I imagine that most likely the tree is a direct descendant of trees that shaded the one who picked up a rock and, with immeasurable talent, carved the arrowhead I now hold in my hand.

The younger generations now present may not be in touch with the storied trees, but when one touches the arm of an ancient tree, or sees the face or profile in its body and limb, the tales of political, cultural, and economic storms, the dancing notes of history's haunting laughter, the silence of sorrow and listening move out into the air. The history of the town is one thing; the complete story of these shading, flowering, shedding, budding, long-living trees is only partially known. But when asked, the trees will share some of their stories.

I grew up a few miles east of the Champion Magnolia tree in Washington, a most celebrated tree which is said to have been brought up from New Orleans and set out by Dr. Isaac Newton Jones in the year 1839. My *Webster's* says that this genre was first so named by a French botanist in 1715, and that it is of the genus of North American and Asian shrub. Webster goes on to identify the magnolia as a popular tree on southern plantations prior to the Civil War.

The catalpa tree laces the city grounds, streets, and back fields of old Washington and the botanist, the environmentalist, and the lover of old trees all hope they could know more about this enchanting tree. Mr. Webster defines this tree as "a small genus of American and Asiatic trees," but seeing that the *New Encyclopedia Britannica* adds that there are eleven species of trees "in the genus Catalpa native to eastern Asia, eastern North America, and the West Indies," the would-be scholar realizes that there is more yet unknown about most beginnings than some writers of dictionaries and encyclopedias and other books may admit.

The catalpa trees in old Washington may have been brought by wagon, along with some of the 'first" magnolias, up from Louisiana with pioneer families who brought the trees they loved with them as they moved west from Florida, Georgia, or Alabama—where the Creek Indians called them kutuhlpa. The Creole name for the tree is atchafalya. How many more names have been woven by the delicious mix of French, Spanish, and African descendants as they re-pronounced words they had heard spoken by people of mixed Creek-Creole descent, while they stood under the wide spread of the old trees' arms?

When I walk along the town streets, I whisper my questions to the trees. How long have the old oaks, pines, redbuds, red maples, sassafras, cottonwoods, sycamores, black walnuts, white elms, hickories, cedars, and sweet gums offered shelter to all creatures of the night and of the air—creatures crawling, devouring, digging, hunting, mating, singing, feeding, weaning, flying, hiding and dying?

In the twisted trunks of so many of the catalpa trees, especially, there are images of face and figure. When the wind brings the music of storm and rain, the trees dance and bow.

In our winter past, the season mocked and imitated the great ice ages, as light snow mixed with the forming of heavy ice, dressing each leaf and limb of all the trees, young and old. Under the great weight of winter's ice, in December, A.D. 2000, the trees lost their music and made no murmur to the hidden moon, no tease to the hidden sun. The birds flew without note seeking a dry place to land. The hibernating creatures lay in the coldest coils. Then the trees began to feel the crack and tearing away of great limbs which fell onto other trees or into the roads.

For weeks, months, the people of the town stared in shock at the broken trees. The Great Magnolia was most seriously wounded, with a great loss of limbs. As the ice melted, the old pines and the baby pines wore broken sleeves of brown.

Then the planet's sun remembered its role of warming, and green returned to the scene. And the people of the town, perhaps without thought of ancient origins of time or place, began to watch the reflected multiplicity of beginnings and endings, images of doubt and truth.

We now wait with our trees for greater understanding of tomorrow.

Bayou Bluff: The Beauty and Darkness of Nature

JOHN CHURCHILL

*In 2001 John Churchill left a long career at
Hendrix College as vice president for Academic
Affairs and Dean of the College to become executive secretary of the Phi Beta Kappa Society. This
essay first appeared in* Somewhere Apart, *an
anthology of collected answers to the question,
"What is your favorite place in Arkansas?"*

Arkansas has a rough sort of beauty that often bears a
sting or an itch. A field lush with wildflowers will turn out to be full of
chiggers and seed ticks. An evening on the porch listening to the crickets and the whippoorwills will be punctuated by the regular slapping of
mosquitos—a process that, when successful, gives us the odd glimpse
of a speck of our own blood, fresh from the guts of another creature.
Beyond the presence of the unsettling, the beauties of Arkansas can
even be fatal. Newspapers are full of stories about people drowning in
lakes and streams, pitching off magnificent bluffs, and struck dead by
lightning in the middle of a spectacular thunderstorm. By providing
plenty of annoying insects, as well as mortal danger, Arkansas saves us
from being lulled into a sappy romanticism about Nature. It offers
instead the opportunity for a rich appreciation of Nature's ambivalences, her webbing of beauty with darker elements.

Arkansas readily offers parallel cultural ambivalences. Little in our
history conjures up a nostalgia untinged by some version of regret.

Our distinctive accents and manners are hard to define. They fade into those of neighbors on every border, just as the land merges with Missouri and Oklahoma and the waters pour to Mississippi and Louisiana. Too often we imagine these mixed feelings as obstacles to an understanding of the state. I don't think so. Because of these ambivalences and not despite them, I count myself lucky to be rooted here and to find my heart fixed to a place that embodies them. My favorite place in Arkansas is Bayou Bluff, a spot at the southern edge of the Ozarks.

About sixteen miles west of Conway, Interstate 40 crests a ridge and the view opens to the north toward White Oak Mountain on the furthest horizon. This country is drained by streams that rise steep, clear, and rock strewn, making their way by bluffs into the lower hills, turning gradually sluggish and moccasin-colored as they join the Arkansas River. The ambiguities of this transition are captured in the place name of Bayou Bluff.

At the foot of White Oak Mountain, the last town with a school, stores, and a post office is Hector. From there, Highway 27 twists through the valley of the Illinois Bayou for a few miles before climbing to the plateau above. Just at the point where the road leaves the creek to go up the hill, there is an old cedar-shaded cemetery and beside it a campgound on a low, ragged bluff. Below the bluff is the bayou, fresh from its descent from the mountain, headed south into canebrakes and cypresses.

I used to be intent on encounters with pristine Nature. That was before I understood that this notion is a dangerous fantasy, a part of the myth that pretends that humans are not at home in the world. But the fact that we are at home here means that the world is freighted with human meaning. Things have happened here. Mossy banks are places where we could lie down, where we have lain, where others, after all, will lie. Here, in a pool of clear, cool summer water, I learned to swim. When my grandfather died and all the cousins ran the well dry, we went to bathe there in the moonlight. I flee to Bayou Bluff from the world of books and committees, and it is the sort of place my grown son refers to when he says, "It feels like where I'm from." Jean and I have taken our three children there again and again in the hope that they would learn what it feels like to be in this place. But it is not a place of benign beauty. Half of what grows is poison ivy, and you must watch where you put your feet. You learn never to put your hand on a ledge you cannot see.

The colors there are oak-leaf green and water green, cedar green and moss, the slaty gray of the rock and the gray-white of lichen, the motley red-brown and weathered gray of cedar bark, and the red of the dirt that runs in seams through the bluff, washing out into a gritty sand and leaving the rocks to fall into the creek in the next storm.

On every visit I find that some new rock, large or small, has fallen off the bluff, and left a hole above where there will be more washing out as the ancient process of taking these hills slowly down and down goes on. In the flood of 1982 the whole creek was rearranged, and my childhood swimming hole was filled with rocks. Someone else might regret these changes. Not me. I like the way the bayou shows the earth itself at work, or being worked on—piling up here, pulling down there. Paying attention to this process can correct our tendency to value only what promises to last forever. Even the mountains are coming down. You can see it at Bayou Bluff, though you have to watch for a long time.

Being in a place like this can help you get a sense for things that take a long time—a lifetime or more. I come here and think of the people who came: the Cherokee who were moved through and my ancestors who followed and stayed only until paved roads made it easy to leave. I think about the academic life I have and the projects I work on, many of which take a long time and embody a dangerous and annoying beauty. I think about my grandfathers who were store-keepers in Hector; my grandmothers who raised families and tended gardens, roses, and chickens; their parents who were farmers; and theirs who came from Mississippi, Tennessee, and the Carolinas. I think about the storms whose waters wear down the land. Cliché or not, it is true: I think of myself as a child lying on a pallet at my grand-parents' house, listening to summer storms batter on the tin roof, and then also of the same storms crashing these last nights around my house in Conway. All this gathers for me at Bayou Bluff, and for that reason it is my favorite place.

Blackwater Reflections

JIM SPENCER

Back in the summer of 1997, Jim Spencer took readers of the Arkansas Wildlife *magazine deep into an east Arkansas swamp in the middle of the night. Jim is assistant editor of the magazine, published by the Arkansas Game and Fish Commission.*

It is peaceful here in the swamp, if you understand that by "peaceful" I mean there are no telephones, no yapping dogs, no boomboxes. Stay here until the crack of doom and you'll never hear the sound of an internal combustion engine. There are no insurance salesmen, IRS agents, or telephone solicitors. There is no yard to mow.

There is only the swamp.

I'll tell you about it, but I won't tell you exactly where it is. See, this swamp is mine—not by deed but by heart—and though I would probably like you if I met you, I don't want to meet you in my swamp. I don't want you there at all. I know that's selfish, but there it is anyway.

I'll tell you this much: my swamp nestles inside a meandering bend of a large southeast Arkansas river. It's accessible by parachute or by a seven-mile boat ride followed by a long, boot-sucking walk through steaming, mosquito-infested woods. This is not a place you can reach without effort.

There are alligators in my swamp, and swamps are better with alligators in them. There's an egret rookery, too, and the sight of five hundred snowys perched in a dozen pale-green cypresses is a vision not easily forgotten. There are 'coons and 'possums, deer and bears, and where the ground is drier you may see bobcat and gray fox sign.

Back in the brush, several beaver lodges rise improbably from the duckwort. But beavers are a minority in this swamp, for here the nutria is king. Toward nightfall you can hear these South American invaders calling back and forth, *"Maaaa-aaa! Maaaa-aaa!"* The sound is reminiscent of calves or lambs. When I hear it, I smile, for it reminds me of the civilized world I've left behind. It's comforting to be reminded of civilization when you're knee-deep in a primordial swamp at sundown.

Sundown is a time of awakening in the swamp. One of the first clues is the bullfrog chorus. One old settler back in the brush will tune up, hesitantly, as though his throat was sore. Gradually he'll gain volume and tempo, until the very leaves tremble. Then another will join in, and another, and before long you know without a doubt why they call them bullfrogs.

This is when I like my swamp best, when the shadows lengthen and the gloom deepens and the bullfrog chorus starts.

There's a blackwater lake in my swamp, and I reach it this day just as I hear that first sore-throated frog. There's an ancient cypress boat on the bank, tied to a tupelo sapling. I have no idea who owns the boat; it belongs to the swamp. In the fifteen years I've been coming here, I've never seen another human.

Sometimes I see signs of other people—a minnow bag left in the boat, a muddy footprint on the seat. But no people. Maybe this is because I'm out of step with the rest of the world. I come to the swamp at night, when saner folk are home in bed.

Whatever the reasons, I'm glad of them. I throw my gear in the boat and slide it into the water, watching carefully for the cotton-mouths that sometimes hide beneath.

Sure enough, one is there. He's a big one, black as death, and he coils menacingly four feet from my thin tennis shoe. I feint at him, and he opens his mouth. The white is startling in the gloom, as evolution intended. I watch quietly, and the snake wavers. Presently he closes his mouth—disappointedly, it seems to me—uncoils, and slides into the lake. I let him go unharmed, hoping he will someday return the favor.

The shoreline brush is thick. It's a matter of opinion where swamp ends and lake begins. A narrow, hacked-out trail weaves through the tangle, and I scull the boat along this familiar corridor. It breaks hard left and then right, and suddenly I'm in open water. The thirty-acre oval lake stretches before me; the only sign of civilization is the Purex jug tied to a button willow behind me, marking the entrance to the boat trail.

My private sea lies calm. For a while, at least, I control my destiny. I am master of my soul, captain of my ship, and that my ship is leaky and twelve feet long bothers me not at all.

Bird, at home sixty miles away, can't understand why I love this place so much. I brought her here once, and the mosquitoes nearly carried her away. Besides, she says, it's dangerous. It's muddy and icky (her words, not mine) and full of things that go screech in the night.

She's right on all counts. Yet I have never felt fear here, not even the inky night I turned the boat over and lost my gear. There have been some neck-prickling moments, but they're more a product of my civilized upbringing than of any real danger. Instead of fear, I feel a calm excitement, a low-key adrenaline rush of utter contentment that recharges my batteries and leaves me pumped, yet relaxed. It's a complex mix of emotions I find nowhere but in the swamp.

I think of Bird now, reading a book on the deck, planning one of her many projects, seeking her own brand of contentment. I know she'll be snug in bed when I get home much later this night, and somehow this makes me feel even more at peace. One of the nicest things about a swamp is that eventually you must leave it and go home.

Fishing is my excuse for coming here, but the real reason is the swamp itself. Sometimes the fishing is good, but usually it's so-so, and even when it's good they run small. Still, I always make the attempt, more from habit than from great expectations. Tonight's pilgrimage is no exception.

The bass are not hungry tonight. Shadows lengthen and merge as I probe the brushline, laying cast after cast into likely looking hidey-holes.

Eventually I do catch a fish. The fight is lively but one-sided. A one-pound bass is no match for a two-hundred-pound man with greed in his heart.

I hold the fish at arm's length, admiring it. I like swamp bass. They're healthy and scrappy, and they're the greenest green in nature. Even the white belly of a swamp bass has a greenish tint.

The bass flips in my hand, still fighting. I smile and turn it loose. I've been known to kiss swamp bass before releasing them, but this one is too small to rate such treatment. He'll be bigger next year, though.

Daylight fades rapidly now. Far back in the woods, a barred owl interrupts the bullfrogs. At midnight in the swamp, when this bird cuts loose directly overhead, he can make you suddenly wish you were home. But at sundown, at a distance, the sound is soothing, the raucous eight-note call providing perfect countermelody to the bullfrogs and nutrias.

Soon it's too dark to see the edge of the brush, so I move out into the lake and wait for moonrise. I cast a tiny white grub to open water, catching a few small crappie to pass the time. But after a while something big and strong takes my little lure away from me, and afterward I just sit and wait and listen.

Nutrias swim back and forth nearby, ignoring me as far as I can tell. Deep in the brush, a beaver tail-slaps the water. Owls and whip-poorwills call, and frogs fill the night with an almost visible noise. There are mosquitoes, of course, but they aren't bad out here on open water. I choose to ignore them rather than stink of bug dope the rest of the night.

At 10:30, the full moon breaks over the trees to the east. It bathes the tiny lake in blue-gold light, light that looks cold even in August. I shiver involuntarily as I ease the boat toward the brushline for round two.

An alligator bellows between the landing and me, and I shiver again. A 'gator's roar is a scary thing, even in daylight. Somehow, a dark row of moonlit cypresses makes the sound even more ominous. I glance over my shoulder, but the 'gator is invisible. It's another one of those neck-prickling moments, exactly what I came here for.

I begin casting again, moving along the brushline, listening to the night and catching absolutely nothing. My lack of success doesn't bother me in the least.

By 3:00 A.M. I've circled the lake. The only thing I've caught, besides the small bass and the few little crappie, is a grinnel as long as my arm—a prehistoric monster too tough to vanish with his contemporaries, the dinosaurs. This particular monster waylaid my spinnerbait as it came by a cypress, and he pretty much had his way with me until I managed to subdue him and turn him loose.

Many fishermen kill these primitive predators, but here again I am out of step. I can't bear to kill one, because a grinnel is the embodiment of my swamp—fierce beauty, strength, permanence, and efficient death in one compact and streamlined package. When I released this grinnel, he lazed beside the boat and eyed me malevolently before swimming leisurely away. Was he unconcerned or merely uncomprehending? I've never been sure, but many grinnel I've released have acted that way. It spooks me a little; I'm glad they're not ten feet long.

The new day is near, and it's time to go. Just before the boat enters the brush, I hold my breath and spray everywhere I can reach with insect repellent. I can put up with the relatively few mosquitoes that venture onto open water, but I'm not tough enough for the multitudes waiting in the woods.

It's dawn when I arrive home. No sense going to bed now. I make a pot of coffee, and while it brews I shower and change. Later, on Bird's back deck, I lift my steaming mug and toast the dawn.

Miles to the east, my swamp is greeting the new day. It will be beautiful under the morning sun, but I don't miss it much during the daytime.

I'll take my swamp at night, with the moon over the cypresses and the owls hooting and the bullfrogs and alligators vying for low note. It's much better that way.

PART TWO

Kentucky Wonders

Stories of Arkansas People

The crux of the entire issue and my own feelings can be summed up in an incident which occurred just last Saturday, four days before this hearing. It was my youngest son's twelfth birthday. He had a morning basketball game in Bentonville, and then we hustled over to Newton County for a hike and to have lunch on the bluff line. We were sitting there scanning the scenery for miles around, feeling the fresh air and the sunshine, and my young son turned to me and he said, "This is the greatest place I can think of to be on my birthday. I want to come back here on my twenty-fourth, forty-eighth, and ninety-sixth birthdays and I'm going to bring my children. Will you come with us?"

At this moment I felt so much pride at having raised a son who appreciates nature as I do, and I really felt the reality of my own vulnerability to the forces of time. I'm obviously not going to be around, but that bluff line can be there for him as long as we leave it alone. . . .

—BARBARA MEYER
Congressional Wilderness Hearing Testimony
1984

Kentucky Wonders

FRANCIE JEFFERY

*Francie Jeffery is an associate professor in the
Department of Writing and Speech at the
University of Central Arkansas and currently
directs the University Writing Center there. In
1999 she wrote "Kentucky Wonders" after a summer spent in the Boxley Valley of Newton County.*

Nothing in the garden was moving as slow as I was.
Bugs and bees and other flying things that I hoped could be catego-
rized as winged insects were motoring busily along the furrowed highways. I entered their space, barreling through a small opening between
the first and second row of corn, a clumsy semi sending the minis and
subcompacts zipping out of the way.

I had waited too late in the day to begin picking beans. No local
gardener would be out thrashing among the corn at the hour I had
chosen. Still, it wasn't like it was high noon. It was 10 o'clock in the
morning—though the sweat forming underneath the headband of my
wide-brimmed hat reminded me why I was to have started this whole
job early.

"Early" is what my dad had said when he was telling me about the
beans. "You could pick the beans," he said, when I asked him if I
needed to do something while he and my mother went to town.
"Going to town" is one of those phrases that's actually code. I now
know that "early" is code too. It means 6 A.M. It means before coffee,
before a shower, before almost anything. "You'd need to get out there
early," he'd said, and I figured he was simply wanting me to get it done

before they got back so my mother wouldn't feel bad about my being out there doing it. But, see, "going to town" is code for either an appointment at a doctor's or have-to-shopping-and-miscellaneous-errand-running which usually includes a stop for feed. With my dad's announcement that they were "going to town," I could figure they wouldn't be back until noon. I disregarded "early" for a second, then a third cup of coffee, the cost of which was now being exacted by the August sun high in the sky.

There are those in the Boxley valley who refuse to let their runner beans do their running up cornstalks. Makes a garden look messy, they say. My father's garden is on rocky soil, though, and will never smooth into neatness. Still, he runs beans on corn because he finds the partnership to be practical. Kentucky Wonders are a fairly late blooming variety, and by the time the beans are coming on, the corn is almost done; unless there's been a big wind to flatten everything, the stalks stand straight as any pole you'd have to pound into the ground, so it only makes sense to use these natural stakes. I'm talking about rational acts here because I do have a working knowledge of rationality. Which is why I can admit that about halfway through the first row of corn-stalked beans, I began to have murderous thoughts about those Kentucky Wonders.

ℳ   ℳ   ℳ

"We're going to need help in the garden this summer," my dad had advised me when we talked about my mother's heart surgery. That was in early June, but way before then I had formed an opinion about gardens. Years earlier, I'd scraped away the Bermuda grass from a small rectangular plot in a corner of the backyard of my very first house in Conway. I'd planted the usual urban patch of salad ingredients plus some vegetables, but the hot summer had fried everything but the okra, which fed on the heat and put out pod after pod. I don't even like okra all that much. Even in that small plot I had learned that everything in a garden is itchy and scratchy. There are tiny fine hairs on garden plants, spines really, and merely brushing against their leaves will release a microscopic shower, tiny archers' arrows flung from a first line of defense. Then there are the sharp edges of things. From far away, the oblate leaves that ladder up cornstalks appear light and wavy, their droopy arms giving softness to the thick stalk. Against a hand or a cheek, however, their serrated edge becomes apparent, a clingy kind of sharpness, like cricket's feet. Except, unlike crickets, the leaves don't jump out of your way.

"You've never had a real garden," my dad had gone on to say. "Gardens are a lot of work."

"Put those two things together," I had said to him and laughed.

I had arrived on Saturday to spend the weekend and all the following week at the farm, mainly to do the house chores my mother couldn't but also to help hay if my dad decided to cut any. One of my brothers had come for the weekend too. When I got up early Sunday morning to fish, I discovered my brother had had the same idea, and so we left together, driving his car through several fields and over to the river that forms the eastern boundary of the farm. He balanced two coffee cups as I jumped out to get the gates. When we got to the ford through Mill Creek, we stopped and fished there a bit, seeing if we could interest any bass in a butter-yellow crickhopper for breakfast. Later, we told my dad about the newborn calf we had seen curled up close to the bank there. The calf hadn't moved when my brother walked past, nor did he scramble up when Bill squatted to stroke his fuzzy hide, a stillness we both thought unusual.

"How you tell when a calf's sick," my dad told me later when he returned from checking on what turned out to be simply an obedient calf "is by first looking at its eyes. If they're running, then you need to look at its . . . ," he paused, "behind." He pronounced it "bee-hind."

"Uh huh," I said.

"You lift its tail and see if it's got the squirts, and if it does, you've got a sick calf."

"Uh huh," I said again.

I wondered if maybe I ought to be writing things down. The day before my father had told me how to plant sweet potatoes.

"You have to mound up hills for sweet potatoes," he explained. I was sitting out on the glider under the big ash, drinking coffee while I watched goldfinches and indigo buntings add primary colors to the

dusty brown seed heads of late summer sunflowers. "Instead of dropping the seed potato into a hole in a furrow, you mound up the dirt
and plant your potato on top."

As he described how to make the mounds, I could imagine it: the
plow's tongue curling the dirt into miniature mountain ranges, the
second pass down the opposite side increasing the elevation. I could
even picture the mule's step, the loose length of straps that tied mule
to man, the grainy gray wooden handles branching up from the
earth-browned blade of the plow. But I couldn't see my hands upon
the handles, couldn't feel the strap looped around my neck like I had
seen it looped around my father's or hear myself say, "Hup, mule, hup
hup."

Who is going to do these things? My brothers? I cannot see them
take these reins either, not so literally. The farm will come to the three
of us, and from talk, I know we can each see ourselves here, somehow,
but does that mean I should see myself out among the cattle? Walking
behind a mule? Planting a garden? What if I don't want to do these
things?

∾ ∾ ∾

I pushed further into the jungle of corn, a green tangle of leaves,
stalks, and vines. Looking for sun, the beans had snaked their way up
the stalks, then spread out along the lengths of the leaves. Some vines
even curled overhead, having moved higher up into the seed heads of
the corn. Beans were everywhere: bony fingers of green clumped in
twos and threes, single beans lurking under leaves, thin pairs of beans
forming parentheses, older arthritic-looking beans way past picking
hanging low to the ground. Unlike the siren ripe-red tomatoes, however, the beans were sneaky, looking like every other green stem or
branch or vine in the garden.

I considered a single theatrical sweep of the stiff leaves, revealing
a hoard of beans. But I'd spy a string of beckoning beans only to have
them move out of reach when I pushed through the leaves to get to
them. They moved when the stalk did, the purse-on-a-string practical
joke. Only it wasn't funny. It was hot. And buggy.

I ducked as a grasshopper choppered its way past me. I bent my head to wipe my sweaty temple against my shirtsleeve and knocked my hat askew. I had two and a half rows to go.

For a while I amused myself by making a game of snatching the beans before they could escape. "Hah hah, my Pretty," I said to a sweet green tendril in my best Wicked Witch imitation. "You thought you could escape but I'm too quick for you. There's no escaping now . . . haaaahhh." I tried a villain voice—nyah ah ah—but soon grew tired of the game. The beans could put up no real defense.

Then to simply get the chore done, I yanked at the next bean and in doing so knocked off a blossom growing next to it, a bean-to-be. Oops, I thought. Then paused. Here were Beans Future, my future, in fact, and I looked more closely at the stalks around me. Small white flowers dotted with yellow-centered suns were on most of the vines. Up high in the tops of the stalks there were whole clusters of flowers and hanging next to them, the tiny apostrophes of newborn beans.

I curled my middle finger to my thumb, held it there for a moment, then flicked it at the closest blossom. The white star sailed out into the air, disappearing somewhere into the green tangle of leaves one row over. I paused.

It's not like we need these beans to feed us, I reasoned. It's not even like we need to put them up this season. With my mother's surgery, she would not be going to the trouble to can beans. We'd eat the ones I picked, and there would be some that wouldn't make it to the pot in time and end up on the compost heap. Maybe I was doing everyone a favor by lessening the number of beans to come. Who would pick them anyway, I thought? I flicked another blossom off into never-to-be-a-bean land.

I wondered about other farm wives. Were there times when it had become too much, too hard? Had they looked across a late summer vegetable patch and thought die, damn you. Or had they all suffered happily, translating the sun and sweat into a welcome winter supper: steaming bowls of beans mounded with small rounds of potatoes.

Flick: I sailed another starry blossom into the air.

Flick: and another.

But I found I couldn't continue. There seemed an essential meanness in the act, coupled with the question of what right had I to interfere in the natural processes of my father's garden. So I quit though I admit I took less care after that in reaching for the pickable beans. If a blossom were to be dislodged when I brushed against it, well, that was something else entirely, simply the consequence of the act of picking. It was hot. I was tired. I stripped the vines with a heavy hand.

I finished before my parents returned. I showered and changed into fresh jeans and a sleeveless shirt. Sitting in a cane-bottomed rocking chair on the porch, I drank iced tea, buckets of beans around me ready for stringing and snapping and simmering. Across the road, the garden was a dense green square. I wondered if I would tell my father what I had done.

Returning

JOHN DAY

*A lieutenant colonel in the Enforcement Division
of the Arkansas Game and Fish Commission,
John Day is a frequent contributor to* Arkansas
Wildlife *magazine. His tribute to his grandfather
appeared in 1997.*

It doesn't seem so long ago in my heart and mind, but
the truth is, the years have rolled by. It would please him to know
what became of my life, and the things I am involved in.

Sometimes, when Dad and I make the run on the Black River to
do some squirrel hunting, I can hear him in my mind. That's not so
bad as it once was. For many years, my grief of his passing wore heavily upon me every time I boated those waters.

Thirty years ago I was a freckled-faced, scrawny boy listening to
Grandpa as he told me about the Black River. I've boated many other
rivers now, but this one still beckons me. It flows though my mind,
calling me back year after year. This is Grandpa's doing. He made it
utterly impossible for me to forget this beautiful stream.

When you see the Black River through eyes that have seen many
rivers, nothing special jumps out at you. But the Black is a deceptive
old thing with many secrets. It holds many lessons for the attentive.
Grandpa was a student of the Black River and passed on to me many
of his hard-earned lessons.

Grandpa fished for just about anything that would bite, but deep in
his heart, he was a bass fisherman. I have his tackle now, and it reminds
me of the many times he and I paddled his homemade johnboat

upstream a far piece, then casually drifted back. Casting Shannon twin spins or deep-diving Bombers, we'd try our luck. I wish I could tell about magnificent stringers of bass we caught, but we never bested that old river. It threw a good fish at us every once in a while, but most of the time we had to work just to catch enough to eat.

In those years, we would fish for hours and never see anybody else bass fishing. We also carried an old fly rod rigged with a Bream Killer and popping bug for bluegills. The fly rod furnished more edible fish than our plugging efforts ever did. Grandpa would get disgusted and talk to the river like a wayward friend. This did no good, but it beat the fire out of sitting in silence dipping water from the leaky boat.

Today when I run the river, I still don't see the numbers of fishermen I often encounter elsewhere. It's not that the river is such a big secret. I believe it has humbled too many egos. It was and still is a challenge, even though it's kinder to me now. After so many years, I know the places that tend to hold bass. This knowledge, plus the fact that my mentor taught me patience, may have a lot to do with it.

Grandpa had an old, beat-up black Bomber plug. Something about that plug was magic. It would have tickled him to see my tackleboxes now, full of plugs and spinnerbaits. My free-spool casting reels and graphite rods would have given him much pleasure had they been readily available to him. The antiquated reels we used back then often backlashed, costing us precious drift time. Our Dacron line would hold any fish we could hook, but it had a way of sneaking up on you and playing havoc with your casting. Fortunately, Grandpa was adept at picking out my backlashes, and he always sculled the boat close to the bank we were fishing. Long casts led to all kinds of problems, particularly if you hung up. Fighting the current to reach your plug was a major achievement with a paddle. And the few plugs we had were precious.

There were electric trolling motors then, but Grandpa feared their noise would scare the fish we were after. He would like the idea of me still bassing the Black River, sculling a boat from the front seat, fishing with the current. His black Bomber still has the quality of mysticism about it and produces when newer plugs don't. I bought two more Bombers just like his and tried to retire the one he gave me, but to no avail. There is no magic in those plugs.

Grandpa had a secret bassin' spot he learned from the man who taught him to fish. That secret was passed on to me in Grandpa's later years. The spot resembled others on that particular bank, but that was the deception. Grandpa would swing the boat just a certain way to get the play of the plug through a small eddy. He didn't always catch a bass there, but when he did it was a good one. When the river is down and running gently, that eddy still produces.

Many men have influenced my life, but my old gray-haired Grandpa played havoc with me. He knew what would happen when he planted those seeds of bass fishing deep in my heart and mind. He created within me a love for rivers that cannot be defined.

More fluent men than I have written about their love for wild flowing waters. Some do not know the origins of their love, but I am more fortunate. I know from where my feelings arise. The grief experienced so long ago is laid to rest. Now I can enjoy those precious activities Grandpa guided me into.

The old black Bomber took a six-pounder from the eddy hole last year. There was one difference, though: I put the big bass back in the river.

I talked to the Black River that day. It was the least I could do for the pleasure it brought and the memories it gave.

Hurricane Creek Wilderness

WILLIAM COLEMAN

William Coleman is a professional environmentalist. He was manager of Environmental Affairs at Arkansas Power and Light in 1983 when he wrote this text for The Arkansas Wilderness, *and he coordinated the statewide RARE II (wilderness review) program as conservation chairman of the Ozark Society. He now lives in California.*

The early frontier days of this great nation were filled with a colorful history which invigorates many people even to the present day. The mountain men, explorers, and scouts were individuals who actually lived beyond the borders of the frontier. They lived deeply immersed in outright wilderness, preferring to leave behind the civilized ways of eighteenth- and nineteenth-century America. It was this group of individuals who learned the ways of the Native American tribes, who became naturalists, physicians, diplomats, and inventors as the only way to guarantee their longevity, and who extended the border of the frontier ever closer to the Pacific Ocean, providing much of the human glue which held together the territories of a growing nation.

The frontiersman was looking for either challenge or anonymity, sometimes even for both. Rarely was there a higher goal involved, such as conducting natural or cultural studies, but there are certain exceptions. In Arkansas, for example, Thomas Nuttall and Henry Schoolcraft were two explorers who, upon setting out on independent journeys during the early 1800s, decided to record their experiences and observations. The several volumes which are handed down to us today are a testimony to the excitement of those early days prior to statehood.

Since having lived in Arkansas, I've come to see that the old frontier days still inspire many twentieth-century outdoors enthusiasts. In fact, many proclaimed "black-powder" enthusiasts have expanded their original, simple interest in early firearms to include a wide variety of wilderness skills—skills that would have been essential to one's well-being if one shared the Ozark Mountains with the handy Osage tribes one hundred and seventy-five years ago. The Arkansas Muzzle-Loaders Association teaches skills which are far removed from space-shuttle technology. Fire with flint and steel? Of course. Skinning and tanning? Natch. Leather and beadwork? Well, sure, if you have the time. Most of today's part-time mountain men buy their clothing from those who make a living sewing together such things—from the reservation Indians, for example.

Old patterns are hard to break.

The original archetypal frontiersman would have been an interesting character to know. Imagine how it might have felt to be the first American explorer, the initial wilderness wanderer, setting out into the woods from some newly established farming hamlet or cabin. You would have wandered west, on foot or ahorse, following topographic features such as the Hurricane Creek watershed. Or you might have chosen a wilderness game trail as your path, hoping that dinner might be near at hand. Nights alone, dark and thick enough to touch. Careful days full of glances over your shoulder or nose raised to the air, sniffing. If the native tribes were not close at hand, then that old sow bear just might have been, or the panther or the snapping wolf. None of these creatures would be necessarily disposed toward hospitality. Fighting, hiding, or running-like-hell would have been other important wilderness skills.

When I think of running wild through the wilderness, I think of my close compadre Don Hamilton. Not because he is used to running wildly from forest goons, but because he has more than once run my legs plumb off during weekend tours to wilderness areas like Hurricane Creek. Don is the preeminent frontier outdoorsman. He is the archetypal scout, the classic wilderness explorer. Belonging merely to the black powder and musket league is lightweight stuff for this fellow; he has managed to become an outstanding authority on eighteenth- and nineteenth-century flintlock rifles and has amassed a collection of originals which deserve to be displayed in some public repository. When he is replete with beat-up hunting coat, powderhorn, and bullet bag slung across one shoulder, longrifle in the crook of one hand, you quickly come to terms with the seriousness of this man's affliction. Yet the only disease here is that biting pain of nostalgia. Don Hamilton lives today for the wilderness of the 1790s; the American dream of gasoline, rockets, and silicon chips has little meaning by comparison.

John Heuston tells me of the time when he was invited to join Don at his fall deer camp not far from the Hurricane Creek wilderness, which is Don's favorite retreat. The rusty yellow and red foliage was near its peak, the air cool and crisp. John recalls his arrival at "Ham's Hollow" in detail. Upon reaching the end of the rocky trail to Don's hand-hewn log cabin, John described the sight that greeted him. There was the man, five days alone in the wilderness, propped casually in a folding chair. He was wearing old, beat-up cords and khaki, wrinkled, with flies buzzing around. A small fire was crackling away in front of his moccasined feet, slowly blackening the leather soles to char. Don watched his friend approach without turning his head; sly eyes slowly followed his movement instead. John opened the rickety gate of Don's split-rail fence and sort of sauntered up closer to the fire. No wave or other greeting. Only the blissful grin on Don's face told John that he was welcome.

Don finally spoke: "Did you know that it takes a hundred years to make one tiny inch of this soil?" He waved his arm in a short arc. "This whole forest is growing here on the dead remains of five hundred years of tree bones."

John plucked a beer floating in the cool water of the nearby creek. He walked back over and hunkered down Indian style, poking the aluminum. "Well, no kiddin', Don. Really makes a fella stop and think, I'll say." I'll bet his face was twisted up tight so as not to give away a grin. As far as I know, that could have been the height of dialogue for the remainder of their trip.

Backpacking with either of these men is a true experience, one of those things normal humans don't forget. Don has taken each of us for tours into the Hurricane Creek wilderness. Despite this I would like to return there someday. Such beautiful scenery as is there can never be spoiled by peculiar friends.

I am so used to carefully judging how my Kelty is to be packed—whether to take this tiny apple or those extra socks—that I am amazed when people get away with less caution. Don reminds me of a walking human cookwagon. He carries a ration of snakebite medicine for winter hazards, for example! He carries in extra, old army boots, a big canvas army tent, whole steaks, and canned hams. There are cameras and lens bags and binoculars, a nine-volt flashlight, and a big old steel shovel—all of this tied on, strapped down, and stuffed in with not a thought to the weight distribution or easy access which is the current sensible vogue among high-tech hikers. Sierra Club, take horrid notice—the man is a wilderness Walgreens!

And me with my toothbrush handle sawed off and discarded to save a puny ounce.

To make matters worse, Don can carry this gear farther and faster than most panicky pack mules. During the two days we had available to us we wowed at every gorgeous beech grove, trundled up every tributary, admired above every bluff line and stone pillar, trudged across each steep hill and *twice* forded the swollen, chilly Hurricane Creek itself. Where were this man's manners?

He and John Muir would have had only one thing in common had they known each other—stamina. Okay, maybe two things; Don loves the wild, untamed forest as much as the eloquent Muir did. Equally as much. He has told me so in flowery, barrister style.

I have a deep affection for this man. Were it not for his legal training, his leadership abilities, and his astute political sense, not to mention his clear, effective delivery of the wilderness ethic, the effort to preserve areas like Hurricane Creek would be lagging, perhaps even lost. Don is a true conservationist in the classic vein, where resource use and resource protection exist in his mind as carefully balanced arms of the land management scale. In this regard he does reflect many of the attitudes of another American conservationist, Aldo Leopold, a man for whom Don himself admits a great respect.

Leopold and Hamilton would have gotten along, and I would have enjoyed the chance to observe their friendship. Leopold the philosopher and Hamilton his advocate: my admiration and thanks will always go out to them both.

The Taste of Dust

MELISSA STOVER

*Melissa Stover is a stay-at-home mom and a
freelance writer and photographer from
Woodlawn. This piece appeared in the University
of Arkansas at Little Rock writing anthology
Quills & Pixels in 1998, when Melissa was
completing her master's degree in Expository
Writing.*

I wake up this February morning feeling summer. The sun pouring through my windows forces me to get up on a Saturday morning when I would normally sleep in. I know I can't possibly stay inside today; today is a fishing day. I reach for the phone to call my cousin.

"Aaron, what are you doing today?"

"Nothing, why?"

"You want to go fishing?"

"Well, I've got to pick up a part for the trailer and fix it, but maybe I could run to Warren before noon . . ."

"No, not all that, let's just go to Papaw's pond."

After my conversation with Aaron, I meet him at Papaw's house just an hour later. Papaw's house is no longer near Papaw's pond, but we decide to meet there anyway, maybe because the pond and Papaw still go together.

"Papaw, we're going fishing; you want to go?"

"Well, I've been feeling pretty bad this week; I think I'll just stay here. Anyway, the weatherman said you won't catch anything today."

As we are walking out the door, my mother calls to me: "Wait, I think Papaw's going with you."

"No, he said he was feeling bad."

"He always feels bad; he's going."

I load up Papaw's lawn chair so he can sit comfortably while he fishes; Aaron and I climb into my truck. I pull out of the driveway carefully so as not to slosh the minnows out of their bucket in the back. This is the first time I've ever driven my papaw to the pond. When we were younger, we drove over with Papaw in the yellow wagon that now belongs to my eighteen-year-old cousin, Aaron. I drive slowly because Papaw is in the car, and that's the way he drives.

Papaw insists that he doesn't want to fish, so I place his lawn chair close by, and we get our poles ready.

"The weatherman said you won't catch anything today; it's still too cold."

"But it's so pretty, I just feel like fishing."

I maneuver the rod and reel until my line is in the water. I miss Papaw's old cane poles we used to use. These poles belong to Aaron, and I don't have one of my own so I have to make do.

The place looks just like I remembered. It's early, but the jonquils are just beginning to bloom. The sky is beautiful and clear, and the air is just warm enough for short sleeves.

"It's perfect," I whisper. I close my eyes, and I can see that old yellow wagon.

$$\text{\reflectbox{∞} \quad \reflectbox{∞} \quad \reflectbox{∞}}$$

The old yellow station wagon creaks down the dusty road catching overgrown tree branches and causing them to slap at the windows. Papaw comes to a lurching stop at the gate and gets out among billows of dust that have just caught up. He opens the gate, and we continue our drive through tall grass that brushes the dust off the bottom of the car and sends grasshoppers out of naps in search of a safer place to rest. When the car stops again, we pile out, carrying what we can, and wait for Papaw at the edge of the pond, eager to get started. After baiting the hooks of four grandchildren with crickets or worms, untangling the younger ones' first cast, and reminding us that if we continue to fuss so loudly, the fish will be scared away, he finally settles down himself.

Across the water from me, I watch my grandfather crouch down, his old, toughened hands shaking, yet familiar with the hook as he works his bait down. A smooth cast sends his worm sinking below and his cork skating the surface. He removes his cigarettes from his breast pocket. He strikes a match on a nearby rock, and the cigarette begins to glow. In this moment of quiet his eyes leave the pond and search the land that is his pasture. He no longer owns cows, but he lets a neighbor's cattle graze here. Beyond Papaw, my eyes take up the rest of the land. An old house sits in the corner, not really a house but a shed with a porch. Papaw built it years ago as a place to stay while they were building their house. Surrounding this shed are green stalks of dried jonquils. They always bloom in huge yellow bundles in the spring, but now, in the heat of summer, they are dried and bent.

Without turning I know that behind me, over the high bank of the pond, is a flat piece of land surrounded by trees. Through those trees I can walk to my parents' house. I like to dream of building my house on that land. It seems an ideal place sandwiched between my parents and my grandparents, the most important people in my life then.

The sun is no longer visible, yet its presence is still felt. The cicadas know the time of day and begin their calling to one another. I change positions and swing my line out to try another spot. After a day of fishing Papaw takes us up the road to the store before going home. We run in, our bare feet stirring up cool, dark dust and tracking in powdery prints on the cold concrete floor. The slam of the screen door behind us and the familiar smell of old things mingle with the taste of dust in our mouths. A coke, candy bar, or ice cream, we can't decide. Papaw sits down in one of the wooden rocking chairs and talks with the store owner, Mr. Rex, while we make our decisions. Afterward we pile back into the wagon and ride at a steady pace of twenty miles per hour, the wind blowing our dirty faces and melting our ice cream.

Now, instead of lighting a cigarette, Papaw fiddles with things in his pockets. He quit smoking last year, right after he turned seventy-one.

"I remember when Mr. Crabb came up to the house and asked if it would be all right if he took his boys over here fishing. I took them over and showed the younger one a spot and told him, 'If you cast there, you'll catch more than your brother.'" Papaw begins telling us the story while we are fishing.

"Later they came up to the house on the way out, and his dad held up a mess on a string. Then the young boy held up his string full. I said, 'Thank you,' and reached out to take them. That boy looked so shocked like I was going to keep them." Papaw laughs, remembering that day, and we smile at Papaw's laughter; he is feeling good.

On the other side of the pond, Aaron is pulling in a fish.

"You got one," Papaw calls.

Once it is out of the water, Aaron holds it up.

"Just a little one," Papaw says; "throw him back."

After three little ones for Aaron and one for me, Papaw is ready to go.

I want to stay and enjoy the day, but I know he will be getting tired, and Aaron has other plans. Breathing heavily, Papaw climbs in with his chair. The truck is loaded, and we start home. The road is bumpy, and the minnow water sloshes. Aaron gets out to open the gates as we come to them.

"I guess I should be more patient and try and take Steve over here sometime," Papaw says, referring to my ten-year-old cousin.

"I'll take him sometime, Papaw," Aaron answers. But I know what Papaw means. Papaw wants to take Steve like he took us when we were kids. Being the first grandchild, I got to spend a lot of time with Papaw, and many of the others did too, but that was twenty-four years ago. Papaw doesn't have that kind of energy anymore, or patience.

I turn to look at my papaw, his pale blue eyes fixed ahead on the road. He's probably wearing the same clothes he wore fifteen years ago. Since he quit smoking, he has begun to gain weight for the first time in his life, although he is still a very small man. Probably no taller than 5' 7", he and I share many features. I have the same narrow chin and sharpness of bones protruding through thin skin. With his idle hands shaking in his lap, his wrinkled face and bald head, he doesn't have the strength I remember.

How will the younger ones remember him? How sad that they won't share the same memories I have. Suddenly I am very glad he decided to come with us today.

When Aaron gets out to close the last gate, I look into the woods. In the side mirror I watch him latch the gate, and I feel the tears coming, so I lean against the wheel, taking a deep breath. I whisper to myself, "Don't cry, don't cry," and I watch Aaron walk to the truck.

Seasoned

WES ZEIGLER

Wes Zeigler teaches English and writing at Southwest Middle School in Little Rock. A teacher consultant with the Little Rock Writing Project at the University of Arkansas at Little Rock, he recently was honored with the publication of his poem "7-11" as part of the University of South Dakota Vermillion Literary project.

I am like the spring
a torrent of becoming
something else,
roots, trunk, bough,
bud, blossom, leaf
reaching out of the earth
year by year
farther, farther up
like a drowned man
after air.

I am beginning to know summer
the slow silence of metallic heat
the timeless click of grasshoppers
in a vacant lot.

Fall humbles me
with the ripeness

of its fruit
at the height
of its vigor
already beginning
to rot.

I eat a decaying apple
in a cold rain
in the gray doorway
of the hardhearted earth
and spit the seeds out
like hate.
A bad death
burns across the earth.
The living
are perpetually
restless,
there is no peace
no relief
from the fever of life
the awesome
burden of being
until we understand
life is too great a grief
to be borne long.

I am getting to know winter
to be a friend of the cold.

The Boy on the Memorial

JOHN HEUSTON

*Veteran newsman John Heuston, a fiery and
articulate defender of the Arkansas outdoors all
his life, played a major role in marshaling public
sentiment in support of the Buffalo National
River. Retired from Entergy in 1993, John continues to update conservationists through his editor-
ship of the Ozark Society newsletters "Pack and
Paddle" and "Paddle Trails." He is the institutional
memory of the major conservation battles of the
past fifty years: the Cache, the Buffalo, the
Mulberry, the Wilderness, clearcutting, Crooked
Creek, and now Bear Creek. But when asked to
provide one single memory, he chose to write a
new story, one he says he'd always wanted to tell:
a memorial to his young friend Warren Mallory
Johnston.*

"Somebody said you could answer a question for me,"
said the unknown voice on the phone. "My wife and I moved to
Arkansas recently, and we've been enjoying some family outings at
Buffalo National River. At a point overlooking the river at Buffalo
Point, there is a metal sign with a wonderful memorial to a little boy.
Who was this boy, Warren Mallory Johnston?"

I've had several phone calls like that one in recent years. So, I briefly told him the story. It's a story every person who draws strength and renewal from a sojourn in the Buffalo River Country needs to know.

Why? Because the tragic deaths of my little eight-year-old friend Warren and his mother, Mimi, in the late summer of 1964, set in motion a series of actions that played a key role in saving the Buffalo River country from being submerged beneath proposed Army Engineer "flood control" reservoirs at Gilbert and Lone Rock. Otherwise, there might not have been any "little corners of this earth put aside by nature to be discovered by and to bring joy to little boys" in the valley of the Buffalo. Here's why.

Warren was the son of H. Charles (Charley) Johnston Jr., a Little Rock businessman who had floated and fished the Buffalo River for many years and wanted to see the river and its unique environs saved from "dam-nation." As a youngster, Charley and his family had enjoyed vacation stays in the old cabins at Buffalo River State Park. He wanted Warren and his brother, David, to also be able to enjoy such outdoor experiences, and they did—fishing, swimming, and exploring all the hidden "hollers" that their father knew so well. During the time of Johnston's own boyhood adventures at the state park, many of the roads leading to it were unpaved and, as he puts it, "you had to REALLY want to go to Buffalo River State Park!" These adventures at the park had a lasting impression on him.

Johnston was also a friend of Ozark native Dr. Neil Compton of Bentonville, who formed the Ozark Society To Save The Buffalo River in May 1962 (a title later mercifully shortened to simply The Ozark Society). However, Compton soon realized it was a long drive from northwest Arkansas to the seat of political power at Little Rock, so Johnston was enlisted to represent the fledgling Ozark Society's operations in central Arkansas, especially when the legislature was in session. Johnston and his associates eventually organized what was to become the Society's first chapter outside of Fayetteville, now known as the Pulaski Chapter.

The formation of the Ozark Society proved to be an exciting and educational experience for many Arkansans and their children. A native of the Ozarks and an avid hiker and 4X4 Scout driver, Dr.

Compton regularly led us into remote hollows, abandoned pioneer settlements, and on hikes to caves and bluff shelters that the general public didn't know existed. Warren was one of the many youngsters who participated in these outings.

At that time, I had yet to experience parenthood—that full-time job for which you get no advance training. Keeping up with Warren was a challenge. He was a tousle-headed, rock-hopping tornado, with a question to ask about everything he encountered! In brief, he was a typical youngster.

On one Ozark Society outing, we were exploring the outskirts of the old zinc-mining town of Rush on the Buffalo River when we found an abandoned one-room school building, complete with school desks, blackboards, and chalk! Warren bounded from desk to desk with enthusiasm. The room looked as though the schoolchildren had just left one day and never returned! He was fascinated with this one-room school that was so much different from his own.

Warren could also paddle a canoe by himself and he loved to fish. Charley and I arrived at the Mulberry River one day only to find it too low for good floating. So we moved further downstream to one of the larger holes of water in search of smallmouth bass. It wasn't long before Warren had hooked one of these scrappy bronzed bombers, an experience he cherished. Talk about youthful joy! I know it strengthened my resolve that what few of our mountain streams we have left in the Mid-South should remain free-flowing so that in the future other youngsters could enjoy this type of incomparable river-fishing experience. Every child should have that opportunity.

The news of Warren's untimely death in what Dr. Compton correctly termed an "unspeakable tragedy" was a hard blow to our close-knit Ozark Society group. Details are not necessary. Our hearts went out to Charley. He dropped out of sight for a while, but returned in time to testify at the all-important second Army Corps of Engineers' public hearing on Gilbert Dam held at Marshall in 1964.

Fate moves in mysterious ways. Some time after Warren's death, while dining at the old dining hall at Buffalo River State Park, the site of many early Ozark Society gatherings, Johnston gazed out across the Buffalo River to see something he'd never seen before. Roads! To his amazement, he could see signs of new roads being bulldozed across the river through some of his favorite places, along with utility poles and other signs of pending development.

"What's going on over there, Delos?" Johnston asked veteran park superintendent Delos Dodd. "I understand some fellow is going to build a housing development and retirement place over there," Dodd replied. Johnston was amazed, and outraged. It had never occurred to any of us that the state did not own the land on the opposite side of the river from the park! Years ago when the state park had been established, the area was so remote that it probably wasn't considered necessary to protect the park's view shed.

This development scare underscored the need for National Park Service protection of the Buffalo River corridor to protect the river from being "loved to death" and eventually degraded by excessive development. This event was just a tiny example of the numerous commercial development schemes that were just waiting in the wings in the event the Buffalo National River effort failed!

The State Parks Commission, also dismayed and embarrassed by this turn of events, tried to raise the $30,000 required to buy the developer out, but fell short of the amount needed. Time was running out. Construction was poised to begin again.

That's when Charley Johnston stepped in.

His gift of $5,000, all of the insurance money from Warren Mallory's death, allowed the commission to purchase the land with the box canyon, the waterfalls, and the springs. After all, there are other little boys, and girls, that need places to explore.

All Johnston asked was that the state place a memorial there for his beloved son, the one you see there today, by the historic old dining hall, written in his own words.

Now consider this scenario: The Battle for the Buffalo River was far from a done deal in 1965. What would have happened if Charley Johnston had not bridged that financial gap for the state and this housing project would have been built as planned—with others sure to follow? The National Park Service had already made as many concessions as they were comfortable with for existing riverside developments that had been built long before the national river was considered (Ponca, Gilbert, Rush, for examples).

A modern housing project with no historic value plunked down in the middle of a proposed "national river" would have given the pro-dam forces a powerful argument that the river corridor was no longer special and worthy of preservation. It could have been the proverbial straw that broke the camel's back and caused the NPS to back away from national river status. Think about that.

The next time you pass by our little friend's memorial, put a flower at its base. He may well have saved the Queen of Ozark Rivers from destruction. So much more than just a name on a sheet of metal, Warren deserves a place in our hearts.

The text of the plaque: *There are little corners of this earth put aside by nature to be discovered by and to bring joy to little boys. The lands over which you look here, across this beautiful river, are such a corner; and the arrowheads to be found there, the tiny box canyon with its waterfall and the spring above, are set aside forever for all little boys in memory of another little boy who did discover freedom and joy here. . . .*

Warren Mallory Johnston

Backpacking with Bill

WATKINS FULK-GRAY

*Swinging a sturdy staff, young Watkins Fulk-Gray
has covered a lot of the Ozarks since he wrote this
account of backpacking in the winter of 1999 for
the Ozark Society newsletter, "Paddle Trails."
Watkins attends Pulaski Heights Middle School in
Little Rock.*

Going on a backpacking trip with Bill Steward is an
adventure. Always. On this trip, we started on a trail that used to be a
narrow country road. Before long we were off the trail and into the
Richland Creek Wilderness! Being only my third backpacking trip, I
did not know that much about Richland, but I do know that it is a
wonderful place.

After we had hiked a few miles, we had lunch at a spot that
resembled Pedestal Rocks, only a lot smaller. We later learned that it
was our campsite. After lunch, Benjamin (eleven), Libby (nine), and I
(ten) tried climbing the rocks. We only found one way up them, and
succeeded in worrying our parents, at least mine.

After we had finished lunch and finished climbing, we put up our
tents. To me, a slow process. Then, Bill called us around to meet in the
middle of our camp. This is always my favorite part of the trip: the
exploring of camp and what is around it. Actually we only explored
the creek bed of Richland, but that was enough to satisfy any couch
potato or nature freak. It was BEAUTIFUL! It was a long trip down
the hill to the creek, which was mostly dry, but it was worth it! When
we got to the creek bed, there were overhanging cliffs that shone in

the sunshine. There was a persimmon tree on the bank, and Catherine and I picked one because it was a low-hanging tree and we each got a sour mouth.

I got a little ahead of the group, so I sat on a rock. After a while I noticed all these little fossils inside the rock. They were everywhere on it. There were really neat ones that are like rectangles split down the middle with tiny teeth-like things. I even thought I could make out some real sharp teeth not connected to anything. That was really neat. As we got farther up the stream, the fossils got bigger and bigger. The biggest one looked like a twisted pasta noodle. The cliffs that were shining in the sun were just magnificent. We stopped to take a group picture by some falls. This is just one of the best places to be in October.

Finally when we found a big enough and clear enough puddle, we filled our water bags and moved up the hill. Now let me remind you, this hill is steeep. It was a hard climb, even with no backpacks (except for Bill, who was carrying the water); it was hard. I was ready to get back to the campsite.

Now for more detail about our camp. To the right of us were the rocks that looked like Pedestal Rocks. There were some big rock towers sticking up out of the ground—actually there was only one, but it was the most fun. I did not get all the way up because Catherine discovered my attempt, and so I got down.

Benjamin and I discovered a big hole or a small cave. There are too many places to be explored on those cliffs. At the bottom of the cliffs (they were not very big) there was a steep downhill which ended in a big basin where several hills met. To the left of us were some big rocks that as you will later find turn into small cliffs too. I do not know what was beyond the cliffs.

After we got back we started a fire and made preparations for dinner. For dinner we had stew, salad, bread, a hotdog (for me), and some'mores. To drink there was wine, water, and hot chocolate. It was all very good. You get tired real easily out there, so I went to bed early.

When I got up there was already a fire going. I am glad because it was cold. We ate Bill's famous bacon strips and very famous banana and apple pancakes. We had hot chocolate and coffee to drink. After everyone had finished, we took another hike along the big rocks on our left. The rocks got bigger and bigger as we went along. Bill had explored this before, so he was showing us "caves" that were holes in the rock. As soon as I said I had found a bigger cave in the cliffs to the right of us, a contest started: who could find the biggest cave? I guess we tied because he found more, but I found the deepest. My favorite that he found was one with about three or four stories; the bottom story had some couch-like rocks and open air so you could go in and out freely.

Once we got to our stopping point, we took some pictures and went back. Then we packed our backpacks, but before we left I had to show Bill my cave. It really was a cave. It went about twelve feet, then curved in another direction, but I did not have a flashlight so I could not go back there. In all, I found two because Benjamin and I both found one.

So then we had to leave a swell backpacking site that was home to my third backpacking trip.

New Water: Baker Creek

STEWART NOLAND

Stewart Noland, a Little Rock environmental engineer, has been a part of the paddling and conservation scene in Arkansas since he was a child growing up in Fayetteville. President of the Ozark Society, he serves as a leading advocate for preservation of Arkansas resources. An ardent whitewater enthusiast, his trip down Baker Creek described in a 1980 Ozark Society Bulletin *illustrates why.*

The paddling day began in a very typical way: up around six A.M., complete last-minute packing, a rendezvous to minimize the number of vehicles taken, and on the road by seven A.M. The destination this particular weekend was the Cossatot River, the whitewater gem of southwest Arkansas. The Cossatot watershed had been pummeled with rainfall the previous week with one reported flow level on Friday, May 16, of eight thousand cubic feet per second, a high level for the Cossatot, experienced only a handful of times each year. But the month was May, and with all of the foliage in full bloom we knew the river would be dropping fairly fast without additional rainfall.

Many of the paddlers that had congregated in Little Rock that morning eventually met at Golden's Store in Athens to top off their petrol tanks and buy last-minute provisions. Having passed over the Little Missouri River on Highway 84 on our way to Athens we had stopped to check its level. The Little Missouri had twelve inches of beautiful blue-green water passing over the old concrete slab below the newer bridge. This level provides a rambunctious run from Albert Pike campground down to the Highway 84 bridge as the Little Missouri carves its steep and narrow path out of the Ouachita Mountains.

Several of us were in a quandary over what to do, especially the open boaters. We didn't know whether to turn back and paddle the Little Mo at this entertaining level, or proceed to the Cossatot, knowing that it was high but not knowing how high. After an excessive amount of hemming and hawing, iffing and butting, and pebble kicking we rearranged a few boats, agreed upon a later meeting place and headed off in opposite directions. Our group's destination was the Highway 4 bridge, the take-out for the shut-ins run on the Cossatot. Just before reaching Highway 4 that morning we crossed Baker Creek, a tributary of the Cossatot, and quickly noticed that the flow in the creek was great enough to paddle it. We immediately decided to try our first run on Baker Creek.

The first time I had ever heard of or seen Baker Creek was in the fall of 1974 when for the first time, and very regrettably the last, I paddled the Cossatot from the Highway 4 bridge to Duckett Ford, a distance of about 4.5 miles. This lively portion of the Tot, as well as several more miles of stream bed, has been acutely changed by the construction of Gillham Reservoir and its resultant slackwaters.

The Highway 4 to Duckett Ford run was at one time the most popular portion of the Tot for open canoeists. It provided a challenge that boaters of yesteryear could meet without the need for a plastic boat and advanced paddling and safety techniques that allow boaters of today to traverse the more rugged upper portions of the Cossatot. The stretch was and would still remain an excellent intermediate skill level boat's delight, culminating in the tricky passages through the offset ledges of Duckett Ford Falls.

Approximately 1.5 miles downstream from Highway 4 the Cossatot turns due east. Before it resumes its southerly flow toward the Little River a large feeder intersects its course from the north carrying the waters of Harris Creek. The flow in the Cossatot increases significantly at this point, perhaps by a third. The mouth of the creek forms a picturesque rock-guarded fiord.

Many times rapids will appear just downstream from the conflu-ence of a major tributary. The influence of Harris Creek at this point on the Cossatot is no exception. Just downstream begins what was described in an early account of the Cossatot as Second Rapids, a fairly long rapid as I remember from my first cruise, that terminates in Tiny Falls, a three-foot ledge that required a diagonally navigated route. No matter, this section is now inundated by the backwaters of Gillham Reservoir.

A little over a mile up Harris Creek it forks. Looking upstream, the right-hand prong remains Harris Creek. The left-hand prong is Baker Creek. Besides a myriad of east-to-west and west-to-east fingerlings, Faulkner Branch is the only named freshet that feeds Baker Creek. The initial rivulets of Baker Creek spring from high atop Porter Mountain in southern Polk County and quickly tumble over one thou-sand vertical feet in eleven or so miles before intermingling with the blue waters of Harris Creek. During its journey Baker Creek passes near two small former settlements of local historical significance, Hartley and Baker Springs. Hartley is the name that has been assumed by a pumped storage reservoir project that has been proposed for the upper portion of the main stream of the Cossatot, the exact status of which I am uncertain. Baker Springs was at one time a resort com-munity that supported several families, one of whose members I recently had the opportunity to meet.

A good paddler and friend of mine from north Louisiana coerced two others of us into backpacking a short distance down Baker Creek this past January on a weekend when the temperature never reached 25° F. The purpose of the trip was to scout Baker Creek to determine whether or not it should be paddled, and if so how much water was required. As cold as it was though, what we were to see and later paddle was absolutely beautiful.

That morning, taking what is known as Ed Banks Road east for about 3.5 miles from where it crosses the Cossatot, we approached a low-water wooden bridge. Baker Creek passes inconspicuously under-neath the bridge. The rains of the previous week had piled rubbish atop the bridge, so we stopped to unload our boats on the west side of the bridge. In all, there were seven paddlers, four kayaks, and three open boats.

As Baker Creek passes under the wooden bridge, it turns and runs due east with the mountains for about a quarter mile. At this point the stream turns southward and cuts across a huge expanse of rock, abruptly exposing to us the first significant cascade encountered during Baker Creek's chase through a spectacular ravine. After leaving the bridge and coming to the end of its gauntlet, Baker Creek drops eighty feet with dispatch in slightly less than a mile. About the second thirteen of those eighty feet occurs at the first cascade in a distance of about thirty feet. The first drop in the falls is about three feet high. The second drop, offset several feet to the left of the first, is about ten feet high. Most of the paddlers dropped over the first ledge, grabbed a left-side eddy, peeled out, and dropped over the second to complete the run. As the water gushes over the second portion of the cascade, it drops headlong into a pool. As one of the plastic K-1's plunged into the pool, the paddler came to an abrupt halt, having nosed the end of his boat under a rock. The boat seemed suspended in air until the force of the water bent the boat in two places like an accordion. After a few suspenseful moments, both the boater and boat were able to work free. Although another K-1 had slipped through unscathed, the two remaining K-1 paddlers decided to carry this one.

After a short respite in the recovery pool below the first cascades, during which time the K-1 was converted from a musical instrument back to a boat, we continued our trip. During the next several hundred yards we scampered among boulders, eddy hopping between the more significant drops and rapids. Our group leap frogged through the canyon most of the way; one person scouting and showing the way while the others darted cautiously past. At one point a slightly broken rock wall extended completely across the creek in a half-moon shape. The water funneled over the seven-foot precipice into a turbulent bowl-shaped receiving pool before exiting between two rocks, giving one the sense of paddling into and out of a pothole, Arkansas style. Before exiting from the steep canyon we were carried past and over several more boulder gardens and drops, some ranging up to five feet high. We all agreed that at higher water this particular mile-long section would create quite a maelstrom.

Before we reached the take out at the Highway 4 bridge, we

encountered several other rapids including some river-wide hydraulics that the decked boaters enjoyed surfing. Baker Creek drops about 189 feet over its four-mile jaunt from the wooden bride to Highway 4. All in all, our first run down Baker Creek was a super paddling experience—one not soon to be forgotten.

If Only Life Could Be a Float down a River

SHARI WILLIAMS

Benton High School teacher Shari Williams wrote this poem as part of her participation in a summer writing institute for teachers, the Little Rock Writing Project, in 1998. She now co-directs the project, which is sponsored by the University of Arkansas at Little Rock.

Shoving off from the shore, the river
pulls us into its flow.
The early morning sun barely
peeks through the swaying tree branches
as a gentle wind pushes us forward.

The peace of the river has not yet
broken from the morning mist
that hovers at the surface
when a smallmouth bass
rises to catch its daily meal.

You grab your rod and cast a line
breaking the glassy surface of the water.
I take control of the canoe
maneuvering it nearer the feeding fish,
the two of us working in rhythm together.

Never in a hurry, we ease the boat
into a still pool where we
can pause for a moment of quiet.
Our reflections in the rippling water mingle
and dissolve as the canoe breaks the stillness.

Deciding to linger in the shade,
we drift to the river's edge
to cast a line into the underbrush
that has fallen in the water creating
a safe-haven for the underwater life.

Almost instantly, you feel a tug at the line
as a smallmouth takes the bait.
Fighting against the pull of the line,
it makes a strong run and
jumps breaking the surface of the water.

Flickers of sunlight dancing through
the branches of the tree-line shore
catch the glistening scales of the
struggling fish as it arches its back
trying to free itself from captive hooks.

At canoe's edge, you bend down
to give back its freedom as you
carefully place your fingers in its mouth
and loosen the hook's deadly grip
letting the fish swim back into the brush.

The contented smile on your face
is enough to give me a satisfied feeling,
knowing that I have shared a fleeting
moment of the pleasure that you find in
this dance between man and nature.

Of Luck and Stupidity

KIRK WASSON

*Kirk Wasson of North Little Rock works as an
IT consultant for Entergy Corporation. He is a
staunch defender of the wilderness ethic and environmental protection of Arkansas lands. "Of Luck
and Stupidity," Kirk's first publication, features his
own wilderness mentor, his dad, on a hunt back
in 1992.*

After I shot, I picked up my cup of coffee and slowly
took a sip. It was still hot and I wasn't the least bit nervous mainly
because I did not have time. I looked over to my right at Dad, and he
had this look on his face like "the boy done let his gun go off." After
all, I was just sitting there sipping coffee with my gun across my lap.
There was too long of a pause before he said, "Did you get him?"

 av av av

I really didn't think I would have time to hunt this year, especially
the opening morning. I had just started a new job and worked the last
two weekends. But there is something about a lot of stress that makes
a guy want to go screaming to the woods.

My hunting partner of forty-two years was always ready. We had
missed opening day the year before because of work on my part and a
bad back on Dad's, but with a little luck that would not happen this
time. Dad enjoys and knows the woods more than any other person I

have ever known and I love hunting with him. He has forgotten more about hunting and fishing than all the Gore-Tex-wearing, four-wheeler-driving, have-to-be-guided, equipment-poor, so-called hunters put together. He especially scoffs at those *Field & Stream* New York writers.

"Do you have any ammunition?" he asked. "I don't want to buy a whole box." I looked around and came up with seven 30.06 shells.

"That's three apiece and we can fight over the last one," I said, remembering how he shot up the woods a couple of years before. He did have a lot better chance this time. His buddy James Herrick had put a scope on his rifle and sighted it in for him. With poor hearing and failing eyesight, he needed all the help he could get.

"What time do you want me to pick you up?"

"About 6:30, that will get us there in time for sunrise."

I thought, "It breaks day at 6:30, but maybe he just don't want to get up so early."

Well, to be honest, I didn't either.

We drove out Highway 10 and onto the dirt road for the eight-mile drive over to Four Mile Mountain. I do not mind telling anyone that there are plenty of deer, turkey, and bear on Four Mile Mountain because they will never find it on a map. We name all our hills, valleys, and camping places to keep eavesdroppers from knowing where we hunt, fish, and camp. I had to put it in four-wheel drive for the last climb, thinking because of our late arrival there would surely be someone parked in our favorite spot at the end of the road. There wasn't. The next piece of luck was that we would have that end of the mountain to ourselves, late or not. We gently shut the doors and hiked to the top of the ridge. Easing out an old logging road, we saw a couple of old scrapes. We knew they would be there despite the fact that we had not done any preseason scouting. I had decided that we would stick together on this hunt but was about to change my mind after Dad kept walking and walking. As we passed a fresh scrape, I asked him how much further we were headed. He described a place past Black Snake Crossing (see!).

"Let's stop here, hunt for while, and then move on down?" I reluctantly asked. I knew he had a plan and hated to mess it up. I just wanted to sit in beautiful woods, and we were in the middle.

"OK," he said after a pause. "You sit down below me and I will rattle up a buck."

"Why don't I sit beside you over there," I said, looking for a large pine tree to settle under.

"That's fine," he said. He hates it when I make decisions (most of the time wrong) about where to hunt. He always knows the best spots, setups, angles, trails, times, techniques, and so on. BUT, I have learned a few things. That scrape just hours old made me want to stay there.

I found a good place where I could see a long ways and cover the old road and a dim trail going to the top. I sat down and heard a "chomp, chomp, chomp" in the woods behind me. "Just a squirrel leaving," I thought as I took off my daypack and got out my Thermos. I loaded my three bullets, keeping the last one in reserve, poured a cup of coffee, and nestled against the tree. Dad had made little noise tying his Tree Seat (patent stolen) to a tree and settling in. I heard him make several grunts on his call when in back of me came more "chomp, chomp, chomp." "That is one big squirrel," I was thinking.

I put my coffee down and looked over my left shoulder in time to see a six-point buck coming down the hill. I eased my gun up and slipped off the safety. I waited for a long fifteen seconds for him to walk out in a broadside view, and I let a bullet fly through his heart. Instant death. Nothing inhuman about that. I didn't even have time to think about the ramifications of killing a deer.

かか かか かか

"Yeah, he's down," I hollered back, getting up and finishing my coffee.

He took down his seat, packed his daypack, and slowly walked over. When he saw the deer he had a big smile and said, "You sure screwed up this hunt."

He laughed and I looked at my watch. We had been in the woods less than thirty minutes. He was proud of me and, I think, *slightly* sorry for the deer.

"You stupid son-of-a-gun," he said as I handed him a cup of coffee. I made sure he was looking at the deer.

"This just wasn't your day," he added, sitting down.

We talked of other hunts and kills, how luck and skill were usually disproportional (luck being about 90 percent), and now we had to leave the woods. I was sorry we had to end the hunt because Dad didn't get to try out his new scope.

"Well, you know what's next?" he said handing me the empty cup and reaching for his always-sharp knife. He carried my gun as I dragged the gutless deer with Dad's Tree Seat (another use they probably stole).

We checked the deer at Williams Junction (a real name), took it home, skinned it, and, for the first time, had someone else cut it up. I had to work the next day, and the effort wouldn't have been good for Dad's back.

Next time we wouldn't have to fight over the odd shell, and I decided that next time I would wait for the second or third deer before I messed up another hunt.

Nature's Draw

RYAN GRACE

Ryan Grace of Dallas is a senior at Hendrix College. He profiled painter William McNamara as his final project for his Literature and the Natural World class.

It was not long ago I took my first adventure into the Buffalo River region and experienced my first taste of the natural beauty of Arkansas. Coming from Texas to attend Hendrix College, I had never been able before to enjoy the beauty this state has to offer. Once I placed my canoe at the launching point in Boxley, I began my tour of the Natural State. I never knew why Arkansas was known as the Natural State until I took my little trip down the river, but I learned. Everywhere I looked I saw animals playing and sometimes coming within arm's reach. I remember distinctly canoeing past a water moccasin sitting on a stump only a few inches away from the canoe I was traveling in. This was a trip I would never forget. No matter how many books you read or pictures you see, there is a beauty in Arkansas that is more amazing than one could ever imagine.

I have had another unique opportunity to have my eyes opened to Arkansas's beauty because I became acquainted with one of the best-known artists in the state, William McNamara. William McNamara has taken to heart the idea of living out a true passion in his work. His move to the woodlands is a common trend among nature writers and artists. I wanted to know why.

Billy was born in Louisiana in a small town outside of New Orleans. Most of his spare time was spent drawing and painting. He found a talent early and has been painting ever since. After high school he attended a small school in Shreveport, Centenary College. Four years of schooling earned him a bachelor's degree, and he moved to New Mexico to earn a master's degree at New Mexico Highlands University. Earning those two degrees still did not bring him happiness. His love in life was painting. While in New Mexico, he found himself driving hours just to find an object to paint.

Billy—which is what everybody calls him—needed a place to call home, a place he could also call work. So after graduation he packed up and moved to Boxley, Arkansas. This was the perfect place for a nature painter. Beauty surrounded him on all sides. Here, he built his home with his own two hands and decided to make painting his living.

Billy always had a love for nature. Now he had moved to a place where he could become a part of his setting. He could step outside his door, sit down in a chair with his watercolors and canvas, and start painting. His paintings were his eyes, painting a beauty surrounding him that he had never seen in his lifetime. The trees were of wide variety, and the leaves turned spectacular colors in the fall, returning to a healthy green in the summer. The winter would bring a breathtaking snowfall that covered the forest floor and became the roof on top of trees. The Buffalo River, with its crystal clear presence, calmly flowed through the mountains, running over large rocks that had rolled down. The wildlife was in its natural habitat: birds, deer, fish, coyotes, and raccoons. This was simply a place that had all the aspects of nature.

One of William McNamara's most famous paintings is the snow-covered Whitaker Point. Once he decided on this setting, he photographed the object to capture the true images he visualized. Obviously the snow melts and does not remain for long. In a case where he painted the running water of the Buffalo, Billy just took his art materials and began painting. Perfection cannot be rushed, he says, and having this much time for just one painting gives him a chance to view every detail possible. If you have never seen one of his works, you will find the painting to be very life-like, a type of painting that has caught the eyes of many art lovers, especially here in Arkansas.

I have had the chance to visit his house and the numerous places he has chosen to paint. They were some of the most beautiful places I have ever seen, miles away from any other neighbor or corner store. The noises I heard were noises you would never hear in the crowded streets of a city, like my home in Dallas. Birds were the music of the outside, while the tune of the tiny spring running under his one-room house surrounded me inside. It was amazing to see the simplicity of his life, for the man did not have to wake up for any other reason but to paint.

I found it easy to connect with his passion, although my passion is of a different kind. Our passion helps us appreciate our everyday encounters. William McNamara has lived out his passion and the life he has dreamed of ever since he was a little kid growing up in southern Louisiana. In finding a passion and choosing to pursue it, he lives life to the fullest, enjoying what nature has to offer. I was reminded that we too could be like Billy, but we often find ourselves living for that extra dollar. Everybody has the opportunity to do something they love; those who act on it are the ones who live life to the fullest.

An Ozark Crusader Leads On

GEORGE OXFORD MILLER

*From his home in New Jersey, George Oxford
Miller roams the world looking for subjects of
interest to travelers, many of which are seen
locally in* Active Years *magazine. This profile of
Dr. Neil Compton comes from George's years
documenting the beauty of Arkansas, featured
in his book* The Ozarks: The People, the
Mountains . . . the Magic, *published in 1996.*

I had thought I would not have any trouble keeping up with an
eighty-one-year-old man until I went hiking with Dr. Neil Compton.
About twenty hikers from the Ozark Society follow Neil down an old
wagon road, across a narrow ridge top, and out onto Point Peter, a
twenty-one-hundred-foot mountain overlooking the meandering
Buffalo River. The view carries you all the way to Missouri. One thousand feet below, rows of sheer limestone bluffs rise out of the Buffalo,
as the channel cuts its way toward the horizon. The scalloped ridge
line of the Boston Mountains frames the wooded valley against the
sky. On this winter day, ghostly splashes of white blooming service-
berry color the gray leafless slopes.

"Can you imagine this valley being a flat sea bottom?" Neil asks the
group. "Millions of years ago, the Ozarkian Sea covered everything.
Upheavals raised the land three times—not a whole lot compared to

other mountain ranges, but enough for rivers to carve into the bedrock. This beautiful valley was formed by the hand of nature."

And preserved in large part by the hand of the man standing before us. Without the efforts of Dr. Compton and the Ozark Society, which he founded in 1962, this inspiring scene would once again be covered by a sea of water. During the decade-long bitter struggle against the dam builders, the society confronted the most powerful political and economic forces in both the state and the nation.

"Everyone thought we were crazy," Neil says as we look across the valley. "The Corps of Engineers had been trying to dam the Buffalo since the early fifties; the state's most powerful congressional representatives wanted the pork-barrel project; and businessmen from Marshall, Arkansas, formed an association to aggressively lobby for the dam."

A classic David and Goliath struggle was shaping up when the Ozark Society stepped into the foray. In the heat of the struggle, Dr. Compton was physically threatened by an angry opponent as he spoke at a town meeting in Marshall, and he was shot at as he canoed the Buffalo with his daughter. On another occasion, extremists felled eighteen large trees across dangerous rapids to block an Ozark Society float trip. Neil also suffered from the stress and frustrations of dealing with Washington politics, as he and others in the Ozark Society tried to swing politicians to the conservationist side.

The Ozark Society grew from a few hundred members to three thousand, and its voice amplified from a whisper to a shout that could not be ignored. The society outlasted two presidents, three governors, and one House member, but the group tirelessly carried on the fight. Finally, on March 1, 1972, President Nixon signed the legislation sent up by Congress that freed the Buffalo River forever from the grips of the dam builders and created the nation's first national river. The city of Marshall now greets travelers with a canoe-shaped sign that proclaims the city as the "Gateway to the Buffalo."

So the view of the broad valley dissected by the free-flowing Buffalo is particularly satisfying for Neil Compton. "It's a special feeling to look at the river and remember all the effort that went into saving it. People thought we were trying the impossible. The Buffalo is a national treasure that we saved for future generations to enjoy. . . . I hope what we accomplished can serve as an example to other groups."

Neil did not set out to be a crusader; he just wanted to preserve the wonders of nature he had come to love in his native Ozarks. Born in 1912, he grew up on Coon Creek in Benton County. He studied zoology and geology as an undergraduate in Fayetteville, and earned his doctorate in medicine from the University of Arkansas [School of Medicine] in Little Rock.

"I didn't really start exploring the Ozarks until I returned from World War II," he recounts. "As the Washington County health officer, I learned from my patients about the natural wonders hidden away in the mountains. I took drive-abouts with my family and explored and photographed what we discovered."

Neil has never stopped exploring the land he loves. He still leads monthly outings for the Ozark Society to some of his favorite places in remote areas of the mountains. His personal experience and historical perspective make the trips far more than just a day hike or canoe ride. He reminisces about his youth in these mountains and entertains with folktales. His knowledge about nature and the people of the Ozarks runs as freely as the river he helped save.

After visiting Point Peter, we head south on Highway 27. "People always talk about scenic Highway 7, but this road is prettier," he says as we wind through a narrow valley. "The Ozarks may not be as spectacular as Yosemite or Yellowstone, but . . . the forces that shaped the planet are evident in the hills and valleys. The Earth isn't frozen in death like the moon or Mars. The surface is changing all the time. . . . We can feel in our hearts that what we see here is the result of tremendous forces at work."

Neil champions the beauty of the Ozarks and crusades to save the sensitive mountain and river ecology at every chance. He finds willing ears among the seven chapters of the Ozark Society, which is established in four states. But one particular area of the wilderness continues to monopolize his efforts. The Buffalo River is just too close to his heart. "I'd like to see the entire watershed of the Buffalo . . . protected. Stopping the dams isn't enough if the river becomes too polluted for human contact."

His point is well made. According to the Arkansas Department of Pollution Control and Ecology, many streams in northwestern Arkansas periodically fail the water quality standards for "primary contact recreation," or swimming and walking, mainly due to bacterial contamination from chicken farm and pasture runoff. The department's list regularly includes the most scenic streams in the Ozarks.

So, the work continues. Through the efforts of the Ozark Society and other conservation groups, four wilderness areas have been established on the upper and lower Buffalo to protect the creeks that flow into the river. Ten other wilderness areas preserve pristine portions of the Ozark and Mark Twain National Forests. Additionally, the Ozark National Scenic Riverways preserves 134 miles of the spring-fed Current and Jacks Fork Rivers in Missouri. Two other legislative designations, the federal "wild and scenic" and the state "extraordinary resource," protect a number of smaller streams in the Ozarks from damming, in-stream gravel mining, and other adverse development.

After eight decades of living in the Ozarks, Neil Compton is outspoken about saving his homeland. "Too many government programs are subsidizing the urbanization of the countryside," he says. "In the sixties and seventies, we had a chance to reverse some of the environmental damage. A lot of farmland was going back to nature. Then the government put power lines across the mountains and paved all the dirt roads so people could move back into areas that never should have been cleared."

Neil motions as we drive past several hundred acres of steep rolling hills recently bulldozed clean and the trees piled up to burn. "Anything overdone is an evil, and we are a nation of overdoers. We overdo paving roads, building dams, and raising chicken and cattle in an area nature meant to be a forest. The government subsidizes farmers with tax write-offs to turn the forest into a monoculture of fescue grass. Bulldozers cause more destruction than clear-cutting ever did in the national forests. What we are seeing is the Ozarkian desert being formed by human folly."

I ask Dr. Compton what he would like to see happen by the year 2000. "I'd like to see the return of the forest cover to the Ozark Mountains. The Ozarks once were the best source of hardwoods in the world, especially the oaks, hickories, and walnuts in the White River Valley. But the Forest Service isn't replanting hardwoods. The only ones planting walnuts are the squirrels."

Neil retired as a physician in 1978, but his years of service have never slowed. His long list of awards include an honorary doctorate in law from his Fayetteville alma mater, the University of Arkansas, and numerous community service and conservation awards. President Bush presented him with the Teddy Roosevelt Conservation Award in 1990. Last fall, the Arkansas Library Association presented him with the Arkansiana Award for his two books on the Ozarks.

The next day, Neil leads the group on a four-mile hike down an unmarked, unnamed trail to a spectacular rock formation known to locals as Buzzard's Roost. At age eighty-one, he shows no signs of slowing down. As members of the Ozark Society attest, keeping pace with the good doctor, on the trail or in battling for the environment, is not an easy task.

(*Ed. Note: Dr. Neil Compton died in 1999, spending his last weekend on this earth hiking in his beloved Ozark Mountains.*)

PART THREE

At the River

Life in the Modern Age

All Arkansans are acutely aware of the value of our natural heritage. Our fathers and our forefathers left us with a deep love for the land, a love that springs from spiritual uplift that one experiences when walking through an unspoiled place and marveling at the examples of God's work; a work that is so abiding that one may feel its comfort in merely knowing that such places are there.

To those of us who must live and work within the confines of concrete and steel marking man's handiwork, such places are essential. We need to visit them from time to time hunting, fishing, camping, hiking, canoeing, to walk beside a clear stream or just to sit under a tree to seek the solitude of these places, to feel a release of tension and to reaffirm our sense of well-being.

. . . I hope that these societal needs for places of solitude do not become critical at the same time that the last of these unspoiled places disappears.

—BOB JAMES
Congressional Wilderness Hearing Testimony
1984

At the River with an Old Friend

KANE WEBB

This piece by Arkansas Democrat-Gazette *editorial writer Kane Webb appeared as an "Editorial Notebook" in March 2001.*

The everydayness of this particular Monday morning had overcome even the most sincere attempts to be productive. Not only that, but word came from the Capitol that the Ledge may be in session for another four weeks, Ellen was still captive at the zoo, the Clintons were still in the headlines, and not even filling out the NCAA tournament bracket could keep you indoors. You had it bad.

So you self-prescribe a reliable remedy: a few passages of Walter Percy, the doctor turned writer turned legend, and a drive down to the river. Just to see if it felt any different there.

You weren't the only ones with this great but less than novel idea. A half dozen cars were parked at various angles, all aimed at the therapeutic undulations of the Arkansas River. No matter how many times you go down to th' river, your reaction is always the same: How lucky are *we* to have *this!*

The folks in the other cars are eating lunch or listening to the radio (the voice of Pat Lynch provides the white noise) or just sitting. And looking. And thinking. Or not.

And as Monday morning muddles sluggishly into afternoon, things begin to look different. Focus returns. Stress subsides. The mental fog lifts.

Still, it takes fifteen minutes of staring at the water before you notice the tree directly ahead—not five feet from the front bumper.

It is not much of a tree. It is old and broken, and its branches are so withered and mauled by the elements that you can't tell what kind of tree it is. Or was. The bark has split to reveal a gaping wound in the trunk. The limbs, though bare and brittle, are raised toward the sky as if to ask, "Why me?"

In the background, behind this dead husk, is the perpetual motion of the river. *Life after death,* you mutter in a prosaic attempt at the profound. Luckily, no one hears you.

Walker Percy did it better:

> I wonder if any writer has ever recorded the observation that most time passes and most events occur without notable significance. I am sitting here looking out the window at a tree and wondering why it is that, though it is a splendid tree, it is not of much account. It is no good to me. Is it the nature of the human condition or the nature of the age that things of value are devalued? I venture to say that most people most of the time experience the same four-o'clock-in-the-afternoon devaluation. But I have noticed an interesting thing. If such a person, a person like me feeling lapsed at four o'clock in the afternoon, should begin reading a novel about a person feeling lapsed at four o'clock in the afternoon, a strange thing happens. Things increase in value. Possibilities open. This may be the main function of art in this peculiar age: to reverse the devaluation. What the artist or writer does is not depict a beautiful tree—this only depresses you more than ever—no, he depicts the commonplaceness of an everyday tree. Depicting the commonplace allows the reader to penetrate the commonplace. The only other ways the husk of the commonplace can be penetrated is through the occurrence of natural disasters or the imminence of one's own death. These measures are not readily available on ordinary afternoons.

To which anyone who has been in peril, or who has just got fatal news, or who watched someone die, might respond: Oh yeah? There are few things less ordinary, as Walker Percy knew, than the ordinary observed well.

Who's to say Walker Percy's thought could rival even the fellow's in the red Chevy truck twenty-five yards away? We live in our own cocoon, and it seems only the courageous or the crazy ever come out. The rest of us sit and watch the water.

At this point, a one-o'clock-in-the-afternoon devaluation, it occurs that your own tree down by the river isn't nearly so dead as you'd been all morning. If nothing else, it has provided a few minutes with nature and Walker Percy, who is still something of a force of nature himself. An ordinary afternoon has changed into a memorable one. The malaise has been shattered by becoming aware of it.

Not one to let an opportunity for symbolism get away, no matter how forced, you climb out of the car and approach the tree, looking for signs of life—a bud or a new branch or sap or something.

Nothing.

The tree is dead.

But the river is still flowing. And you hear Walker Percy still talking.

In a minute, you'll go.

In a minute.

River Travel

LOUISE BARDEN

*Louise Barden, a freelance writer in Charlotte,
North Carolina, penned this poem about a Buffalo
River trip she had made in 1965 before the Buffalo
was designated a national river. "River Travel" first
appeared in the* Chattahoochee Review *and is
included in Louise's chapbook "Tea Leaves."*

The summer after we married
when our jobs disappeared and left us
with no place to live for weeks
we loaded bread and dried beef
in your dad's dented canoe
and headed down the wild part
of the Buffalo even though the season
was wrong and the water low.

With days feathered out before us
we drifted like leaves through July heat,
empty pastures and woods, stopping
at each curve to crack open the bindings
of your new guides to wildlife, add discoveries
to your list. Fat-lipped Monkeyflowers,
Mimulus alatus. Vervain, verbena stricta.
Snowy egrets in the shallows.
A pair of ruby-throated hummingbirds,

he leading, she following. At one sharp bend,
we floated in the shadows of a limestone wall
eating peanut butter sandwiches,
then scrambled up to look for caves.
Farther on it was Wild Senna,
False Pimpernel, a giant bullfrog.
Now and then a cabin on the bank.

Evenings we camped on gravel bars,
stirred soup and rice over driftwood flames,
watched stars pierce velvet,
and crouched beside black water scrubbing smoke
from a Boy Scout mess kit. Cicadas rattled
above a whisper of cars crossing distant bridges.
After a row of nights spent on river-polished rocks,
the evening we lay on sand felt soft.

Years later I still see mornings opening
like phlox on the banks, sometimes feel
sun loosen my shoulders, knotted
with pulling a paddle over and over.
I remember how often the clear stream spread out,
leaving us within inches of the bottom,
how when the river wouldn't carry us
to the next pool, we stepped
into the brief shock of cold and walked.

Gates and Fences

LISA MONGNO

*A former small-town reporter, Lisa Mongno now
teaches writing at the University of Central
Arkansas, where she also co-directs the Central
Arkansas Writing Project. She has won the
Alma K. Daugherty Award for her poetry. This
piece was written in the spring of 2001.*

A fencepost. A bird of prey perched on its top, silently watching acres of land gone fallow, looking for a stir in the grass, a field mouse, a rabbit. Our white jeep whizzes by in the delta dusk, sweat gathering among the concave areas of our heat-ridden bodies. Gnats coat the windshield as air whips around my husband and me. Fifty miles an hour down an old country road. Through squinted eyes, I watch for the mice who dart back into the underbrush, scurrying to unseen burrows, leaving small clouds in their wake. The smell of the lake diminishes as dust fills the air.

As stars begin to pepper the sky, I wish we would pull over, quiet ourselves and the engine. I wish my ears could capture once again the sweet, rhythmic sound of the cicadas. How many nights they lulled me to sleep on the farm, their collective voice ambient even through a closed bedroom window. Perhaps they would transport me to a more simple time, when frogs in the swimming pool and raccoons in the sweet, molasses-laced grain were the topics of conversation around my parents' dinner table, when my brother and I squabbled and bickered like normal children do.

The food was always simple. A meat, usually chicken. A tuber, often a baked potato. Green vegetable. Dessert, typically Jell-O. My favorite was orange, with canned tangerines on top, some cream swimming in tiny eddies in its tidal pools. My mother made an art of economy while raising us. Our diets seemed as stable and practical as the grain in the barn: life-sustaining. As predictable as the way that night fell over the land, which was especially appreciable from the kitchen window. The farmhouse, you see, was itself perched on a hill, tucked against its basin, a pragmatic defense against floods and tornados.

And there were plenty of both: They seemed to rage upon our land in consort; first the ominous thunderstorm, rolling in from the flat, western land, with its winds and, too often, a funnel cloud. The next day, the rain would often continue for hours; first, the creek bed would fill, and slowly, we would watch the water creep onto and then up the road. Most times, it stopped at a big oak, the one that signaled the second of three bends in the long gravel drive: one-quarter mile of darkness that I ran up many nights when I had stayed out too late playing as I chased my older brother's shadowy silhouette.

The playing was the usual childhood sport, if considered from the early part of the twentieth century. As far as my ten-year-old assessment went, time did not touch this land. Jumping from hay bale to hay bale. Running from the notorious Black Angus cow. Climbing the spindly arms of trees. Exploring the creek bed. Hunting for box turtles, occasionally finding a snapping one. Throwing flip-flops in the pond, fishing them out with a dime-store rod and reel. Trying to keep up with my brother, to convince him to acquiesce to a ride on his mini-bike, to show him how to ride a horse. I was always the horsewoman, while he owned manufactured items: BB guns, knives (big ones, not like my handy Swiss Army knife that stayed scrunched in my dirty jeans pocket each time I left the house), motorcycles, and, later, cars. Well, more cars, more than the 1930s pickup he somehow convinced my father to tow back from California when we moved to the farm. My father always indulged him in his loves.

It was 1976. My father was thirty-seven, and just retiring from twenty years of military service. A Brooklyn boy raised in the Italian section of the city, he had seen enough of city life, and decided to buy this sixty-acre patch of land with his own brother in 1963. They divided the property into two tracks, and my father had worked two jobs in California, each month making the payment for his portion of the land and the Civil War–era house that stood upon it. My grandmother, meanwhile, lived on the farm in one of the two houses while we traveled the world. As the days approached his retirement, he filled my head with stories of the animals I could have there, the guinea hens. How I could raise them and harvest eggs. How our Great Dane, who always seemed somewhat cramped in suburban "Cali," would run free. As he described the rock-lined road we'd live on, I pictured European cobblestone streets. He described the barn, too, how many cattle it could house, the colors of the Hereford cows that my family kept there now. I had been many places in my short, air force–centered life. I had lived on a tropical island and a British isle. I had seen the Black Hills of South Dakota, and Spain (I remembered the beaches of Spain). But I had never really seen a farm. My young mind was active with live-action footage of what my new life would be like. I anticipated the move.

As our loaded-to-the-ceiling-it-took-three-days-to-fill U-Haul finally rumbled up the long drive of our farm, my eyes were wide. It was February and cold. Tall, bare-branched trees encroached on us as we slowed to negotiate the pothole-filled drive. These were not cobblestones! I was frankly scared as darkness covered us. I listened intently during the night as the house slept. The next morning, I walked slowly to my grandmother's picture window to survey my new home. My quaint, English-village imaginings did not prepare me for what I saw: Land stretched before me as if it were alive. The other house, obscured from this view, was not visible. No structures were visible. No humans. No cars. Only land and, eventually (I didn't know how many city blocks away), trees. Trees. Tall trees. I looked out at it for a long time. My grandmother came to stand behind me, told me sometimes deer walked across the fields.

I started school. A girl at lunch asked me if I was a redneck. I was not prepared to respond, went home and asked my father what a redneck was and if I was one. He laughed. I didn't know what was funny. He laughed again, said maybe I should tell them that I was, but that I really wasn't. And they might be able to tell by the way I spoke. I was scared to speak.

Winter rolled into spring, and the farm became a place I explored. The old Civil War house, which a previous tenant had used as a chicken coop, had to be torn down. My father began construction on the new house. He had an architect draw up the plans, and then he put it together, piece by piece. My brother and he rolled out the insulation in the attic, working together for a day. My mother took pictures of the process, made tea for us all at my grandmother's house, about fifty yards away. Brought it over on a little tea tray. I explored. Dug holes and started fires in them. Wrapped potatoes in tinfoil and baked them in the earth. Asked my parents about the different types of trees. Bugged my father for a pony.

We moved into the house, and years folded in to one another. I showed horses with my dad, and my brother graduated from high school, joined the navy. Electronics technician. I should have known. He married his high school girlfriend, and my parents and I drove to Texas to visit them when they had a baby girl, Sophia. I was fifteen, and no one listened to a thing I said. I sat in the backseat of the red Chrysler and complained that I would throw up from the smell. The baby's mother yelled at me that there was nothing in her diaper, I was a spoiled brat. I decided she had a bad temper.

A day later, when we stopped for gas, my brother found the bait-shrimp he and my father had forgotten about in the trunk. Everyone nearly choked on its noxious odor as we quickly drove away, leaving the reeking plastic bag in the gas station trash. There are certain smells I associate with people I have known. My high school boyfriend smelled like cheese sandwiches. My brother, his smells were rotting bait and alcohol.

By the next summer, mother and child were living with my parents and me. My brother's marriage was failing. My parents helped her buy a trailer down the road, and she worked the morning shift at the local fast-food restaurant, came home by early afternoon smelling of grease to pick up Sophia. My mother had Sophia all day, five days a week. We sat out in the hot summer sun by the black walnut trees in my parents' front yard. The child gnawed on the bill of my leather cap, giggled, played in the blue plastic pool my parents bought for her. In the fall, she and I walked the land, collecting leaves of all shapes and colors. We took pictures and went to the circus and she giggled as the wind whipped through her crazily curly hair.

ᘯ ᘯ ᘯ

And that is where I want this story to end. A happy baby. My parents, newly doting grandparents. A marriage that might mend. A giant gentle white space, for the rest of our story.

That's where I want to pull the Jeep over and listen to the rhythm of the bugs. To remember my childhood, a gift that my parents centered their lives around. To think of shaggy Shetland ponies, horse shows, and pet frogs. The names of trees, they comfort me. What follows—sometimes I tell myself it is not worth remembering: that they finally divorced. That my brother remarried. That he gained custody of Sophia, and she became a shadow in a window to both my parents and me.

But there it is, every time I walk to my mother's kitchen window, rest my hands on her hands on her sink, and look out. The land is scarred by fences. Fences and gates. The five acres my father helped my brother buy is fenced off, separate from the rest of the land. I remember the day we watched him digging the postholes: he, his new wife, and their assembled children. How they didn't look up toward the house on the hill. They must have felt our eyes upon them. Did his angry words toward my father fuel him that day? " I'll shoot your horses," he had said, "if they come anywhere near my fence. It's my fence on my land, five feet in from my property line. You build your own damn fence."

When they finished working, my father came out on his tractor, the one he'd had for twenty years. He built his own fence, ten feet away from my brother's so that my father's horses couldn't fight with the new gelding that grazed in the five acres. Male horses will fight, gelded or not.

I remember my father watching from the window, shaking his head. "I told that boy if he bought a mare . . ." His words trail off. He walks into the living room to watch television. Months later, when my brother's stepdaughter has lost interest in the horse, and riding in circles around the five acres, my father begins to feed it, sneaking over when no one is home. They must know, though, because the horse stands at the gate and whinnies at my father as he works outside. In a few short years, they sell the horse. The daughter needs the money for a car, a new Pontiac. She is not home when the people arrive to take him away, but my mother watches his white rump disappear as the trailer jolts down the driveway, which is now filled with more potholes than ever before, since my brother won't help pay for gravel. It must be three years since my parents and brother have spoken, longer for my brother and me.

This May, my niece Sophia, the one who stayed silently in that house for years, waving at my mother through her bedroom window as my mother walked her dog on a leash, is getting married. She wanted to have the wedding out on the farm, in front of my parents' house, on the hill, looking out over the fields, the fences, and gates. She thought better of it after her father said he would not attend the wedding unless she apologized to the stepmother she'd filed a police report against for battery. "No."

She's moved the ceremony to a wedding chapel in town. The guests will sit in white plastic chairs under fluorescent lights. I wonder if the day will be sunny. I feel too old to be her bridesmaid, but I offer to get a photographer for the wedding my parents are paying for. I want her to have a record of this day, her day. I wish the photographs could replace years of fragmented memories, of things she doesn't share. If I could, I would give her the way I remember the farm: the vision I have of her father as a boy, of her grandfather as a vibrant, thirty-seven-year-old man building a home for his family on the land that he loves. I would give her my stylized, view-finder-like memories of this place.

The years have rolled over me, season after season I have looked out of that kitchen window. I have watched the fields, seen the fences and gates erected. Like a stone in a river, I have moved little. I bought an old house surrounded by tall oaks in a city not far from my parents' farm. Some nights I stop by on my way home from work, and we talk about the fat squirrels that are in the horse feed, about trapping the raccoon in my attic to free it on the farm. My brother's old chair is there, empty. If I talk about him and his family, I say, "The people next door."

My friends from high school, the ones born here, many of them have moved far away. They ask, when they come back once a year from the Meccas of the south, places like Houston and Dallas, "Are you going to stay in Arkansas?" They look at me incomprehendingly, mystified. But on summer nights, when my husband and I drive out in the country, I feel it, a stirring, this love of the land, deep in the center of my body. And I know, I know how the land can claim you, can make a place for you as infinite as the human heart.

My Father's Dream

JON LOONEY

Jon Looney is an Arkansas native now working for AARP in Colorado. In addition to many articles on the students of artist Thomas Hart Benton, he has published three books of verse but says his favorite, which remains unpublished, is called Thirteen Ways of Looking at Mt. Olive, Arkansas. *"My Father's Dream" first appeared in* Headwaters *in 1978.*

Over there
where that barn
extends the hillside
to the sky
was
a stand of hickory.
And that goat-
shed
shares memory
with oaks
that once shaded
him there
as his forehead
and chainsaw cooled.

This cleared
forty
was woods
till
afternoons and Saturdays,
mounting up
like beads
of perspiration
on my family's faces,
cut them down.
Rick upon cord.

And those two
ponds,
not natural.
Dozer.
Saved what
might have been
otherwise
lost.
But runoff pooled
into surplus
(and prospective fishing),
reserved to serve again
during drought.

And here
where
you are standing
that is where
my father will build
a big picture
window
on the west
looking out
over
this last wooded slope.

Old and new
in him join
on this farm:
all over
these hills are
the insides
of my father's head.

Why We Hunt

JIM SPENCER

Jim Spencer of the Arkansas Game and Fish Commission, assistant editor of Arkansas Wildlife *magazine, goes on the offensive in this essay written in 1998.*

In today's cyberspace society, hunting seems as obsolete as the buggy whip. Our jungle is asphalt, not cellulose. Some 97 percent of Americans live in cities. The average citizen is as far removed from the natural world as from the North Pole.

Even so, many of us still embrace the hunt. Now that large predators are mostly gone, hunters assume the role of top-of-the-food-chain animals such as the mountain lion, bear, and wolf. Sometimes we use that as an excuse. We tell our critics, and ourselves, we're keeping nature in balance. We are, but that's not the whole truth. Nature doesn't need us to play that role. Nature keeps her own balance, more ruthlessly and with greater population swings than wildlife managers do.

The truth is, we hunt because the hunting instinct is in our DNA. We can't and shouldn't deny that or try to change it. Hunting took us from the four-limbed gait of our ancestors to an erect, bipedal posture. Hunting rotated our eyes to the front and gave us binocular vision, the better to see our fleeing prey. Hunting forced us to perfect our opposable thumbs, to better hold our clubs and spears. Hunting enabled us to prosper in hostile landscapes—the Arctic, tropical rainforests, deserts. Man is a hunter, period—always has been, always will be.

"The hope is sometimes expressed that all these instincts will be outgrown," wrote Aldo Leopold, the father of modern wildlife management. "This attitude seems to overlook the fact that the resulting vacuum will fill up with something, and not necessarily something better. It somehow overlooks the biological basis of human nature. We can refine our manner of exercising the hunting instinct, but we shall do well to persist as a species at the end of the time it would take to outgrow it."

In other words, man is going to hunt. He may not hunt animals, but he will hunt something. Michael Jordan hunts; he's king of the heap when it comes to sponsorships and good basketball. Jordan has refined his "manner of exercising the hunting instinct," but he's a hunter, make no mistake. Mark McGwire and Sammy Sosa are hunters, too, as they chase after Roger Maris's homerun record. And don't tell me Bill Gates isn't a hunter, though he may never have owned a firearm in his life. He's one of this century's best hunters; he'd have made a good mountain man.

Get the idea? You don't need a gun to be a hunter. All you need is the instinct, and we all have it. Show me the most rabid animal-rights fanatic in the history of Western civilization, and I'll show you a hunter.

Look in the mirror; you'll see a hunter there. You hunt for a low golf score, maybe, or a faster time in the next 10-K race. Or perhaps you do your hunting in the workplace, like Bill Gates. "Bringing home the bacon" isn't just an idle term, you know. We all hunt for a spot at the top of our personal food chain; some are more successful than others, but we all hunt for it. Maybe, like me, you hunt the old-fashioned way, with a gun and a raggedy set of camo. I don't need Freudian substitutions; I'm just a hunter, in the old, original, outdated, politically incorrect way. I don't apologize for it. Matter of fact, I'm proud of it.

The Fancy of the Ouachita Trail

LINDSEY THOMSEN

Lindsey Thomsen was a student in the University of Arkansas at Little Rock in spring 2001 when she wrote this piece for Dr. Andrea Herrmann's advanced expository writing class. Lindsey recently graduated from UALR with a degree in Professional and Technical Writing.

I loathe running on pavement. Not only is it hard on my body, but I find it monotonous. My saving grace is finding the trails scattered around Little Rock, like those in Alsopp Park or at Pinnacle Mountain, but I find my best solace on the Ouachita Trail. I can take a twenty-minute drive from my house and get into the woods. There, I feel far away from the bustle of the city and my life and have the opportunity to process my thoughts and discover my feelings.

Beginning at the Visitor's Center at Pinnacle Mountain State Park, the Ouachita Trail weaves for 236 miles across the western half of Arkansas into Oklahoma ending at Talimena State Park. I would love to backpack the whole thing one day, but at least three times a week, I frequent the first six miles, giving me about an hour's escape, depending on how strong I feel and how fast I run or hike.

I embark on my running meditation late afternoon on an early spring day. The first section is the steepest; it leads me practically straight down a bluff, offering my legs and spirit a hasty warm-up. The slope eases at an intersection with the access road to a launching ramp on a backwater cove of the Arkansas River, and I begin to pick up speed. Passing boulders on my left, I enter a rock garden that focuses my attention on my feet. Here, the trail cuts into the hillside swerving around and up, finally dropping me at a sometimes bubbling, sometimes stagnant brook.

I usually see more animals than people on the trail, but I always remember passing photographers or fellow runners and hikers near that watering hole. Most people stop to offer comments about the weather or a basic hello. However, the Sunday after St. Patrick's Day, about a month ago, I came upon a father with his daughter apparently searching for something in the woods. The sandy blond-haired blue-eyed toddler innocently presented a gold sack filled with chocolate gold coins to me as her father cleverly remarked, "The leprechauns must have been busy last night."

The trail continues switch-backing through the woods and eventually spits out on a slightly larger dirt road. As my muscles warm up, my legs feel lighter, and I catch my stride. Trying to pace myself, I pick the most groomed tire track as I peek through the trees checking out the boats and people fishing on the curve of the river that parallels my run. After I pass a clearing where a cliff juts skyward, blue arrows direct me back on the trail where it begins a gentle ascent. I slow to ponder a lone lilac bush that has shed its purple flowers and scattered them on the trail like confetti.

This part of the trail is the easiest, and I usually just let my mind wander, replaying the day's or week's events. However, when I walked this with my mother one time, our slower pace and her new insight helped me notice the strange capabilities of nature around us. "Trees can grow into such interesting shapes," she stated as we passed a pine tree born on the trail's shoulder, S-curving upward for its share of sunlight. And I realized that spring had sprouted five-petal daisies that bordered the trail and mocked my wish to play he-loves-me, he-loves-me-not.

As the trail crests, I enter a field of power line towers crackling with the flow of electricity. With the abundance of rain and the dawn of spring's growth, grass and weeds strive to cover the path as flying insects come out of hibernation. The trail, still worn, jumps over rail-road tracks emitting the warm scent of friction and tar. I rarely worry about encountering a train, but now I hear a buzz that makes me wonder if a C-130 is on a test flight out of the Little Rock Air Force Base. As I progress, the chugging whistle becomes more obvious.

The trail falls into the muddiest section yet. After passing a pond in the field behind one of the ranger's houses, I skirt the path on a rut that has been formed to the right side by others like me trying to avoid the quicksand nature of such sticky mud. Using a line of rocks, I carefully cross a runoff creek that has eroded its way through the trail, bringing me to an intersection with Pinnacle Valley Road at Pinnacle's East Summit parking lot. Here, I have the choice of three trails to take: the Base Trail, the East Summit Trail, or the Ouachita. A ranger stops me to ask which one I plan on doing. He warns me that a friendly looking female cocker spaniel is lost on the Base Trail and has been snapping at people. He asks me to report if I see her. The thought of a ferocious golden Lady makes me chuckle as I continue on the Ouachita.

This portion at the base of the mountain is fairly rocky, so once again, I pay special attention to my foot placement so as not to stumble on shaky rocks or massive tree roots that snake across my path. There is a new smell here, not necessarily as simple as pine, but a fresh, not-too-perfumey, green scent. As I turn around to backtrack to my car, I try to think of ways to bottle it and store it as my own.

I always encounter the rustle of animals, whether it's a lizard scurrying under my feet, a squirrel running through the fallen leaves, or someone's dog tracking new scents in the woods. On my return trip, I hear the excited crunch of leaves under the feet of two deer who hop the trail ten feet in front of me playfully chasing each other. I thankfully remember a sign I passed on the drive in: "State Park, No Hunting, All Plants and Animals Protected."

Once I reach the Visitor's Center, I climb the wooden steps to a scenic overlook. From there, looking east, I can see down the river to Jimeson Creek. To the west, Lake Maumelle spreads itself, ducking in and out of the Ouachita Forest where Pinnacle and other hills roller coaster across a kaleidoscope landscape. The breeze from this height washes my body, rippling my running shorts and soothing my six-mile morale. I am in a dream state. I have left my burdens on the leafing trees of the Ouachita where they will evaporate to replenish the next soul fortunate enough to enter its splendor.

Catching More Than Fish

STEVE TAYLOR

Steve Taylor is part-time freelance writer from
Little Rock with credits in Field & Stream, Sports
Afield, *and many other outdoors magazines. He*
is a frequent contributor to Arkansas Wildlife
magazine in which "Catching More Than Fish"
was published in 1997.

So, I'm fly fishing near an Arkansas River boat ramp one morning, where I often stop before work to catch a few bream. This fellow walks up. Like lots of folks, he says he "always wanted to learn how to work a fly rod." Wants to watch awhile.

We talk a little. Says he's from Detroit. I think about big cities I've seen; Little Rock's big enough for me. It's got this river, and trout streams that aren't too far away, and camping spots within an hour's drive where my buddies and I find deer and bear tracks along the creek below our tents.

The man from Detroit is in his fifties. Says he's a general contractor, taking a vacation to "rest my achin' back." I'm thirty-six and work at a computer terminal. My back aches from work only when I don't remember to sit up straight. He's black; I'm white. The minnow bucket by his car proves he's a bait fisherman; I usually fish with a fly rod. Not much in common, but he's friendly enough—for a guy from up north—so I keep talking.

"You catchin' anything down there?" I ask.

"Yeah," he says. "I don't get to fish much back home, so I've been here all night. Caught a few catfish, but I let 'em go."

I remember days when I've seen the sun both rise and set on the Little Red River, when I squeezed every minute of fishing possible into a precious vacation day. Been close to a year since I killed a fish to take home. I like to catch 'em for fun, too.

"What brings you to Little Rock?" I ask, casting my popping bug toward a stump.

"I'm visitin' my buddy, but he doesn't hardly fish," he says. "I don't understand it. How can a fella live around all this and not fish? Water's so polluted around Detroit, there's not many places like this to fish."

I follow the sweep of his arm as he indicates the endless acres of water, the trees, the birds. I feel fresh appreciation for my fishing spot through his viewpoint. A bass rips through the shallows, scattering minnows.

"My wife, she thinks I'm crazy stayin' out all night on this river-bank just to catch a few fish and throw 'em back," he says, chuckling. "She just doesn't understand."

I understand. "There's more to fishing than just catchin' fish, huh?" I twitch the little fly across the water's surface.

Detroit smiles. "Man, just bein' out here! You know, when I'm working, it's the daily grind. But I can come to a place like this, and it really relaxes me."

I look at him and nod. Of course, a big bluegill explodes under my popping bug just then, and I react too late to the sound, setting the hook only into the windless morning. We laugh and decide that fish everywhere—even the big-city fish in their polluted water—always strike when you're looking the other way.

"That doesn't matter, does it?" he says, still smiling. "Another one'll be along soon."

I speak the tired old line, full of truth: "If you caught 'em every time, they'd call it catching instead of fishing." We both laugh again. I tell him, "Seems like I forget my problems out here—or solve 'em."

"Yeah," Detroit says. "You focus on tying knots and baiting hooks and casting. Or you just watch the clouds go by if the fish aren't biting. But when you're through, all the stuff you've been worrying about always seems better."

I think about the pleasant work of solving fly fishing problems. How hours slip by as you try different flies, figure how to drift them into just the right spot where you think a trout might be, fiddle with the boxes and gadgets in your vest. I always leave a river tired, but clear-headed.

He walks back to his rod and bait bucket, vowing (like so many do) to "get me a fly rod and try that out." It's time to go to work, so I put up my rod and get in the car, waving goodbye.

As I drive away, I think about the common threads running through the lives of people who fish as an excuse to enjoy the outdoors, who daydream on riverbanks—and who don't really care that big bluegills always seem to strike when you're looking the other way. It's a rich way to spend part of your life, especially when what you catch is a new way of thinking about folks who aren't so different from you, after all.

Letting Go

GIBANN TAM

GibAnn Tam co-directs the Little Rock Writing Project and teaches in the Department of Rhetoric and Writing at the University of Arkansas at Little Rock. In "Letting Go," she reflects on her move to the "city" in 2001.

I turn into our drive and listen for the familiar sound of gravel crunching beneath the tires. Gently I ease through the opening in the trees where the black wrought-iron gate marks the entrance to our land. My eyes are drawn immediately to the bright yellow gargantuan sign with its five-inch red and blue letters. It still seems so out of place tacked on the trunk of a towering oak.

"It's a real eye-catcher," I remember the realtor attempting to reassure me.

He was right. The very next day the cars that normally whizzed past our land now slowed to read the eye-catcher sign: "For sale, house and acreage."

The sign's presence had surprised me a few weeks ago—I didn't know the realtor had posted it already. An uneasy feeling overcame me as I studied the sign then. I wondered, as I wonder now—were we doing the right thing?

How would I let go of this house and this land? Eighteen of my twenty married years had been lived out on this land. My children had grown up here.

Today as I walk the perimeter of our land, I notice the leaves are beginning to turn. This is my favorite time of the year. I love the cool mornings and nights that seem to herald the brilliant fall colors. I love the sound and feel of the autumn breeze moving through the trees, rustling the leaves. It's a whispering sound that is both faint and distinct at the same time. It is an unforgettable sound.

I move on through the acre of Christmas trees and remember that we once held lofty ambitions for these overgrown evergreens. Five years ago, six hundred saplings—most of them eight or nine inches long—were delivered to our door in a tightly wrapped bundle of burlap. My twelve-year-old son and his dad then spent three back-breaking days digging six hundred holes to house the trees that would form the beginning of our Christmas tree farm. Some of the trees are over ten feet high now, all growing thickly and unevenly, vines and briars twisting tightly around their neglected trunks and branches. Only the birds and other small animals venture into the dark thicket of trees these days. Our dreams of a family Christmas tree farm never materialized.

I head toward the bank of our fish-stocked pond. What great fun we'd experienced out here. I fling the crumbling dog food I'd been keeping in my pocket out over the water's surface. In less than a minute, the quiet pond awakens. Whiskered catfish begin splashing noisily to the surface, swallowing the crumbs with loud slapping, plonking sounds. I love watching this.

We don't swim in the pond anymore, but when the kids were younger, many of their summer days were spent playing here. They lived for the flying leaps off the wooden dock that extended out over the water. The leap commenced with a running start and finished with a screaming body sailing through the air, bent on hitting a float strategically distanced from the dock.

One particular summer day comes to mind. Anya and Andrew and two of their best friends had been playing in the pond for most of the afternoon. Since they were all strong swimmers, I was not keeping a close eye on them. In fact, I had returned to the house for a few minutes.

I had only been inside for ten minutes when I discovered Andrew standing beside me. As the pond water dripped off of him and puddled in concentric circles around him, he proceeded to tell me in his matter-of-fact, quiet way that he had almost drowned. I'll never forget the serious look on his face and the shaky but calm sound of his voice as he told me how he had fallen off the float and couldn't reach it, how he had forgotten that he could swim, and how he had almost drowned. I held him very close, and all I remember saying to him was that I was so glad my little boy didn't drown.

I circle back toward the Christmas trees and the house, and two wild ducks fly over my head landing at the water's edge behind me. They paddle completely around the pond, keeping close to the bank, repeatedly thrusting their bills and heads into the water. I crouch down in the tall grass hoping they will not detect me. A moment like this makes me wonder why we would ever even think of moving to the city.

"Mom, it was an accident. Marcus was trying to hit the tree." My son cradled the dead duck in his two hands and continued to unfold the details of the duck killing in his matter-of-fact tone of voice. The boys had been target shooting with the BB gun and accidentally shot the duck down by the pond. Our last duck—the first duck had been eaten by wild animals; the second eaten by a stray dog, probably one of those dogs that city people drive out to the country and let loose for one reason or another; and the third duck flew off.

I was really upset—our last duck! But I did take some comfort in the boys' obvious remorse. They discussed the need to give the duck a proper burial and left me to carry out their funeral plans. Two hours later, Andrew was hollering at me from the front porch. Marcus had gone home, and Andrew had continued playing alone outside. In both his eleven-year-old hands, he fingered the duck's remains.

"Mom, look." He proudly held up a mass of duck entrails between two fingers. "I decided to dig the duck back up." He brought his other hand toward me, "This is the heart, and I think this is the stomach—I can tell because when I cut it open, I found some grainy-looking stuff, like it eats."

"Andrew Kahai!" I felt faint. I'd never been much good with dead animal parts—always let my husband deal with such unpleasantries. I did recover from the duck dissection after a few short moments and decided that Andrew's exploration was really completely natural for a curious eleven-year-old.

I conclude my duck-killing reminiscing and notice right away that the wild ducks had disappeared. Don't blame 'em, I think. I continue my trek.

Beyond our two-story house, the land slopes gently upward, then steeply, just as it kisses the tree line. On the hill's crest, I stop to catch my breath. I had been following a steep and rocky path overgrown with wildflowers of golden rod and white aster, and now I am deep into the trees. An army of pines, hickories, oaks, and dogwoods surrounds me. Peering through the trees and down over the pasture where our house is sided by oaks and hickories, I am overwhelmed by the striking array of color that spreads before me.

Almost nineteen years ago, when we first bought our land, the section of road that runs alongside it was a mixture of gravel and dirt. From top to bottom, the trees lining the road were always a chocolate-brown from the dust swirls raised daily by cars driving past. Across the road lived Mrs. Inman and her thirty-something-year-old son, Russell. Nineteen years ago, this was their land.

Mrs. Inman was elderly and eccentric. I remember our realtor, Miss Jean, warned us about her, "She's strange, now. One minute she'll go along with you, and the next minute, she won't. Just because she's verbally accepted your second offer, doesn't mean a whole lot." Taking her warning to heart, my parents and my husband and I decided to pray together that all would go well when we visited Mrs. Inman. We really wanted the land.

Mrs. Inman's house was dark with small rooms, narrow hallways, and not many windows. The temperature inside was oppressively hot, probably from the woodburning stove in the corner of the darkly paneled den. After polite introductions, we sat down and Miss Jean brought out the acceptance papers to sign.

"Now listen here, I'm not about to . . ." Mrs. Inman's scratchy voice started into the first of many objections about us buying the land. I sat through maybe ten minutes of her ranting, then excused myself. I was only twenty-one then, and patience was not one of my finer qualities.

I went outside and began to wonder if Mrs. Inman really wanted to sell her land. I stared across the road at the land we so much wanted to own. My Chinese husband who'd grown up in a Hong Kong high-rise dreamed at night about owning this much land. The trees blazed with leaves of orange, red, and gold. Their beauty seemed to call out to me. For the second time that day, I called out for God to help us own this land.

After a few minutes in the chilly fall air, I returned inside. Mrs. Inman was signing the acceptance papers.

One year later, we sold our tiny nine-hundred-square-foot house in the city, bought an eighteen-hundred-square-foot doublewide trailer with vaulted ceilings from Big Mac Mobile Homes, and moved out to our land. I was nearly eight months pregnant with Andrew, my second-born child. Anya was two. The day we attempted to drill our own well, my husband and my dad were using a three-hundred-dollar, do-it-yourself well-drilling kit from *Mother Earth* magazine. The kit was from a company named Deep Rock. About fifteen of our friends were there to watch the groundbreaking event, everyone estimating how deep the drill would go before it reached water. An expensive bottle of champagne was promised to whoever came closest with their guess.

Mr. Carnation, our realtor's husband, was traipsing around our woods with two witching rods in hand. This was truly an odd sight. For thirty minutes this seventy-something-year-old man wearing tan-colored coveralls and Kabota Tractor cap obeyed the wiggles of an ordinary-looking brown stick while a small crowd of semi-intellectuals and white-collar professionals tagged along.

Within thirty minutes or so, Mr. Carnation identified a suitable location for the well. The drilling began.

And it continued on and on and on. Hours passed, but we hadn't even reached the first guess of twenty feet. The Deep Rock driller hit hard rock at twelve feet, and although my husband and father promised that the drill would most definitely pierce the rock, our disheartened friends left one by one. We drank the expensive champagne ourselves, and the next day we arranged for professionals with very high-powered equipment to drill our well. They hit water at seventy-four feet. The well cost us fifteen hundred dollars, not including the cost of the Deep Rock driller from *Mother Earth* magazine.

The day I went into labor with Andrew, trenches were being dug to lay the water line. I remember sticking my head out the tiny bathroom window, yelling to my husband and six other men that my water had broken, and we should probably go on to the hospital.

I experienced eight hours of excruciating back-stabbing labor in the birthing room at Little Rock's Baptist Hospital. One hour after my eight-pound son was born, I wanted to return home again, back to our land, back to our own place in the country, in my own bed, my mother at my side. My mother was there every day by my side for two weeks, preparing meals, tending to housework, and caring for my two-year-old Anya.

My parents had a small house, or a shack as we called it, just thirty yards from our doublewide. As the years passed and my children grew, they visited their grandparents daily. Nene and Taata were their special friends. Andrew followed my semi-retired dad around, helping him tend to the rabbits and chickens and pigs and the garden in the pasture. Many days, both Anya and Andrew would play in the shack with my mom. They held tea parties sipping Earl Gray tea in real china cups, munched on peanut-buttered apples and cheese and crackers, while my mom read from *Winnie the Pooh* and *Peter Rabbit*.

My kids spent a lot of their time outdoors. Between the playhouse and the fort in the woods, the tree swings, the egg gathering and feather-clipping, there was always plenty for them to do. Our chickens and guineas and geese roamed freely, and although we kept the birds primarily for their fresh eggs, we did occasionally eat one or two as well. I remember the first time I watched my husband and Anya butcher a chicken. Anya's small hands held the chicken still while her dad stretched its neck across a tree stump and quickly cut the head off with a small hand ax. Chicken blood spattered and smeared their faces, and the chicken ran around, dancing headless. I felt pretty nauseated and never watched the chicken killings again.

Goose chasing was a great thrill for Anya and Andrew. I always knew when the chase was on. High-pitched squeals echoed through our doublewide from one end to the other, my signal to assume a watchful position from the front porch. The goose chasing was at times a bit unpredictable. Occasionally the geese would allow themselves to be chased for only a few yards. Then suddenly they would turn the tables and chase the chasers. Whenever this happened,

Andrew and Anya turned on their heels, their squeals escalating to screams, and they made a beeline for the porch where I stood with arms outstretched. The thrill of their little legs just inches from the snapping beaks of the geese excited them to no end. I doubted the sensibility of the goose chasing many times, but I allowed the risky play to continue. The goose chasing continued for a couple of years until one winter morning the geese up and disappeared.

Nine years ago, we began building our twenty-five-hundred-square-foot house in the pasture. Back then we could only afford to have the shell of the house built, so when we moved in, we lived only in the partially finished downstairs. The completely unfinished upstairs we partitioned off with huge sections of ugly black visqueen. After one year, we had completed about 80 percent of the house.

All four of us hammered in the tongue-and-groove wood ceilings in the four rooms upstairs. In the very beginning we worked at a snail's pace with hammer and nail only, but after one hour we'd nailed up only five boards—that left another two hundred and sixty boards. It was eight o'clock at night and we were eighteen miles from Little Rock, but my husband made a run to Sears and Roebuck and brought home a high-powered nail gun to finish the job. It was the first of many power tool acquisitions.

The whitewashed floor in the downstairs hallway is covered by one hundred and twenty pieces of oak flooring that my crazy-to-find-a-bargain Chinese husband salvaged from an abandoned house in downtown Little Rock. Along the sides he stenciled burgandy-colored diamonds and slate-blue curlicues. In contrast to this finished floor art stands the unpainted door of the hallway closet. The door's surface wears faint pencil scratches that mark our children's growth through the years. The marks begin toward the middle of the door and climb upward across the smooth wooden panels. Out to the side of each line, a name and a date is penciled in.

This morning I peered down at the overgrown pond from my study window and saw two deer standing motionless and silent in the pond's morning mist. I called Andrew and Anya, and together we watched the deer, our three heads crowded together, noses pressed against the cold glass, waiting for the deer to move away.

Standing there, it seemed like time had frozen for us, like it was standing still. I wondered if there would still be moments like this in our future.

It was then that I understood something.

Letting go of this house and this land is not really about letting go—it is about holding on, too. Holding onto my almost-adult children. Letting them go. Holding on to the times and memories that have made our lives wonderful. Holding on. Letting go.

Magic of Nature

DEE BRAZIL

Dee Brazil is executive director of Caring Friends
of Arkansas Hospice. As one of its two founders,
she helped open the only hospice inpatient facility
in Arkansas. "Magic of Nature" was written as a
speech to a local women's organization in 1998.

What do we mean by "magic of nature?" Is that the same as "miracle of nature?" And what is our place in it? Many of our species assume nature was created for us, but I think we must have been created for it. Perhaps God made nature to get our attention. I imagine the Creator surveying wondrous creation and having to bring conscious beings into it, someone to contemplate his grand design and be aware of the Creator's great works. And then, to really appreciate this golden, rich banquet, we were made mortal and given awareness of our mortality.

At the risk of being perceived as a "wacky environmentalist," is it that God and nature are one?

When in our lives do we really see the magic and miracle of nature? For me it was only after the great grief and loss of a child. I remember the moment the "magic of nature" intervened in my life. I was working as a counselor at a substance abuse clinic. My office was in a small, dark corner of a day-treatment facility. There were six alcoholics waiting to be interviewed, and as I rose to call the next client in, my eyes caught the photograph on my desk of my son. He had been dead for two years, but that afternoon, the hammer of grief hit full force and I doubled over in pain. In that brief moment, I was transported somehow to a beautiful place and was given beautiful words; a moonlit ocean and warm Santana wind, and the words, "Timelessness perceived for an instant in nature's mirror." I straightened up, filled with wonder, went on with my work that day, amazed by the depth of that experience and that I could function with my normal activity but with a new and sustained sense of wonder.

Later when I had become disgusted with myself in my extended grief and decided to try to live my life as a testament to a remarkable son's life, I took up his passion of backpacking and came to know the mountains intimately, becoming an outdoorswoman and a photographer. Did that moment in my office lead me there?

Joseph Campbell said, "If you see your path laid out step by step before you, you know it is not your path!"

Since time began, that is, since man became conscious, nature has been our teacher. This northwest Indian teaching story rendered into poetry by northwest poet, David Waggoner, shows us the depth and breadth of nature's teachings. It is titled "Lost," and it is the child asking the elder, "What do I do when I am lost in the forest?"

Waggoner reminds us of the wisdom of nature as he answers: "Stand still / The forest knows where you are / You must let it find you."

The Urban Paul Bunyan

JIM ALLEN

Retired insurance agent Jim Allen and his wife,
Pat, left career and home in North Little Rock to
establish a new life in Mountain View. The chain
saw is in constant use.

Our new house had a fireplace. Our dreams of romantic evenings before an open fire were about to be realized. But we had to have wood for our fireplace, and that meant I needed an ax. The salesman in the hardware store convinced me that the beautiful red-handled Plumb ax is the woodsman's choice. I could hardly wait to get home to show my prized purchase. As I held it for my wife to see, the head slipped from my hand and proved how sharp it was. It cut through the new rug and cut a deep gash into the hardwood floor below. We were able to turn the rug so the cut was under a chair. When we were ready to sell the house, we hoped that no one would want to examine the floor under the carpet.

While I made an excellent choice in the purchase of an ax, it soon became evident that we were not going to have many fires if I had to cut all the wood with an ax. It looked so easy in the movies. I learned later that they were cutting softer woods than the oak trees in our area. We purchased some firewood, but that was against my principles. It became an ego thing. Somehow, I had to find a way to cut my own firewood. That is the way a real man would do it!

I met a man in our church who later visited our home. He noticed our fireplace and asked if I would like to get wood with him sometime. He had a chain saw, splitting tools, and a trailer. He proposed that I load the wood as he cut it and we would each take half of the wood. This seemed like a great deal for me, and I jumped at the chance. Using a chain saw looks like hard work, and it is. However, a cutter can wear down two or three helpers in a short time. I tried to keep up with him, but that was not possible.

We cut wood together several times, and he taught me the best ways to split with a splitting mall and with a sledgehammer with wedges. He would never trust me to use his chain saw. It was only after buying my own saw that I understood his reluctance.

I finally tired of being his helper and decided to get the tools and do it myself. I figured to get all the firewood picked up. My first chain saw was not the quality of my friend's, but it was a good starter saw. I read the instructions in a do-it-yourself book and took off for a building site where there were some freshly downed logs just waiting for me. Putting to use my newly acquired knowledge proved more difficult than it looked. My first cut was too deep, and the log closed over the chain so that I couldn't remove it. I jacked the log up and removed it easily. Lesson 1 had been learned: Don't cut too deep in a log on the ground.

Lessons 2 and 3 came quickly. When I cut through the log, I noticed some sparks flying from my chain. When I tried to make the next cut, I realized the sparks meant that the chain had hit a rock. The chain was so dull it would hardly scar the bark. I had to go buy a sharpening tool and then made one of my wiser decisions: I bought a spare chain. If that happened again, I would only have to change the chain and could do my sharpening at home.

With the new chain I was able to cut up the logs and take a load home. I was so proud of myself; it was a hard job, but I now kept 100 percent of the wood. My pile of wood was very impressive. My ego and sense of independence soared.

Lesson 4 came when I started splitting my wood. I struggled for almost an hour to split the first log. The second was just as difficult. I couldn't understand why I was having so much trouble. The wood my friend and I cut had split very easily. Burying my pride, I called my friend for help. Without even a glimmer of a smile, he asked me to demonstrate what I had been doing. I repeated the procedure on another log. An hour later, he told me my technique was good. He asked me what kind of wood I had cut, which of course I had no idea about. He went through the motions of studying my wood. At that point he couldn't control himself any longer and burst forth with a laugh that almost shook the foundation of my house.

When he finally quit laughing, he told me I had a gum tree. The only way to split gum is with a hydraulic splitter. In an attempt to help me recover some of my damaged ego, he confessed that he had once done the same thing. Later, while sipping a cold beer, he loaned me his tree book and explained how to identify trees. Today, I cut only oak and hickory. If I can't identify a tree, it is left for someone else to get their Lesson 4.

Buffalo River Friends

KIRK WASSON

Kirk Wasson is a modern woodsman who has devoted much of his time to issues concerning wilderness protection, whether by hands-on training of campers in the ethic of "leave no trace" or attending legislative hearings to defend issues such as roadless designation. He works as an IT consultant for Entergy.

In the middle of March 1998, I had the fortunate luck to travel the Buffalo River with good companions. The mission was to bid farewell to good friends Marny and John Apel and share the love of river and wilderness.

This was my first solo paddling in years and first ever in a thirteen-foot white-water canoe. The gauge at Buffalo Point read 5.8. At such a good flow, one only had to keep the boat straight and perpendicular to the plane of the water. Soft pillows hid the canoe-grabbing rocks. The rapids and shoals were flat and fast. I got dizzy and hypnotized watching the bottom move by at six to eight miles an hour. A definite lack of pools to catch gear, boats, and people in the event of a capsize. I decided to keep the boat in an upright and locked position.

> *It was a riotous ride*
> *with a frantic man at the controls*
> *Down the watery slide*
> *through Clabber Creek Shoals*

To solo a boat
with your ruin in your hands
on a 26 mile float
through remote wilderness lands
Just one of the delights of life

We put in at the historic zinc-mining ghost town of Rush on a cool, clear morning. I made it through the only real rapids (Clabber Creek Shoals) and soon caught Marny and John, who had left the day before. They were easy to recognize as I came around the bend since they are the only folks I knew who try to keep a beagle (Leroy) on a leash. It was good to see these hardworking wilderness managers at rest.

We took a long lunch at Big Creek, and I met two nice young guys who work with John at the National Park Service. They quickly got out fly rods and disappeared. After catching up on wilderness talk with Marny, wilderness manager for the Ozark National Forest, I headed out, knowing the tandem boats would soon catch me.

I really wanted to be alone with the river for a while. Other than passing or being passed (going up stream) by fishermen in johnboats, I did not see another soul. I blocked out the motor people except for having to turn into their wake to keep from being flipped. I was not going to become worked up about why "*THEY*" allowed motors in the largest wilderness area between the Appalachian and Rocky Mountains.

I just took a deep breath, squatted in my boat, took in the scenery, and enjoyed the free ride, thanks to recent rains upstream—much-needed rains that would better the budding trees. Only a week before, the river level had been at ten feet and closed. I glided on and thought of a hiking trip back in November down to Big Creek. The river level— at eighteen feet—had been fast, muddy, and full of trash. Now I could see the high-water marks and wads of leaves, "bird nests" as some call them, high in the willow trees. It was also interesting how the gravel bars change with these floods. I hoped there were still plenty of rocks upstream to keep supplying the beautiful, multicolor, and perfect camping, gravel bars.

Like the changes to the river, I thought of John and Marny's big move to Idaho. They needed the change, but we (wilderness, Arkansas, and I) will miss their love of and dedication to protecting the sparse wild areas in Arkansas. I would wish them good luck and hoped they could work their way back to Arkansas someday.

Continuing my one-man wilderness experience, I jumped wood ducks out of an eddy just feet away. I watched them circle and land back upstream at the head of the pool. I could not keep my eyes on the road for enjoying the terrain without a cover of leaves. I saw new-sprung (to me) rock formations, bluff lines, hollows, and contours. I wished for time to pull out at every drainage, put on hiking boots, and climb each hollow and overlook.

My friends caught me just before Leatherwood Shoals. Another spot I was a little concerned about, but it too was washed out. We camped at one of the nicest places on the river. It came with flat, packed gravel, close to the water, High Burr Bluff to gawk at, a full moon shortly after sundown, and our very own comet (Hale-Bopp). After some whiskey, a great chili supper, and a good visit, we enjoyed my friend Bill's birthday cheesecake with strawberries, and a little more whiskey. Good conversation and comet watching ensued until a late eight P.M. when everyone was ready to retire.

Those who slept out under the stars woke dusted with a nice layer of frost.

River water coffee
on a morning frost bound
slowly stirs me
from a night on the ground
A large banana pancake
one last cup of Joe
Time to pull up stakes
and join the river flow

Coffee warmed bellies and banana whole wheat pancakes, with a side order of peppered bacon, made for happy paddlers. We started for Shipps Ferry, which was five miles down the White River from the mouth of the Buffalo. There was a full release from Bull Shoals Dam, which had backed water up the Buffalo a couple of miles, and made me worry about the dam-ruled, electricity-generating, flood-controlled, ruined White River. I was bolstered by the shot of whiskey in my last mug of coffee. My friends peeled out into the cold, fast, slick water and shot on down like a dart. They must have had confidence in me or did not want to listen to me bemoan the "White Shiver." I worked my way across river trying to stay out of the eddy currents close to the bank. Some of which made sucking noises as I paddled to keep the boat straight and away from boil-ups that wanted to dump me. The water was frigid, fast, and deathly artificial. Even still, people flock for the pond-grown, artificially inseminated, nonnative fish. I was even wondering why electricity was such a good thing.

Safely on the bank, goodbyes exchanged, we went different directions knowing we would continue on the same paths toward protecting wilderness; how to love it and when to leave it alone.

Floating with good friends
Gathered from frazzled ends
for the love of remote places
and wilderness' many faces
to savor the sunny solitude days
knowing soon we must part ways
The fire remains in our hearts
"Like Thinkers" are never far apart.

You Find It, You Keep It

CINDY PERLINGER

Cindy Perlinger of Benton is a senior in the
University of Arkansas at Little Rock Department
of Rhetoric and Writing where she wrote this
account of diamond mining in fall 2000.

I have always been a treasure hunter. The idea of finding something unique or valuable is such a fascination to me that I
have been known to go anywhere that might hold a chance of discov-
ering something. I love to rummage through old antique shops and
flea markets (*old* being the operative word here—new, fancy shops do
not appeal to me because those items have already been discovered
and are priced to prove it), and I love to go to garage sales. I have even
gone dump and dumpster diving. This was a friend's idea, and
although it was kind of interesting, I found the smell revolting and
only did it once. I'm not that much of a fanatic, but I do have an insatiable desire for treasure hunting.

Arkansas has some of the most unusual and beautiful rocks in the
world, and it offers geologists a virtual gold mine (or shall I say, diamond mine) to study. One of the unique state parks in the world is the
"you find it, you keep it" Crater of Diamonds State Park, which has
been dubbed "The Crater."

I heard about the Crater when I first moved to Arkansas fifteen
years ago, but I never found the time to go. Finally, this spring, the
treasure hunter in me stood up and demanded to be satisfied. I gathered up some gardening tools, my seven-year-old daughter, Bailey,

some clean clothes, and drove the eighty-five miles from Benton to Murfreesboro to dig for diamonds.

The Arkansas State Tourism Web states that "The crater is the only diamond site in the world where the public can pay a fee to dig and keep any gems they find, and it is the only productive deposit of the precious mineral in the United States." However, diamonds are not the only gems that can be found in the Crater; there are other semi-precious gems and minerals that can be found also: amethyst, agate, jasper, quartz, calcite, barite, and as my daughter said, "all kinds of pretty rocks."

According to the Crater of Diamonds State Park brochure, two diamonds were found in 1906 by "Diamond John" Huddleston, who bought the property for one hundred dollars and a mule. He sold the farm for $36,000 because he had six daughters and felt that a $6,000 dowry apiece would be sufficient to get them married off. The brochure also stated that Huddleston died a pauper, which I found very interesting, because there have been more than 70,000 diamonds found at the site since he discovered those first two diamonds.

An informational sheet from the park explains that there were forty acres of diamond-bearing soil that were owned by Huddleston's neighbor M. M. Mauney. Mauney tried to mine his property and even allowed visitors to search for a fee; this is where the finders-keeper's idea got its start. Of course, there have been several attempts to commercially mine portions of the diamond-producing soil, but for many reasons shrouded in mystery, lawsuits, fires, public opposition, and other reasons, they have been unsuccessful.

"In 1969," the sheet continues, "General Earth Minerals, of Dallas, bought both properties and continued the tourist attraction of public mining for a fee until 1972 when the State of Arkansas purchased the land for $750,000 and turned it into the Crater of Diamonds State Park." Today visitors pay a small fee to hunt for gems.

I found that it is best to bring your own tools to dig with, but there are some that can be rented at the site. Small garden tools work great, and a screen is recommended also. A screen is made out of wood and window-screen material. Just take four pieces of wood and make a square frame out of them, then take the screen material and stretch it across the bottom and secure to the wood making a box. The soil can then be sifted through the screen to reveal any larger objects. The only regulations concerning what tools can be brought into the site is that they cannot be motorized or have wheels.

I had read that the Crater's best time to go diamond hunting is after a heavy rain. Basically because diamonds have an oily, slick outer surface that dirt or mud will not stick to, making them easy to spot, and the lamporite soil is lighter than a diamond so the soil washes away, exposing them. The day my daughter and I went it had been raining for two days and was still raining that morning, so I figured we might have a chance to find a diamond. I knew the rain had already left the area that we were going to, so the weather didn't concern me. However, it was barely fifty degrees, and I wasn't looking forward to sloshing around in cold, sticky mud. Mud is hard enough to maneuver in as it is, and it's down right miserable in the cold. On the positive side, my daughter's excitement and my desire to squelch the treasure hunter in me made me convince myself that it was a good idea and that hopefully, I wouldn't get too cold. And, I couldn't disappoint her; this was her only spring break outing.

We arrived at the park around one in the afternoon, and I was surprised to see that we weren't the only ones foolish enough to brave the cold, sticky mud. There were about fifteen other people slipping and sliding through the muck looking for the treasures that hid in the volcanic soil. I asked the park attendant at the office if they had visitors at the park everyday, and he said that as long as the weather was halfway decent they did. I jokingly suggested that I thought we picked the worst time of the year to dig, and he surprised me by saying that we actually had come at one of the best times. He said that the worst time of the year was in July and August when the temperature reached triple digits and the sun fried you like a worm on pavement. I wasn't sure if I agreed with him though—I can handle the heat, but I can't handle the cold. I know what he meant about the heat though: in Arkansas, it is stifling in the summer, and there are no shade trees in the mine field.

We paid our admission and toted our sack of tools down the hill to the grayish-greenish muddy field. The color of the earth was different than any I had ever seen before, and this intrigued me. I guess I hadn't fully believed that there really could be diamonds here until I saw the soil. The field is plowed regularly to keep it pliable for easier hunting, and it looked like a huge garden plot. The rows were even mounds, and the rain drained down a gentle slope between them. Scattered throughout the field were pools of water that immediately fascinated my daughter; before I could stop her she was knee deep in one of them. What looked like a clear shallow puddle of water to her turned out to have a foot or so of mush at the bottom that sucked her down into its grip. To her, this was the best place in the world to play; she laughed and giggled while I fought with the mud for her and her shoes.

I finally rescued her, and my stern warning of staying out of the pools of water apparently floated away with the wind because I had no more than turned my back on her when she yelled that she was stuck again. I realized that there was no way of keeping her out of them; she was so ecstatic about all the pretty rocks that she was finding that she just couldn't help it.

Surface hunting is the best way to find diamonds, according to the park attendant, and that's what we did. Surface hunting is where you basically look on the surface of the soil or dig shallow holes, but all holes have to be covered up when you are finished. The second method is screening, which I described earlier. The third is wet screening and is done by using water to wash dirt through the screen. I'm sorry to say that we didn't find any diamonds, but we did find some jasper, crystal, calcite, and other "pretty rocks," and that made my daughter happy.

By the time we got ready to leave, a group of young teenagers appeared over the hill. They were literally covered in mud. One of the boys looked like he had just lain down and rolled in it, but they were having a blast. There is an area where you can use water hoses to wash off, and it took them almost an hour to get cleaned up. By this time I was freezing, although I wasn't wet anywhere, but my daughter was, and by the time I got all the mud washed off us, she was freezing.

We changed into dry clothes and looked around in the museum and gift shop. That's when we learned that a diamond had been found just before we arrived at the park. The attendant in the gift shop said that there are two or three found each day; they are usually about the size of a match head. In the museum visitors can see various diamonds found on site and get tips for diamond hunting. According to a display in the small museum, "The largest diamond found at the park is the 40.23-carat Uncle Sam diamond, which was discovered in 1924, and in 1994 a 5.25-carat diamond was found. The largest in the past year was a 4.36-carat brown diamond found in August 2001."

Soil erosion from the diamond mine's surface has been calculated to average about 64 tons per acre per year over most of the mine (or a vertical loss of about half an inch per year, or about 12 inches since 1972). Because recent studies have shown the diamond deposit is at least 669 feet deep, there should be diamonds available for many generations to come. I have already decided to go back when it gets a little warmer and dryer. The treasure-hunting demon inside me hasn't been squelched yet, only delayed by cold, wet mud.

Ice Storm

VICKI BENNETT

*An attorney for Arkansas Children's Hospital,
Vicki Bennett is at work on a historical novel. "Ice
Storm" was inspired by a record-setting December
2000 winter storm.*

We had an ice storm yesterday. The weathermen and
women predicted it, and for the second time this year their dire predictions of a "major weather event" came to fruition. Despite the hazards (slick roads and downed tree limbs) and inconveniences (power
outages from the downed tree limbs and a twenty-eight-hour shift at
the hospital where I work), I found a certain beauty in the outside
world and a wonderful camaraderie at work.

I didn't get much sleep night before last. In spite of my almost fifty
years on this planet, I remain as a child when it comes to fireworks
and snowstorms. Bleary-eyed, I lay within my warm cocoon of blanket at five A.M. and heard not the concentrated silence of a world covered in snow, but the scritch-scratch of sleet hitting the window. It
didn't look bad enough to justify staying home in defiance of the edict
that all directors *would* find a way to get there, so I glumly headed for
the shower. By the time I dressed and reinforced myself with hot coffee, the sleet had turned to freezing rain. Surprisingly the roads
weren't bad, and I managed to get to the hospital in just over the normal commute time.

I reported to the command center and was dispatched to the hospital cafeteria to help fill in for the people who couldn't make it. My
"supervisor" was a cheerful woman named Earlene, who patiently

taught me the fine art of cooking for a crowd—several hundred to be exact. Earlene is in charge of the salad bar portion of the cafeteria and each day prepares a variety of salads, sandwiches, and desserts that I had heretofore taken for granted. In spite of my ineptitude (I rarely cook for myself, let alone a hundred strangers) we managed to get out all that was needed for the day.

It was, to me anyway, backbreaking work. After only a few hours I was ready to scurry back to my cushy desk job, thankful that my parents insisted that I go to college and "make something of myself." And yet, all the cheerful people around me did this sort of thing every day. When we finished for the day I found that I really didn't want to leave; I realized a sense of accomplishment in the mounds of vegetables I had chopped and sandwiches I had prepared that I rarely sense after a day of filling out forms or talking on the telephone. As I turned to go, I was inordinately pleased when Earlene told me I had done a good job and asked with a warm smile if I would "please come back tomorrow."

By midafternoon it was apparent that the evening shift would be short as well, and I headed home to pack a bag. When I emerged I found myself in a crystalline world of ice. While a snowstorm creates a blanket that seems to envelop and soften everything, ice intensifies the appearance of everything it touches. As I trudged gingerly to my car, I noticed how all the trees stood out in relief against the leaden sky. Each limb, branch, and twig was coated with a quarter-inch layer of ice that worked as a magnifying glass, making them appear larger than they were. The yellowing blades of grass stood stiffly in clear coats that crunched underfoot. Even my car, much in need of a wash job, glistened red and shiny beneath its icy shell.

Although I had little time to spare for communing with nature, as I drove home I couldn't help but notice how the ice transformed everything it touched. The flags at the Capitol hung in stiff, disconsolate folds instead of snapping smartly in the breeze. A chain-link fence became an inviting crystalline lattice instead of a cold barrier saying only "keep out." Different varieties of trees responded in their own ways to the icy layers that coated them. Some stood defiantly beneath their burden of ice and refused to yield to the weight. Others, particularly the pines, bowed their rime-covered heads nearly to the ground as if praying for the strength to survive. Still others, unable to withstand the load, stood broken with their shattered branches littering the ground around them.

I returned to the insular world of the hospital, not ready to leave the strange beauty of the world outside. There were more small tasks to keep me busy as I reported back to the command center. Here I found my everyday colleagues doing unfamiliar tasks and, I suspect, enjoying it as much as I had enjoyed my stint in the kitchen. When I finally crawled gratefully into my sleeping bag to catch a few hours of sleep, it was with a weary body but an easy mind.

On the second day, when my chores in the cafeteria were done, I escaped into the cold once again to find most of the ice still in place but beginning to melt. Everywhere there were sounds of running water and the plip-plop of droplets falling from every horizontal surface. I heard the scrape and clatter of a window-sized sheet of ice as it slid down the side of the building and hit the pavement below. Stopped at an intersection, I noticed a sheet of ice slipping down from the backside of the stop sign it had recently coated, a perfectly clear octagon. In the Target parking lot I arrived just in time to see the layer of ice surrounding a light pole fracture and slip to the ground like a glass dropped from a careless hand. Elsewhere I saw icicles hanging from the eaves of buildings, looking for all the world like the pipes of a miniature organ. Everywhere I looked there were wonderful sights that I could not have imagined.

Part of me wishes I could have played hookey and spent the day wandering in the woods, but then I would not have had the opportunity to see how others live. Instead I found enough time to stop and smell the roses both inside and out. You can't ask for much more than that from a single storm.

Catch and Release Smallmouth Therapy

MILTON JOHN STEPHENS

This piece by Milton John Stephens first appeared in the University of Arkansas at Little Rock Rhetoric and Writing Department collection PYX. Milton was completing a degree in Rhetoric and Writing at UALR at the time of his death in 1996.

Her sensitive side peeked over the shoulder of her usual, serious grad student demeanor. "Don't the hooks hurt their mouths?"

"You mean pain them, or do you mean injure them?" I muttered, teetering on the edge of an almost hypnotic state.

"Well, first of all, *does* it injure them?"

"Not so they can't function as fish," I said. If I hadn't lapsed into such a meditative mind set, I might have felt somewhat bothered being coerced to communicate. "Old fishing lore has it they don't have much feeling in their mouths, but science dictates since they eat with their mouths, it's a good bet they're a little sensitive there. I guess hurting the fish's mouth is like a moral issue you've got to resolve if you're going to fish. But go ahead and reel in that tired old crankbait and lie back here, and we'll talk about how much fun it is to take a nap on a flat rock on a sunshiny fall day."

A certain part of her mind wandered, while the determined part concentrated on her next cast, and she whispered back to the waters, "This really is therapeutic." Already she had incorporated my favorite catch phrase into her new perspective on the art of angling for small-mouth bass. She dangled her canvas hightops off the edge of the rock, in the cool rush of Richland Creek, and eagle-eyed a fishy-looking stir near the bank. With a simple flick of the rod tip, she zinged the balsa wood crankbait with pinpoint accuracy beneath an overhanging limb next to a rock. She cranked the reel slowly a few times, and, "Bam!" she said.

Her eruption had little effect on my requiescence.

"*Good* one! Ooooh, I got a *good* one. Look. Oh look. Look . . ."

This was too good to be true. On just our fourth date this woman had trusted me enough to put stereotypical notions of bearded rednecks in big bass boats aside, and an activity that had repulsed her the day before had now been used as an excuse to ignore me. But even being forgotten about was wonderful on such a fine day. Stretched out on the warm rock, like a cat on the sidewalk, I allowed the water rippling all around us to lull me back into the deepest recesses of my shallow ruminations. The irony of being alone again, but this time with a beautiful, intelligent woman beside me, struck me as pretty funny, and I managed a faint smile. I had created a monster.

The sensitive one was having a little difficulty controlling her new-found passions. "Oooh, ooh, look! Look! Oh! Look! Look!"

With my eyes closed against the late morning sun, I began to swoon, a good vibe, vertigo, a roller coaster of positive effect, a phenomenon I call mellow determinism. Nothing could go wrong.

"Look!" she fairly bellowed.

"Get her," I chuckled, never opening my eyes, never stirring from my spot in the sun. "Get her in quick and pick her up."

"No. This is a really nice one, and I don't want to lose it. I've got to play it until I can get her in."

"Why? You're going to let it go anyway," I said.

"I *will* catch this fish."

"You owe it to that fish to get it in as fast as you can. The longer you play it the tireder it gets; the more stressed. Catch it; remove the hook; place her back in the water; let her gently go; and you'll have done minimal damage to that robust fish's health and psychology." I remained flat on my back, more at ease perhaps even than in my sleep.

"What's that trick you said to immobilize them?"

"Stick your finger in its mouth and pinch the lower jaw between your thumb and forefinger."

"Yeah, yeah," she said, "just like that! Look. Look, look, look, look. *Please.* Please look at my beautiful fish."

I assumed she was hoisting her trophy, but I continued playing hard to get. "If it's a beautiful fish, lay it on the rock beside me here so I can hug it up real close and we can take us a nap together." However, my new friend's therapy was going so well I found myself ignored once again. The moment was hers alone.

"I really don't think I hurt her mouth at all since those barbless hooks come out so easy. Where do you buy lures with barbless hooks?"

"You've got to file the barbs off yourself. That's what the little bitty file I keep in the little bitty pocket box is for."

She eased onto her stomach, hung off the edge of the rock, and lowered the fish back into the water. Like a child letting a tadpole back out of the jar, she watched as her trophy glided from her cupped hand, realized it was free again, and then darted back under the rocks. "All your stuff is little bitty," she said.

"Hey!" I sat up on the rock and smiled at her. "That's the beauty of fishing this way; minimal expenditure of finances as well as physical effort. No boats to haul around. Not only is it inexpensive, but we've carried everything we've needed on our backs. We've afforded ourselves the privilege of sitting right smack-dab in the middle of this beautiful little crystal clear creek flowing between these quaint little Ozark hills. We pitched our little ultralight tent in the pasture and watched the sun go down, and the stars come out, toasted the Greek gods with a little ouzo, then got us a little sleep, got up in the wee, wee hours, had a little breakfast, and a little coffee, put on our little packs with our five-piece breakdown rods and ultralight reels with super sensitive four-pound test line, and a couple of big, fat peanut butter and jelly sandwiches, and our little water purifier, and we hiked beside the creek and chatted a little, and waited for the fog to lift off the creek so we could see a little, and then we waded a little, and the water was just a little cold, but our wool socks kept our feet nice and warm inside our wet Chuck Taylors, and we've thought absolutely not once about a single one of our little personal problems. And you said you hated fishing. And no, not more'n a day later, you've not only forgotten that I exist, you've also forgotten all about your problems."

She interrupted, "You know it *is* funny," she said. "I forgot all about the deadline for my thesis and all that; wasn't even thinking about it, and suddenly the solution to my little calculation problem just popped into my head. I had to stop and go, 'Whoa, where'd that come from?'"

"That's it, *exactly*," I said. "Any time you're out doing the nature thing, you're focused on each and every moment. You've never seen these hills under quite these same circumstances. Squirrels are barking. Deer are in the rut. Turkeys are blending in with the fall foliage. Owls are hooting, and crows are cawing. The woods are alive, and you're just *inundated* with nature's full assault on your senses. The aromas of the woods and the waters. The warm sun in the crisp autumn air. Every step is new. You're totally caught up in precisely how you're going to put your foot in between those two slippery rocks while the current's pushing against your legs. There's no time to think and worry about your mundane problems back home. You're just lost in the moment, and nothing else matters. And when you throw out that lure, your focus is even more intense; you're so into it nothing exists but that bait at the end of that very fine line. And when a smallmouth hits, and, 'Bam!' as you put it, hey, you're one on one with nature just about as close as you can get. And then it's like flying a kite in a thunderstorm. The water's so clear you can see the whole drama. The lure wobbles toward you just below the surface when from nowhere that big old smallmouth comes busting out from under his rock and snatches up the bait. He fights, and he flails, and then he comes flying out of the water and skips across the surface on his tail, again, and again, until finally he gets tired, never gives up, mind you, because for him it's the everyday business of life and death. He just gets tired. And when the storm is finally over and you take the fish off the hook and hold him in your hand and admire him for a second, it's like looking at a glistening piece of God's fine art. Your problems . . . have ceased to exist. And when you come out of this trance, you're still glowing with positive effect, and you've got a whole new perspective on things. You've given your mind a break: it's fresh; it's rested, rejuvenated."

"Smallmouth therapy," she mused, and she scooted to the other end of the rock and prepared to cast to a new spot.

For most people I would guess that lying on your back on a flat rock in the middle of a babbling Ozark brook, daydreaming in the clouds against a blue sky through the autumnal boughs of oaks and maples would seem a common-sense approach to stress reduction. But we forget so easily the simplest of common-sense approaches. That's where the smallmouth comes in. Because he can thrive only in nearly pristine conditions, it's hard to find an ugly place to locate such a fish. The excitement of a tail-walking brownie is the best reminder I have found to search out a tranquil spot in which to live out my Huck Finn fantasies and reacquaint myself with my carefree childhood. The smallmouth is my excuse.

PART FOUR

Disturbance

Creatures of the Land

*I speak today in favor of wildness,
that uncorrupted state of bobcat,
deer, raccoon, and moose; hickory,
maple, walnut, and oak; ferns,
orchids, jointweed, and soapweed.
Not a land cut by roads, rowed with
pines, or ripped open by mines. A
land not for conspicuous consump-
tion, but rather for charging one's
soul—for connection to the Earth
force.*

—TOM MCCORMICK
Congressional Wilderness
Hearing Testimony
1984

Disturbance

MATT FORESTER

Raised on a farm in northeast Arkansas, Matt
Forester now lives in Gainesville, Florida, teaching
writing courses at Santa Fe Community College
and the University of South Florida while enrolled
in the English doctoral program at the University
of South Florida. He wrote "Disturbance" in 2000
as part of his Master of Arts degree at the
University of Arkansas at Little Rock.

"You thank the seep ditch is dried up yet?" The seep ditch was dug many years before to provide dirt for the levee, so it ran parallel the entire length of it, which was about twenty miles. Delta Farms owned the land, and they were draining the seep ditch because it took up valuable space that could be leveled and farmed. Willow trees draped on each side of it. In the summertime water moccasins crawled everywhere, and my brothers and I often went there to throw rocks at them or chase them with sticks.

"I guiss we'll see when we gi' thar." My cousin Nathan lived about eight miles away from us down a different gravel road. He was already driving a tractor sometimes. I wouldn't be able to drive one until I was his age. He was practically grown. His approval was important to me. Everything he liked was something that I should like. Everything he said was something I should believe. Everything he did I wanted to do.

We made it across the field to the narrow gravel road that crossed the seep ditch over two giant concrete culverts. We paused on the road above the culverts and looked down the seep ditch. The draping willow trees almost touched above the middle. The bottom of the ditch was dark green and murky and the water was gone.

"Looky thar. Thank 'at's a beaver dam?" He pointed down the ditch. About a quarter of a mile away was a pile of sticks and rubble that crossed it.

"I bet it is."

"Le's go." We scrambled down to the ditch bank and decided to run down the middle of it because the trees on the bank slowed us down. Our feet sank ankle deep into the dark gray mud beneath the top layer of murky green. The mud would not let go of my feet a couple of times, and Nathan had to pull me out. We moved over to the edge where the mud wasn't as thick so we could run better. Soon enough we made it to the beaver dam. We crossed up onto the bank and around the dam. The beavers had dug a network of trenches about two feet wide to preserve the water that was so essential to their survival. Their industriousness amazed me.

"Look in the water. See 'at beaver?" In one of the trenches was a brown, furry beaver back moving slowly toward the dam.

"There's another one."

We saw three in all.

"Buck Taylor told Daddy he gets twenty-five dollars for a beaver skin." Buck Taylor was a farm hand who always called my dad and my uncle "sharecroppers." He ran traps for animal skins.

"Twenty-five dollars? Wow! That's seventy-five dollars in all."

"I wish we'd 'a brought a gun. Quick, git a stick." Nathan picked up a big stick and started running toward the trenches. I picked one up too and smacked my way across the green murk. We stood by the trenches and waited until the beavers emerged.

We were accustomed to killing animals. This was a source of pride for the men we knew and a rite of passage for boys. The bigger the animal the better. Our fathers took us deer hunting every year, and Nathan had already killed one. We knew that our fathers would be proud if we killed the beavers, and seventy-five dollars was more money than I could imagine spending.

Crack! A beaver back appeared in the water in front of Nathan. He smacked it with the stick. The cold water splashed over both of us, and the beaver disappeared under the water. Another one or the same one—it didn't matter—appeared again a little further down. Nathan ran to it and brought the stick back down with a loud grunt.

"Thar's one down thar. Don't jis' stand thar." I ran down to the other beaver back and smacked it with the stick. It broke.

"It's rotten. Git a stick 'at's greener 'n 'at one. Don't you know nothin'?"

I threw down the stub I had left in my hand and ran back up on the bank to find another stick. I heard the water splashing again and again as Nathan continued beating the beavers. I found a better stick this time, one nice and solid. When I got back to the trenches, we stood there waiting. But the beavers had caught on by now and disappeared into their dam.

"This ain't gonna work. We need a gun."

"We can go back to the house and git my twenty gauge." This was the gun I hunted deer with. My father had had the stock of the shotgun cut short to fit my arms.

"Okay, let's go back 'n git it." We dropped our sticks and clambered back around the dam and trudged back down the seep ditch, running as best as we could in the mire. The fields were muddier now that the frost had melted, but we were too excited to care. We talked about what we were going to do with our share of the money. Nathan said it would be more than thirty dollars for each of us. All I had saved in my piggy bank my entire life was about forty dollars. We decided on the way back to the house that we would not tell anyone. We wanted to surprise them when we carried the dead beavers back to the house.

We were panting when we burst through the door.

"Stop! Take those muddy boots off."

"Mama, would you git me my shotgun?"

"What for?"

"We wonna target practice. Thar's a bunch o' crows flyin' around the levee." It was okay to kill crows anytime we wanted because they ate the grain from the fields.

"Is that where y'all been all mornin'?"

"Yes, ma'am," Nathan said.

"Well, y'all need to eat some lunch first. Take your boots off and come inside."

Nathan and I looked at each other, and he shook his head.

"Can we take it with us? We don't won't the crows to be gone when we git back."

She thought for a second. "Well, I guess so." She went back into my bedroom where I kept my gun and brought it back to me.

"I need some shells, too."

"Where are they?"

"In my underwear drawer."

She disappeared again and came back with a box of shells. They were #6 birdshot, but that should be powerful enough as close as we would be to the beavers. We took the shells from the box and loaded them into the elastic in our hunting-coat pockets. Between us we could carry eighteen shells. That should be plenty. I gave the box with the remaining shells back to my mother.

"Now wait there and I'll git y'all a sandwich."

We took the sandwiches and headed back across the fields. We took turns carrying the gun while we ate our sandwiches. Nathan would stop and point it every now and then at a bird that would fly by.

"Bang!" He would say, just as he thought he should shoot if he were going to kill the bird. But we were well trained with firearms, and we knew not to load it until we were at the levee.

As soon as we got back to the beavers, we saw one floating in the water. We thought it might be dead, but it sensed us approaching and disappeared under the water. Nathan loaded the gun, and we stood beside the trenches. We waited silently for what seemed like hours, when finally a beaver back emerged in the water a few feet away from us. Nathan aimed the gun and fired.

"Did ya git it?"

"Of course I did." But the beaver disappeared under the water. We thought it might have sunk. We took a stick and felt around in the trench for it. We didn't know that beaver fur is very thick and their hides are tough. We gave up trying to find it and waited quietly until we saw another one. Nathan shot it, but we could not find this one either. We stayed there until the sun was going down and we were out of shells. We shot eighteen times into beaver backs, but never killed a single one.

Disgusted, tired, and out of ammunition, we trudged dejectedly back across the field to our home. It was well after dark when we got back, and my mother was angry. She had my dad whip us with his leather belt for staying gone so long and making her worry. We didn't care about the whippings. We were used to them, and we were too disappointed about the beavers and our lost fortune.

Three days later, Nathan came back over with his dad. This time he brought his deer rifle.

"We're going to the levee!" we told our dads.

"You'll git another whoopin' if you ain't home by dark."

"Yessir!" we yelled.

Nathan's gun was a 30.30 and could kill a deer from a hundred yards. We knew for sure that we would be coming back home in no time with three dead beavers.

We crossed the gravel road. By now the top layer of soil in the ditch bottom had started cracking open in patches like dry skin, and our tracks from before were dry casts in the dirt. We scrambled around the dam. Suddenly we were overwhelmed with the putrid smell of death. I recognized it immediately. One of our dogs had gotten stuck under the shed behind our house once. Before we found it the stench was unbearable, and its swollen carcass was stuck between the pipes.

Flies swarmed around four dead beavers, swollen twice their normal size. They had crawled out of the trenches and died on the banks. One of them was opened, and the redness of its insides was exposed to the cool air. A coyote had probably eaten it. The stench of death made me nauseous.

"We cain't do nothin' with 'em."

The smell seemed to stick to my clothes, to my skin. I didn't want to open my mouth for fear the smell would get inside me somehow and make me rot. We turned and headed back down the seep ditch. This was not the last time I would kill an animal, but it was the last time I would enjoy it.

Between a Rock and a Hard Place: Gardening in the Ouachitas

TOM W. DILLARD

Tom Dillard is curator for the Butler Center for Arkansas Studies at the Central Arkansas Library System. "Between a Rock and a Hard Place" first appeared in the Mountain Signal *in April of 2000.*

My back hurts and my knees ache. But, I have a broad smile on my face! The explanation for both the smile and the pain are the same—wildflowers. I spent the last weekend preparing an area for a wildflower garden, which involved brush clearing, trying to kill briars, and damming up a small stream in order to create a "bog." I think the pain was worth it—because in the future I hope to be the proud owner of a woodland wildflower "dell."

A dell is a small wooded valley or hollow. I have just such a place, replete with a seasonal creek that meanders through it. The soil is deeper than one normally encounters in our neck of the woods. And it has just the right kind of shade—meaning deciduous trees such as oaks, with the lower limbs removed so as to have "high shade." Most woodland wildflowers like high shade, good moisture, and a soil with lots of organic matter.

My attention was drawn to this area in the first place because I discovered native irises growing there. Last year, around the first of April, I was walking through this small hollow, and out of the corner of my eye came a glimpse of something blue. Upon closer inspection, I discovered several blossoms of the crested iris (*Iris cristata*), a miniature that seldom reaches more than ten inches in height. The flowers are a lavender blue, and they sport a wonderful foliage that looks good all the way up to the first killing frost. The crested iris is on my short list of favorite wildflowers.

Another contender for "favorite" is the trillium. The Ouachitas are home to at least four species of trilliums (also known as "Wake Robins"). As the name implies, trilliums have leaves and flowers that are made up of three parts. They grow in sizable drifts across my property, but I'll have to relocate them to my new "dell," as they don't grow there naturally.

One well-known wildflower that does grow in my new garden is the May apple (*Podophyllum peltatum*). Most people do not realize the May apple has a flower since it sports only one blossom per plant, and the flower is always hidden down beneath the foliage. But, the bloom is irrelevant since the really nice thing about this plant is its lustrous foliage. The May apple, like many wildflowers, is a transient in the garden. It puts up growth in the spring and then goes dormant when the hot weather of summer sets in.

What the May apple lacks in showy flowers is made up for by the beautiful blue flowers of our native Sweet William (*Phlox divaricata*). This phlox is found widely throughout Arkansas, and the plants produce foot-high mounds of radiant blue flowers during late spring.

I have saved my favorite (at least my current favorite!) wildflower for last: bloodroot (*Sanguinaria canadensis*). This tiny citizen of damp woods bears a solitary white flower that lasts only one day. Plus, it is such a short fellow that it often escapes notice. Why, you might ask, would this inconspicuous plant be my favorite wildflower? One reason is that it blooms early. This year, it had already finished blooming by mid-March, but our spring has been early. I like plants which produce flowers early in the spring for they are signals to me that the winter is dying and the rebirth of spring draws near.

Another reason I like bloodroot is its foliage, which is a nice velvety green. But, the main reason I'm a bloodroot fan is its ease of cultivation. Plants can be dug in full flower and moved, and they don't even wilt! How can anyone dislike a plant with such a will to live?

Bloodroot gets its name from its fleshy root, which contains a bright red liquid. Native Americans reportedly used the liquid to make dyes. It is that fat root, by the way, which makes bloodroot so easy to move. The root stores water, allowing the plant to be yanked up and moved about without worry.

The Ouachitas are a haven of wildflowers, another good reason to garden here.

The Mystery of the Horsehair Worm

LARRY DON FROST

Larry Don Frost sent along this piece just after
he retired in 2001 as professor of English at
Henderson State University. He writes that he now
divides his time between working on his first novel
and fishing and hunting deer, hogs, and duck close
to home near Lake DeGray.

"Didja know you can put hairs from a horse's tail in a fruit jar of water and they'll turn into worms?" I didn't know that, but the country boy in my first-grade class said it with such conviction, how could I doubt? Then he actually brought a jar full of hairs to school one day, but they just lay there curled in wet strings, looking nothing like worms.

Our teacher let the jar stand on a windowsill in the sunlight for a couple of weeks for a "science experiment." We examined them daily, but nothing happened, and then the jar disappeared.

My family moved to Benton, and I neither heard nor thought about horsehair worms for years. Then one day I saw a rain puddle in our gravel driveway literally crawling with them. They looked exactly like hairs from a horse's tail or mane, but they were weaving from one end of the puddle to the other—obviously alive. Now, I was puzzled. How did a horse get into our driveway in town and shed hair into a rain puddle? I looked the next day, and the worms had evaporated with the water.

My next encounter with a horsehair worm was a real shocker. My wife and I had moved into a rent house in south Arkansas, and our tap water was pumped from a well. I didn't much care for the smell or taste of the water, but I assumed it was safe to drink. One night I started to step into a bathtub of hot water and stopped, poised on one bare foot in horror. There it was—a horsehair worm, about twelve inches long, swimming vigorously from one end of the tub to the other. It was just as thin as a hair, but it had one black spot at each end, about the size of a period on a typed page. Also, a black cricket floated on the surface. I drained the tub quickly and watched both creatures wash down the drain.

That worried me. I could not drink the water in that house after that. What if I should look into a glass of tea and see a hair sporting around the ice cubes? That would spoil my whole meal.

I took the encounter with my unwelcome pests to Dr. Kelly Oliver, a biology professor at Henderson State University. When I mentioned that a cricket was also in the tub, he smiled, puffed his pipe and nodded.

"The worm came out of the cricket," he said. "The cricket picks up a parasitic egg by drinking from a puddle somewhere. Once the egg has hatched and the worm has grown to maturity, something compels the cricket to go to water. As soon as the cricket gets into the water, the worm comes out and lays its eggs. Another cricket swallows an egg, and the cycle is repeated."

"I just want to know one thing," I said. "Is it safe to drink out of that well, or will I fill up with horsehair worms?"

Kelly laughed. "It's safe. That cricket probably jumped off a curtain into the tub." So that explained the origin of the schoolboy myth about the metamorphizing horsehairs and also explained how the creatures got into our driveway puddle in town. While we may sometimes feel a sense of loss when a cherished myth gets debunked, again the truth may prove to be as fascinating as the myth.

Return of the Peacock

MELISSA STOVER

*Written in 2001, this is a previously unpublished
piece. Melissa Stover is a former teacher, a freelance writer and photographer, and a stay-at-
home mom.*

The return of the peacock after the long, breaking winter seemed a sign of hope. Though winter still hung on, and the evidence of its harshness was everywhere. The ice storm left behind
broken and bent trees, branches snapped out of their tops; pines still
sagged though the ice was long melted. He pecked on the French
doors as if he'd never been gone, demanding food. So, now there
might be more spring days with his loud, honking mating call pierc-
ing the air.

So many other things had begun to change, end really. When Mom
started talking about tearing down the old egg house, I ignored her.
Finally I decided to look into it, see what I might salvage from the past.
Granted the tin roof had caved in under snow, or maybe it was the tornado that came through last spring. It had uprooted two of the huge,
ancient oaks and completely taken away the crabapple. No doubt that
the years and the weather had taken its toll here too. Water had ruined
much of what was inside. Tools, tires, metal objects I had no name for,
all of these cluttered around, hugging the sides of the small area. So
much to go through that none seemed worth saving. A white metal
bucket caught my eye. We used to feed the dogs in that. I tossed it out
to keep. A wooden box with a handle and "Pete Bailey" painted on its
side. I had no idea where that came from. It was something I might

use. I noticed the windows. Paint peeling off, old, Dad may have put them in, I couldn't remember. I wanted those. I climbed up on the shelf, resting my knee on tools and metal, and pried away the nails. I worked at it, pushing and pulling, using the flat metal pieces around me to work it from the frame, trying not to damage the window or break the glass. When I had two windows out I stopped. Two was enough. My old easel was under some tires. I couldn't get to that today but I wanted it.

I decided to walk the land. I left the egg house and headed to the back. The old chicken house nearly covered in vines, grass, bamboo, still held the rabbit cages. The chicken houses were already in poor condition when we moved to the Kimmell place, and we didn't use them for chickens. Dad put the rabbit cages in there to keep the rabbits dry and cool and built a chicken coop, too. Later came the deer pen and then the quail and peacock pen. Animals, always something for me to feed, look at, and pet. Toto, my dog, and I walked back here daily to feed. When I moved out and married, Dad tried quail and got rid of the rabbits. Then came the peacocks.

He said you had to keep them penned up for a few years until they knew their home. Then you could let them out and they would stay around the yard. He was right, but the peacock never seemed happy on the outside. He paced back and forth in front of his old cage, wanting to be back inside with the other peacocks and quail. At night he roosted on the chicken house and sometimes during the day would venture up to the porch. In spring the mating calls of peacocks and the gentle cooing of quail were familiar sounds. The spreading of the brilliant feathers usually followed the sound, rustling and stretching like a fan, the eyes at the tip of each tail shining. Dad captured that on film once.

When Dad left he killed the quail for eating and sold the peacocks, all but one, the one on the outside. Mom spoke of selling him, and I told her he couldn't be caught, something I hoped was true. Tearing down the egg house, selling the peacock, all part of wiping Dad's memory off the place.

In January their divorce was final, in March the land and house were settled. It stayed with Mom. One sunny March day Mom told me she hadn't seen the peacock in a while. I knew it had been roosting in the open quail pen, the place it always wanted to get back to—only now it was empty. I decided to look there first.

Inside was foretold what had happened. Long, blue-green feathers were scattered inside the door. I felt a sinking feeling as I picked up the long ones to keep. We'd done this so many times before. Each season when the feathers were shed Dad brought handfuls in and Mom kept them in vases. Where were all those feathers now? We didn't seem to have any left. Out of the cage and toward the woods were more. A struggle maybe, perhaps the peacock gained strength here and got away. I even maintained hope that he was alive and maybe only injured. Brilliant blue feathers got smaller and fewer. Finally I reached a pile of tufted gray-black and blue feathers in a scattered pile where the feast was taken. Not a beak or toe left.

I clutched the long feathers in my hands and walked back through the yard. The rough ground, once a pea patch, still held the semblance of rows and made walking hard. I passed the dog pen, now home to mice, long unused. I saw my mom and my daughters in the yard and swallowed back tears. I went forward to report the news.

Communing with Black Bears

AMYLOU WILSON

Amylou Wilson is a staff person for the Arkansas Environmental Federation. This article first appeared in the Federation's Environmental News in March of 1994.

At six A.M. on a pitch black Friday morning in February, Stan Jorgensen, his son Colin, two educators from his school in Little Rock, Tonie Patterson of Governor Jim Guy Tucker's office, myself, and several other people piled into two rented vans in Little Rock and headed west on Highway 10 through Perryville, Danville, and Waveland to the rocky, rough terrain of Hogan Mountain in Yell County. We were searching, along with employees of the Arkansas Game and Fish Commission, for a certain black bear sow, known as Darla, and her four male yearlings. The young had been born the previous winter and now would be in the range of forty to sixty pounds. They would be hibernating in a den somewhere, and we were going to find them via a radio collar attached to Darla's neck.

After waiting over an hour on the logging road where the Game and Fish Commission employees had left us so they could hike in and determine the bears' whereabouts, we were finally led on a journey I will never forget. After about an hour's hike that included descending a seventy-five-foot cliff and crossing a creek bed, we finally made it.

Wildlife biologist David Goad and others sedated the bears with a jabbing stick poked through openings in the den. In the process, one of the three cubs (the fourth had not survived) got spooked and ran out another opening in the den and up a tree, where it peered at this crew of human invaders for about thirty minutes while his siblings were gently pulled from the den so their ears could be tagged.

I held a bear cub's head in my hands and stroked its amazing body, while the professionals worked at measuring the cubs' length and weighing them for the purposes of tracking them later to attend to their progress.

All of this is being done to monitor the black bear population in Arkansas, once known as the Bear State, for a very good reason. Settlers all but eradicated these great beasts in the early part of the century. Then, in the 1950s and 1960s, 250 black bears were brought from Minnesota and Manitoba, Canada, to the Ozark and Ouachita Mountains of Arkansas to boost the population.

Ongoing studies to monitor the black bears and track the population are supported through contributions from companies such as Environmental Systems, which has donated five thousand dollars annually for the past several years. Jorgensen is the company's director of environmental affairs.

The trek back to the logging road seemed to take forever (about an hour and a half to be exact) and all up hill. Some of us were faster than others, and we patiently waited at the vans, slugging down the last of leftover soft drinks and eating whatever food was left from the morning. (Lucky for us, Jorgensen's wife, Renae, though not well enough to join us on the trip as planned, had taken the time to make some homemade tuna salad sandwiches the night before. There was certainly no fast food to be had in this remote setting.)

In the meantime, I found myself thinking how this particular hike rated in difficulty only second to the time I spent three days at ten thousand feet hiking in the mountainous terrain near Laramie, Wyoming, where I had slowly sloughed off more and more of the supplies in my backpack because the weight proved too much for my 105-pound body to carry. But in spite of all the hardships on that Wyoming trip, I will never forget the vision of a herd of fifty or a hundred mountain goats that blended in so expertly with rocky whiteness and a light dusting of the first snow of winter. Like the "trick" drawings in the panel of the newspaper that ask you to identify the difference between the two pictures, it had been hard to distinguish goat from rock from snow from cloud, and when the snapshots of that scene were developed, I proudly showed off this "trick" of nature to all my friends.

In much the same way, this adventure with the bears will not soon be forgotten, for there are the endearing snapshots of these creatures that might have torn us apart had they been awake, and the forever sensation of the bear's silky, bristly coat against my hands, and the "trick" of nature that allowed me to enter the lives of bears for such a brief moment.

Mad Scientist

GINA KOKES

*Gina Kokes is an aspiring writer living in
Little Rock. She began this "first-ever" poem as a
student in an Arkansas Extended Learning Center
class in the fall of 2000.*

---

i've never thought of myself as a cruel person,
but I do remember a time in my childhood
when experimenting with my playmates
captivated me with the glue of curiosity
and the delight of playing god on a summer day.

i grew up in a city neighborhood
slim on kids my age,
so I had to make do . . .
i found my world littered
with quick, wiggly dots and dashes of life.
i recruited them to be my "special friends."
they empowered me.
i strutted through the neighborhood
like royalty,
the only girl on the block—
who would look at,
touch,
and even pick up—
a bug.

my first venture into research
coincided with the start of the space program.
NASA placed ads in newspapers calling upon citizens
to collect millions of lightning bugs.
the glowy goo of their tummies
would be mashed and spread
on some type of satellite antennae.
armed with a glass jar
and brimming with patriotism,
i fearlessly crept into the vast and scary darkness—
of my own backyard.
i filled my container with dozens of night lights
and ran back to the safety of the porch.
i watched my own fantastic private light show
then hid the jar under my shirt
and watched myself blink . . .
but did my friends have
the "right stuff" for NASA?
outer space was so cold and icy—
perhaps an hour or so in the freezer
would test their mettle.
unfortunately,
my mother needed ice cubes.
her loud, angry disapproval of the scientific method
let me know
my friends were not NASA material—
any longer.

my favorite project hatched
during a plague of grasshoppers.
these hopping, spitting, wily creatures challenged
my young hand-eye coordination.
it was a shame to place such worthy opponents
in an ordinary glass jar.
my grandmother's white tin breadbox with the red lid
called my name as I walked by.
i placed a stunned captive inside,

then stood back to hear the wondrous ping
of a grasshopper hitting the inside of a tin box.
i collected at least fifty more.
placing the box on the kitchen table,
i listened in rapture to a symphony of dings.
my grandmother heard the lively music too—
and didn't like it one bit.
i begged her not to open the music box,
but in one quick move she flipped the lid open—
my orchestra joyfully jumped out and away to freedom.
i spent two days catching grasshoppers in her kitchen.
my grandmother had much to say.
fortunately,
she lapsed into her native tongue.
i didn't understand her foreign words
but my imagination translated.

my final experiment
followed a thunderstorm
on a warm summer evening.
spooked by the rain,
the earthworms stampeded
in a wiggling panic onto the sidewalk.
they were easy to round up.
i piled them high in a mayonnaise jar.
i wasn't too sure what to do with them—
until my dad passed with an empty plate in hand.
hmm . . . grilling burgers . . .
i was pouring the last of my friends
out of the jar and onto the grill
when my dad returned to flip the meat.
i'll just say . . .
i didn't sit for the next hour—
nor did I have any supper.
come to think of it . . .
neither did my parents.

after the "grill incident,"
my research supplies dwindled.
each request for a jar, container,
or use of a breadbox
met with a solid "no."
lacking equipment,
i drifted into the funeral business
burying every dead baby bird
that fell out of its nest and hit the pavement.
sometimes,
i think my budding conscience
nudged me into undertaking,
atoning, in some way,
for the untimely deaths
of my special friends.
one day,
the boy next door
slapped on a new pair of roller skates,
and big science died.
hello, new passion.
flying through the neighborhood
on my brand-new skates,
i swore I heard a collective sigh of relief
coming from my playmates.
look! the mad scientist has moved on—
the world is safe again
for an ordinary bug
on a city block
in the neighborhood.

Birds: Humanity's Barometer

GLYNN HARRIS

*Glynn Harris is a freelance writer, book author,
outdoor radio personality, and newsletter editor.
His reflection on birds first appeared in* Arkansas
Wildlife *magazine in 1998.*

Jack Miner has been dead for more than half a century.
Called "the Father of Conservation" for his pioneering work banding
ducks and geese and in providing a sanctuary for migrating waterfowl,
a statement attributed to him still rings as true today as it did then: "If
I can get a child to love a bird, that child will love his fellow man."

God in His infinite wisdom knew what He was doing when He
placed birds on the Earth. Some birds were placed here for man to
harvest; to allow humankind to experience the essence of nature in the
hunting of wild fowl; for the bounty they afford on the dining table.
Others are here purely for ornamentation; for their ability to stir the
senses with sweet trills and warbles; for the sheer fun and enjoyment
afforded by spending a few quiet moments simply watching birds do
what birds do.

I am indeed fortunate. My father taught my brother, sister, and me
the thrill and suspense of hunting ducks when we were just youngsters. Watching a pair of wood ducks come barreling down through
the cypresses at dawn is something that still gives me goose bumps.

Later, hunting doves and quail would be added to my menu of fun
things to do outdoors. In recent years, the pursuit of the wild turkey
has been a consuming passion.

As much as I enjoy hunting various species of wild gamebirds, another childhood experience has enabled my fascination with birds to be more than one dimensional. As much as I enjoy hunting, the gentle sport of bird watching, something I learned from a wise and sensitive mother, has given me untold hours of delight.

For ten successive Aprils, I watched in wonder as a male painted bunting visited my backyard feeder, occasionally joined by a shy female. They were predictable. Tax time meant painted bunting time.

It has been two years now since I last saw a painted bunting. None came last year, and so far, I haven't seen one this spring. I find a measure of solace, albeit small, in hearing from neighbors and friends who report that they are enjoying watching painted buntings on their feeders.

As a consolation prize, my feeder is dotted with a splash of color— the bright vermilion of the male cardinal; the metallic blue of indigo buntings; and this week, the black, white, and red combination of rose-breasted grosbeaks passing through.

Down on the creek there is color. Yellow predominates. Shy, secretive hooded warblers pop up on a branch overhead and just as quickly flit away. Prothonotary warblers, their yellow as brilliant as melted butter, skim low over the water flying from tree bole to cypress knee.

My gaze has not missed the nesting birds around the yard. On the pond in the pasture across the road, a pair of wood ducks is rearing half a dozen fledglings. The babies follow their mother over the pond's surface, darting like wind-blown thistle down.

In the box on the utility pole, fledgling bluebirds are ready to leave the nest. In the bowels of a hollow post across the road, brownheaded nuthatches have made their nest for the umpteenth straight year. And in the garden, a clutch of tufted titmouse babies are almost full-feathered and will be soon out of the box and on their own.

"One key to the human heart is in wild creatures." Jack Milner said that too.

I wish I could have known him.

Plugging Turtles

DANA STEWARD

Dana Steward is editor of this book. This piece was written in her Hendrix College composition class in the fall of 2001, where everyone is expected to write, even the teacher.

Before my husband and I were married, he taught me to shoot a pistol. Although I was always the tomboy, my dad had injured an eye on a barbed-wire fence as a kid, and so, unable to sight a weapon, he had nothing to do with guns other than the conscriptive experience of World War II; consequently, neither had I.

But I loved them, especially "my" gun, a twenty-two-caliber High Standard cowboy-style revolver. Although it would never have the accuracy of my Ruger automatic or the artful design of the Smith and Wesson revolver I would eventually own, I shot the High Standard pretty well. We drilled away at paper targets at a local range, and I loved to plink aluminum cans lined up on a sawdust backstop in the woods, but my forte was turtles.

We would snake the little powder blue Fairlane around the concrete barriers and out to the end of the bridge under construction across Fourche Bayou in Little Rock, park at the unopened intersection of I-30, I-430, and what is now I-530 where it peels off toward Pine Bluff. Then we'd walk out onto the bridge span, hang our legs over the side, and look for the brown round disks atop the logs. The muddy waters a hundred feet below were full of turtles: big ones, little ones, grandmas and grandpas and all the kids, sunning in polite conversational rows on cypress knees and tupelo snags. The bayou was a curious contradiction of swamp (with cypress, lilies, cattails, green brackish water) and flowing stream, feeling its way around all the interstate birms, the elevated railroad bed, backing up as far southwest as the old Big Rock Quarry and running freely through an open burn garbage dump at Arch Street.

I don't dislike turtles. In fact, I remember as a child trying to keep a dandy marked box turtle as a pet when Mama wouldn't let me get a dog. Still, there is just something about the way the creatures present themselves as targets—poised as if for a family portrait and yet allusive to the kill. At the first report of the pistol, they're gone, *plop, plop,* only the briefest ripple revealing they ever existed. I can't even remember how I knew at the time I had hit one. We certainly never attempted to retrieve them, wouldn't have wanted them if we could, having been raised too long in the city to consider the meat a delicacy. I just remember Bill's shout in my ears, "You got one!" and my internal response of, "YES!" I have never been a fast, from-the-hip type shooter, and I can still feel the practiced way I lined up my sights on my quarry, the careful stance my feet took, the solid report of the revolver moving into my arms and shoulders, and the joy—make no mistake about it, that's what it was—when the turtles dropped from the log like a rock in a paper sack, rather than gracefully sliding into the ooze. I'd made my shot; the turtle was dead, I was alive, and that was the end of that.

I had quit shooting turtles long before it began to bother me that I had ever hunted turtles at all. The quitting was circumstantial. Not many women of the late sixties took time from their three small babies and a household to run in order to make a shooting expedition. Bill even traded the High Standard for a deer rifle at one point, but I cried so hard, without being able to say why, that he bought it back again.

The freeway opened, and over the two score years since, our family has buzzed countless times above the bayou, seldom looking down to the waters below. The Big Rock Mountain has continued to inch away, just as our children grew up and did the same. The open fires of the dump were smothered, that whole area filled, even into the wetlands, and a neighborhood ballpark was built on the sight, complete with ten zillion kilowatts of halogen lighting that eerily pierce the swamp nights.

Last spring we paddled up Fourche Creek headed toward the old Coleman Dairy land south of Asher Avenue. It is not a pristine wilderness experience, but concealed beneath the banks burrowed out over a time frame that easily predates our statehood, the creek remains thrillingly wild. Birds of prey, snakes, beaver, mink, and, of course, turtles are at home here, oblivious to the skyscrapers and the international airport as their neighbors. Speaking softly as we floated drowsily back down stream, we speculated as to the effect of the impromptu twenty-first century dams impeding the flow, constructed of thousands of plastic drink bottles, fast-food styro containers, and all the detritus of the city south and west of Main. So far the creatures mostly seem to have survived.

An exception is Arkansas's largest turtle, the prehistoric snapper that used to guard the bayou, frequently growing to monster size in old age. The days of sepia photos showing proud men preening around rows of giant snappers, some measuring two feet and more along the carapace, their flat backs barnacled by more than half a century of living, are over. The largest, the alligator snapping turtle known as loggerhead, whose toothless snout can take a man's arm, is practically extinct in this area of the state.

Ironically, the day I saw my first snapping turtle, caged in a large trap, with grown men poking broomsticks at his eyes to watch him strike, is the day I consciously quit shooting turtles. It's also the day I realized just how complex and interrelated the choices we are required to make can be and that sometimes the fact we make those choices in innocence or ignorance does not lessen the result. The turtle must be among the bravest of beasts because he literally raises himself, hatched from an egg laid by a mother who then moved on. He makes it in the world on his own, but he is no match for Man (or for a woman with a High Standard pistol).

Recently, inspired by some grant money being made available by the Game and Fish Commission, the city fathers had been talking about setting aside what's left of this Fourche Creek area as a nature preserve. Unfortunately, the idea did not gain purchase, upstaged by a flat sterile piece of earth that provides an additional piece of the crazy quilt called the Clinton Library Project.

Now the project is being discussed with the Audubon Society. I think it will happen, this Fourche Creek Preserve—this place where people could bring their binoculars and field guides, or just their urban souls and feast upon what has been left to us here. No doubt, the interpretive sign will read "No hunting."

Bamboo Grove

LAURA NEALE

*Laura Neale is a student at Covenant College. She
wrote this poem for Sandy Bakke's class at Walnut
Valley Christian Academy in Little Rock in 2001.*

---

in the late morning
the cackling night birds are gone
so I am not an intruder here
sometimes they have left a few glossy
black feathers lying
among the papery leaves
ivory brown and golden
that have spiraled down from their green brethren swaying above
to rest close together over the moist earth and
to quiet my footfalls to a gentle rustling
under the bamboo stalks that grow side by side
lancing their way high over my head into the canopy
a loose weave of smooth jade blades
through which diamond points and
bright silver streams of daylight fall
and are scattered like water drops on my face
as I look up
my eye catches the outline of
a single narrow leaf
glowing in the light alone
for a moment
before it is drawn back among the others

where the air under their whispering shelter is cool and
through it glide invisible currents visiting each living stalk
assuring the young shoots
slender and pithy and arrow-straight with ambition
they will become through faithful years like
the towering seasoned ones
whose green is ashen streaked
thick and strong and
beautifully crooked with time
natural and noble shafts rising together
keepers of stillness
keepers of peace
in this place I have come
to just
be

Botany Notes

MAXINE CLARK

*Along with her husband, Joe, Maxine co-edited a
nationally award-winning magazine called the*
Ozark Society Bulletin *for almost two decades.
"Botany Notes" was Maxine's monthly column
educating her readers about the native plants of
the Ozarks. The distinctive three-lobed sassafras is
the Ozark Society symbol.*

As the days grow shorter, autumn approaches with the glorious kaleidoscope of coloration in foliage and grasses. There aren't enough days to visit all our favorite places in the Boston Mountains to enjoy the mosaic of gold, red, and bronze that covers the hills. One scene that flashes back in my memory is the magnificent view across the mountaintops as seen from a high lookout on Highway 7 above Jasper.

If I were to choose the one tree that typifies autumn for me, it would be the hardy sassafras. *Sassafras albidum.* It is the only member of its genus found in America. Only two other species exist in the world—one native to the island of Taiwan and the other to mainland China.

Sassafras belongs to the Laurel Family. Two other members of this family that grow in Arkansas are spice bush, *Lindera benzoin,* and the rare pond berry, *Lindera melissaefolium.* All of these are dioecious, meaning that male, staminate, and female, pistillate, flowers are borne on different plants. We have a male spice bush which never produces the brilliant red berries that are on the female plant.

For a number of years we have enjoyed seeing a beautiful grove of sassafras as we drive Highway 16 west to Siloam Springs. In early spring the sinuous branches are topped by a cloud of small golden flowers. Sassafras is usually found in colonies since it sends up root suckers freely. All the trees will have the same general shape, branching habit, and sex as the parent tree.

Small tender greenish leaves appear along with the flowers. Three different leaf shapes are common on the tree, and all may appear on the same branch. They may be one lobed, oval shaped; a mitten shape with two lobes; or they may have three lobes, similar to the mitten shape but with an additional lobe. The latter was selected as the Ozark Society emblem and was first printed on page two of the [Ozark] Bulletin, spring 1973 issue. Embroidery shoulder patches and decals for canoes, cars, and luggage are available for Ozark Society members.

By early autumn sassafras trees begin to brighten the landscape with bright splotches of color, changing from pale orange, yellow, or salmon to orange-red. It is during this time that the fleshy, one-seeded fruits ripen. They are about one-third to one-half inch long, ovoid, dark purple, and held in small red cups at the end of scarlet stems. Usually the seeds are dispersed by birds who often eat them before they fall. The minimum seed-bearing age for trees is ten years, and a tree will produce a good crop every other year. It is almost impossible to transplant a sassafras. It can be accomplished with a small tree and a good ball of earth.

Sassafras became known as a medicinal wonder in the early 1500s. French colonists were repeating Indian tales about the wonderful healing power of the liquors made from the root bark. Early expeditions to America to bring back furs and cedar logs also carried a load of sassafras root. Captain John Smith included it in the cargo of his first exports to England from the newly established Jamestown colony.

Eventually its popularity in Europe declined as its curative powers failed to produce miraculous results. Only on the American frontier was it still regarded as a spring tonic to revitalize the body before the summer heat set in. The Indians continued to use the powdered leaves on wounds and solutions of the juice to relieve sore eyes. In the 1800s sassafras root bark was used to flavor candies, medicine, and drinks.

The oil of the root bark of *sassafras albidum,* safrole, is now regarded as toxic and a carcinogen. It is a natural ingredient of sassafras tea. Until recently safrole was used as a flavoring agent in root beers but its use there was withdrawn after it was noted that prolonged ingestion of high levels (0.5 percent of the diet) of safrole by adult rats led to the formation of liver tumors.

Sassafras wood is highly aromatic, and the early pioneers figured that anything that odoriferous just had to repel insects, particularly bedbugs. So they used it to build the floors and walls of their cabins and their bedsteads. The same theory applied to mites in the chicken house. Sassafras sticks were preferred for stirring the kettle when making soap. Pioneer women boiled the bark to make red and orange dye for cloth.

Louisiana, with a French and Spanish heritage, is famous for its Creole cooking. One of its original creations is gumbo. From *River Road Recipes,* published by the Junior League of Baton Rouge, Inc., Baton Rouge, Louisiana:

> A Word About Gumbos: Gumbo is an *original* creation and a cherished possession in South Louisiana kitchens. The word "gumbo" comes from the Congo "quin-gombo" which means okra. It may be made with okra or with filé as a thickening agent. Filé is the powdered sassafras leaf made long ago by the Choctaw Indians. Whereas okra is cooked with the gumbo, filé is added *after* the gumbo is removed from the heat. Never add filé while gumbo is cooking because boiling after the filé is added tends to make the gumbo stringy and unfit for use.
>
> You may make your own filé. Just dry and crumble some sassafras leaves, or string them on a thread to dry and keep a supply handy.

If Turkeys Were Monogamous

JIM ALLEN

*Jim Allen retired from the insurance business in
central Arkansas and settled on a mountaintop at
Allison outside Mountain View to enjoy the hills
and write. His turkey tale first appeared in the*
Ozark Mountaineer *in 2001.*

He is closer now than the first time he gobbled—I can
feel my excitement building. This was my first turkey hunt, and a
gobbler was coming to my call. I was sitting on the ground with my
back against a large pine tree just below the ridge line. I was facing
west hoping to have the sun behind me. My father-in-law had invited
me to join him for the spring turkey hunt. This was my first trip in the
area, and I was not optimistic for success.

I called to the tom again but did not receive a response. As I sat
there, afraid to move, I was concerned the tom might have changed
his mind. Suddenly, his gobble filled the forest! He was behind a fallen
tree about thirty yards to my right. He fluffed his body feathers and
fanned his tail feathers into a majestic display. His beard almost
touched the ground. I was spellbound; it was the most awesome sight
I had ever witnessed.

He raised his head and sent forth a gobble that shook the ground
and made the trees sway. He strutted, searching for the hen he
expected to come running to his magnificent display. He was on my
far right, and my shotgun was on my lap pointing to my left. Since I

am right handed, my only chance for a shot would be to bring it to my shoulder and swing to my right. I hoped to shoot him before he realized what was happening. I overestimated my ability—and I underestimated his reactions. My shot went to the spot he had already vacated. He was gone before I could fire a second shot.

If turkeys were monogamous, I would not be sitting here with a smoking gun, an empty shotgun shell, and a sore shoulder. If turkeys were monogamous, I would not even be sitting here.

If turkeys were monogamous, entire industries would not exist. These are industries that cater to hunters seeking to claim this elegant bird as a trophy or else a meal, or maybe both. Visit the sporting goods section of your local sporting goods store in the spring. You will be serenaded by a cacophony of yelps, cackles, and gobbles emanating from some of the most unusual instruments imaginable. There is a cedar box that if manipulated in one fashion imitates a hen and in another way sounds like a tom.

A cedar stick rubbed on a slate or piece of glass imitates the hen. These are old styles that are still popular today.

The newest calls are mouth diaphragms that with practice can duplicate virtually any sound made by turkeys, hen, or tom. While they are promoted to be the best, there are some of us who have never been able to master them. I have found it impossible to use the mouth calls with a wad of Red Man chewing tobacco in my mouth.

If you can tolerate the noise, walk further through the sporting goods displays to find camouflage pants, shirts, hats, gloves, face masks, and camouflage skin creams to conceal you from turkeys—and from other hunters. Have you ever wondered how a turkey hunter gets shot just sitting in the woods? It is because they were making turkey noises and some low-life "sound shooter" comes along and shoots in the direction of the sound. Nobody likes "sound shooters!"

Look in the store for the turkey decoys: they are life size and look like the real thing. A friend told me about a hunter hidden in the brush next to a field where he had his decoy placed. He was making yelps like a hen when suddenly a coyote streaked in front of him. It grabbed his decoy and was gone in an instant. Imagine that coyote's reaction when he tried to eat his dinner.

Browse some more, and you will find shotguns just for turkey hunting. Our grandfathers used their single-barrel shotguns to kill squirrel, rabbit, quail, ducks, geese, deer, and turkey. We have been led to believe we need a special shotgun just for turkeys.

Call it salesmanship or gullibility, the results are the same; we buy these products in an attempt to outsmart a bird with a brain about the size of a pea. Old-timers talk about how smart turkeys are. They are probably no smarter than the hunter; turkeys buy into the same clothes, decoys, and calls as the hunter does. That is how they get fooled and lose their lives.

It is not my intention to badmouth this noble creature. I just want to set the record straight. The turkey has excellent eyesight that distinguishes colors, has good hearing, and is constantly alert. We have only a short season to hunt, but the turkey is hunted all year by his other enemies. They must always be on guard. Turkeys roost in tall trees to avoid four-legged hunters while it rests.

There is no turkey that is smarter than I am, but there are some very lucky toms out there. I have called others in since that first experience, but I have never succeeded in killing one. They seem to hang up before they are in range or they approach from an angle that I can't get a decent shot. They are quick and are experts at putting a tree between us.

For all his skills, the gobbler is vulnerable in April because he is not monogamous. That old boy may have a large harem, but he can't resist the call of another hen he believes is seeking his companionship. Like many other male critters, he never seems to realize that what he has may be better than what is calling to him from the bush.

There are many that think the wild turkey should be our national bird instead of the bald eagle. It is hard for me to imagine inspiring patriotism with the image of a turkey on our money, flags, and posters. We tend to respect the eagle, while "turkey" is sometimes used as an unfavorable description. I am happy to keep the eagle as our national symbol and to have the turkey as our edible symbol of Thanksgiving, a national holiday.

If turkeys were monogamous I would have missed that first experience on the hunt with my father-in-law, a cherished memory of a great person and a wonderful trip. God did it right the first time—I would not want to change a thing.

Wild Wisteria

VALERIE DUNN

*Valerie Dunn became a fellow of the Little Rock
Writing Project in 2000 when she taught high
school in the Little Rock School District. She is
now a Graduate Dean's Fellowship recipient
attending Southern Illinois University at
Carbondale in the Rhetoric and Composition doctoral program. She wrote this poem shortly before
her move in early summer 2001.*

You grew so fast, thick and twisted
Wild, Wicked Wisteria
clutching, climbing, clawing your way
to the wicked waiting Sun
No dainty vine were you
but some mad determined wench
grabbing any pole and post
sprouting leafy shoots;
curling your eager tendrils just for him.
Flashing,
fragrant,
falling,
Dangling clusters of deep rounded purples
shamelessly before his rapacious eye,
impetuous,
insatiable,

resplendent in his light
Every part responding to his seasoned touch
Try as you might,
you never could overleap that distance to the Sun
hoping to entwine his muscled thighs.
Did he turn in disappointment or disgust?
When he left,
you withered as fast as you had come.
Stooping naked now like some old arthritic one—
gnarled, alone and bent.
Then came the night his minions fell
pattering from the sky
so that now you glisten—entombed in crystal light.
Perhaps a last embrace—
but more for spite
and to preen at his own reflection
in icy morning's light.

Terror Hangs in the Trees

BOB LANCASTER

Bob Lancaster's column in which "Terror"
appeared in 2000 is a longtime fixture of the
Arkansas Times, *where he is associate editor. Bob*
is equally well known for political and cultural
commentary on Arkansas in his books such as
The Jungles of Arkansas.

I lost track of the presidential campaign and all the big political doings last week because something more important came up. Something more unnerving than the thought of George W. Bush with a couple of Bud 40s aboard as president. Even more unnerving than George W. Bush sober as president. Totally creeped me out—the first thing since the movie *Psycho* that wrought a fundamental change-for-the-worse in my way of looking at the world.

I've been squirming around uncomfortably ever since; had trouble sleeping nights; wary of venturing out of doors. One of those bits of knowledge that you wish to high heaven you'd never heard about, that you know you'll ever after regret not having remained blissfully ignorant of. I only heard this third-hand now, but here's what it was: A Fayetteville herpetologist who's done a high-tech rattlesnake study disclosed his findings at a big scientifico-snakelovers' gathering in Fayetteville last week. His project involved implanting little tracking sensors in a slew of rattlers, then turning them loose in the wild. He learned a good deal about their private lives, including their roosting habits, one of which turns out to be profoundly unsettling indeed: that they spend a lot of their leisure time hanging around in trees!

This was stunning news, shocking news—the prospect of a side-winder the size of a pulpwood billet launching at me from one of my backyard mimosas some moonlit night is just intolerable in this geezer phase of the long journey—but it wasn't a surprise somehow. I sensed the truth of it, the horrible unnegotiable truth of it, and felt that I might've known the truth of it at some primal, lily-livered level since way, way back when. It was almost like I'd always known they were up there. Looking down, watching, heat-sensing the fool human waddling through the brush, ready to drop on him at some mysterious signal from the snake deity, slither over his collar and down his back, and with a quick ripping fury of fangs end his lifetime of bothersome intrusions into what was once and someday surely will be again the rightful reptilian domain.

In the creepiest recesses of my being, I've been aware of this awful snake secret for a good fifty years. Pap used to take his boys fishing on the Saline River in an old aluminum boat, and he liked to minnow for crappie ten or twelve feet out from the bank, paddling from the bow, which swung the squared-off stern (where his terrified offspring cowered) into the streamside willow bushes hanging out over the water.

There might have been one or two of those willow bushes over fifteen years' time that didn't have snakes lying up in the branches, but of the quarter million others, as the boat brushed through their limbs and banged their cottony trunks, at least half of them shook out their snakes and at least half of those snakes fell into our boat. By that conservative reckoning, my brothers and I had to fight off 62,500 snakes.

We were impressionable youngsters so warped by the experience that we carried the consequent phobias and complexes traumatized into our old age. Pap did not sympathize with us as we flailed and shrieked. If anything he took the snakes' side. "You're not afraid of a little old moccasin," he'd scoff. "Why, you're twict as big as he is."

If all those willows had snakes, no reason in the world why the bigger trees on back away from the water shouldn't be snake-draped too. Of course they were, and always had been. Didn't the original tempter serpent scale up into the appley boughs so he could make his pitch to Eve eye-to-eye? And the monster snakes of "Tarzan"—did bwana ever see them writhing along the jungle floor? No, they undulated down at him along smooth-barked vinery from high above. So much safer up there: they didn't have to worry about patriots treading on them, about Fat Broads happening along to club them to mince. Why wouldn't our rattlesnakes recreate there too, out of harm's way, given their druthers? So much of my life I've spent traipsing around the Arkansas woods, an eye out for snakes on the path ahead, in trail-side brushpiles and behind fallen logs: living in a fool's paradise in that the whole time they hung there just above my Stetson in wads and strands and windblown curtains of snake. Trees as snaky as they were avian in that last great scene of *The Birds*.

Pap also took us squirrel hunting. Mostly our method was "still hunting," which required hitting the woods a full hour before the faintest glimmer of dawn to wait quietly in some squirrelly-looking glade for the bushes to start moving in the high branches in the first smears of morning gray. One of our haunts took us in along an abandoned railroad track for what seemed like three or four miles, whereupon he would station me in a little stand of hickories and go on ahead taking the flashlight with him. Leaving me enswamped in a dark as heavy as flannel. What else to do but hunker beside one of the trees, lean back against the base of it, gun across lap, waiting for break of day? An eternity before I could make out gun, frosty breath, hand in front of face. Then another half hour before objects around me began to take shape—hickory nuts, clumps of sumac, pieces of driftwood, including the one just about a yard long and big around as a vacuum cleaner hose. Lying between my feet as I sat there, not an arm's length from the crotch. It never did move, but soon after I learned what cold terror was, what Emily Dickinson meant by "zero at the bone." Years passed, though, decades, before I realized, having heard of this Fayetteville snakeologist's research, that the thing had probably tumbled down out of the inky treetops—one copperhead among no telling how many of them spaghettied up there in a kind of snake skybox or snake condominium or snake Y.

Groundhog Lying Dead

ELAINE MCKINNEY

"Groundhog Lying Dead" was written as a part of
a thesis for the Department of Rhetoric and
Writing master's degree at the University of
Arkansas at Little Rock, where Elaine McKinney
graduated. She frequently continues to write from
the UALR campus. This piece takes its title from
the Richard Eberhart poem, "The Groundhog."

I did not understand the word "death," although I knew what it meant to be "killed." To be killed was simply to vanish, to disappear, to be there one moment and not there the next. People who were killed were zapped by people and things, as on the radio shows "Captain Marvel" and "The Shadow" and "Gangbusters." People had been killed in the war by something called the atom bomb. Indeed, my father's work on war planes, his little booklets with illustrations of fighters and bombers, and his model planes given as rewards for his service in the nation's defense fed my imagination overtime, and the sight of any kind of aircraft going over our house would often send me scurrying inside screaming that the Nack-zees were bombing us. But what happened to the bodies of people who were killed I did not know. I had no idea that people could sicken and die or that death was something that happened eventually to everyone.

My father came in that evening with the news.

"Well, I hate this, but there's nothin' we can do. A car hit Spot and knocked him way over in the corn patch. He's dead."

Spot was a stray cat that my parents had taken in, a beautiful white cat with large, round black spots on his back. I liked him but had not yet become attached to him.

"When I found him, his eyes were wide open." My father looked a little pale. He was fond of animals.

"I'll go get him. He may be scared," I said, starting for the door.

"You can't. He's dead. I'll bury him sometime this evenin'." He did not explain, and left the room to sit with my mother at the kitchen table and talk.

I decided to go see for myself what had happened. The corn patch across the road was not large, but I wandered a long time among the huge leaves of the cornstalks before I found Spot. He was lying outside the last row I searched, on a carpet of grass mottled by the interplay of light and shade. He lay on one side, his lovely spots bright in the glow of the afternoon sun, every hair glistening and defined, not a mark of imperfection to be seen on him. However, as I stood at an angle I could see his wide-open amber eyes that seemed to regard me lazily, and the trickle of blood from his mouth that had congealed in small droplets on his whiskers, and below the wide crimson spreading stain. With a shudder I suddenly knew what death was. I longed with all my heart to run away from this mockery, this seeing that was not seeing, this life that was not life, but I stood frozen, unable to move. I heard my mother's call, but could not turn around to see where the call came from. Only when her hand seized mine and led me on my unsteady feet toward the house did I realize where I was and the meaning of what had happened.

I followed my father everywhere he went that summer. Whether he was saddling up Alan, our old white horse, or taking the cows to pasture, or digging postholes, or putting up a stretch of barbed-wire fence, I was at his heels, with Tib usually trotting along behind us.

One day my father and I stood in a part of the pasture far from the house and gazed down at a strange, white structure, something I had never seen before.

"That's a skeleton," my father said, in answer to my question. "That's one of my cows that died. That part there's the skull—you can see the eye holes."

Standing beside me, my father towered above me. His shadow was long in the sun. The skeleton seemed to reveal the hard clear edge of death, to have a cleanness lacking in the too-lifelike death of Spot. I felt a relief and sniffed the air. It seemed that everything around us, the meadows, the distant hills, referred to the Skull, the Central Fact. The winds coming over the hills seemed to blow toward us and suck through the eye holes and sweep beyond us toward the outermost stars. My father and I stood each in our own worlds, yet both occupied the center of the stillness at the heart of the world.

Many years later I described this experience in a poem:

Skull Song

Still fields. Late afternoon.
In laughter's grip we wandered.
The small brook rambled after,
Humming a sad old tune.
And the sun had done with blazing.
And the bones lay white on the ground.
The Skull sat, and the Eyes
Were two round hollows gazing.
Flesh and the fields were one.
The Skull said: "Eyes are winds
Fresher than peacock dyes
That flash and fold in the sun.
Know this: All joys made One
Are found in passing things,
And the moons that tug at the night,
And the suns that scowl at the day
Blow through these hollow rings.

I had a child's usual fascination with feces and loved to follow a trail of cowpats and to watch their progressive desiccation, from steaming to crusty to dry powder, no longer even an allurement for flies. I loved to kick the dry ones, shot through with grasses and cockleburs, and watch the powdery substance fly in all directions. One day, in one of these meanderings I saw by the side of the path a small dead animal. I did not know what it was. It was merely an unidentifiable handful of fur. I did not dare turn it over. Months later, when I examined the same spot, much of the fur was gone and I could see the skeleton beneath. Fascinated, I bent down to examine the tiny skull and eye holes: I could see the sharp incisors, pathetic in their negated ferocity, and the tiny, fan-like claws. Later on that year, in the late fall, I passed by the same spot and saw nothing, though the skeleton may have been hidden by mud and rotted leaves. I looked at the place where the animal had been. Then I knew, with a child's wordless thoughts, that the rays of sun, which disappeared when I stood under them, but which stood out as a clear shaft of beauty when I stood a little apart, was the Father; I, the Son who received the blessing; and the Holy Ghost, the Infinite Nothing which lay at my feet. I stood for a moment naked in the quivering leaves of autumn. Then, with all the blessings of that day on my head, I walked on.

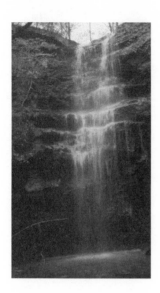

PART FIVE

Should've Built the Wall

The Varied Voices of the Conservation Movement

Mostly I'm here today because I am really afraid, afraid of what this world is going to be like in thirty, forty, or fifty years. I guess every generation has had its fears for the future of the world, but no generation has ever had to contemplate the environmental disasters that we face today. And it really scares me because if I can't go out and enjoy the simple pleasures of a clear view, green trees, healthy forest, free-flowing streams, then there really won't be much pleasure left in life at all.

—KATIE GUION
Congressional Wilderness
Hearing Testimony
1984

Should've Built the Wall

RICHARD ALLIN

Arkansas Democrat-Gazette *columnist Richard Allin is known for his fascination with trains, good food, and his Helena roots. Here in his "Our Town" column written in 2001, he reminds us all of a familiar Arkansas boast.*

I loved to hear our teacher tell us in grade school how you could build a wall around Arkansas, and that we would still have everything needed to sustain a civilization. She said we'd have all the diamonds, coal, and oil that we would need. We would never run out of resources to build houses and buildings.

Railroads ran all over the state. Helena, my hometown, had an airport dotted with three or four planes. Buses ran in and out regularly. Actually, we didn't know absolutely everything that it took to make a civilization, but we couldn't think of anything we needed.

We never discussed whether we could come and go in and out of the state if they built the wall. Maybe we would have to live here as an eternal experiment, just to show the outside world how rich we were in natural resources. And could visitors from other states and countries come in and partake of what we had? We didn't try to answer these questions.

When we went to visit relatives in Ontario, I told my two cousins—Gerald and Ruth—about Arkansas and the wall. It puzzled them. They thought in terms of provinces. Ontario was one of the biggest political subdivisions in the world, bigger than several of the states in the United States.

"Say *what?*" Gerald would ask in puzzlement.

I was too young to get into much of a debate, so we left it at that. He then showed me the only ice rink I'd ever seen. It was near his house. I wondered if Arkansas had one within its walls. He also showed me a hockey stick that made no sense to me whatsoever.

I told him how we said the Pledge of Allegiance to the flag every morning. He said his class sang "God Save the Queen."

I still thought we were luckiest in Arkansas. Ontario was too big to build any kind of wall around.

One night the sky glowed red. It made me nervous. I thought it was forest fires.

"Northern lights," Gerald said. "Do you have northern lights in Arkansas?"

I didn't know. Anyway, they didn't fit into a state with a wall around it.

Time has passed since those days. Before we could get the wall built, timber corporations discovered our forests. Millions of our forested acres have since been clear-cut, the lumber shipped off. Other trees have been planted, but the forests don't look the same. Where are the old hardwoods? Anybody can plant a pine tree.

So, I guess Arkansas's wall turned out to be a parable about conservation. We would be able to last perpetually in Arkansas as long as the resources were conserved, and nobody got greedy.

It hasn't really turned out that way.

Residents of Arkansas noted with interest a few days ago when a group of county residents wondered if the Clinton Library Foundation might not fork over enough millions to help build the River Rail project. The project is a couple of million dollars short. The Clinton Foundation had just offered to help former president Clinton meet his rent payments in Carnegie Towers in New York. It made us wonder whether the foundation might not also fork over some money to the city of Little Rock to help it pay for the land the library is to rest upon. Arkansas is (or was) the Clintons' home, after all.

City leaders, you see, managed to divert tax money away from other projects to buy the library's land without a vote of the people. They did it this way figuring that a vote of the people would put the kibosh on buying the land for all eternity, and that would embarrass the former president.

Since then, Clinton has forsaken the glitter and glamour of midtown Manhattan for the clamor and clatter of Harlem, the most famous nearly all-black neighborhood in the world. So, with the savings, maybe some Clinton money could be cut away for use by the new streetcar line.

Downriver: Reflections on the Lower White

KEITH SUTTON

Keith Sutton, who wrote "Downriver" in 1999, is the longtime editor of Arkansas Wildlife *magazine published by the Arkansas Game and Fish Commission. His latest book is* Hunting Arkansas.

"The White river is beyond all dispute the most beautiful river of Arkansas."

So wrote Frederick Gerstaecker, a German adventurer, after visiting the state in the late 1830s.

I wonder what he would think now.

I sat in a johnboat last summer, where the waters of the White meld with the Mississippi. On shore, several bulldozers worked, clearing timber for a new road. I watched as they ravaged the area like a slow-moving tornado. Huge trees toppled before their blades. Some had sprouted in that swampy ground hundreds of years before Gerstaecker's visit. Workers pushed them into rows and torched them.

So much for respecting your elders.

Across the river, scores of people wearing hard hats scampered here and there. Cranes pivoted on floating platforms as they gouged at the river bottom. Huge pilings were taking shape in the river, each big enough to house a high-rise hotel. A network of monstrous pipes drained the flooded bottoms so the men could work unhampered. Fish gathered in huge numbers where one pipe spewed its dusky load into the Mississippi, feeding on the thousands of small bottomland creatures being sucked from the swamp and vomited into the dark water.

This chaos originated with the construction of Montgomery Point Lock and Dam, the first on the lower White River. When the river is low, barges have difficulty entering the mouth of the White, the starting point of the McClellan-Kerr Navigation System. The U.S. Army Corps of Engineers came up with a solution: build a dam at the river's mouth so the navigation system can function during rare low-water periods.

People hoping to preserve this remote island of bottomland habitat fought the project for years, but to no avail. The work continues. The dam will be completed in 2002.

When I first visited Montgomery Point fifteen years ago, I found myself surrounded by near-wilderness. Small, barely passable roads snaked through the bottoms, but visitors rarely came. The only people you were likely to see during a week-long stay were residents of a few shantyboats, occasional hunters and fishermen, and men who worked on riverboats passing through. It was a peaceful realm then, where one could find refuge from the hazards of the outside world.

Construction of the paved highway to the dam site changed that forever. A constant stream of traffic now infests the once-peaceful woodlands. There is no freedom from crowds of hurried, harried humans. Wild animals once commonly seen along the river have retreated to more remote areas. Hundreds of acres of trees have been cleared, or buried beneath mountains of sand heaped upon them by dredging operations.

Those of us who valued the area for its wildness consider it devastated. The landscape is gut shot.

All along the lower White River, things are changing. The shantyboat culture, peopled by generations of Arkansans who made their living from the river, is all but gone. The fish don't bite like they used to; some species once common here are gone. Beds of mussels that covered miles of river bottom have vanished. Civilization increasingly compresses the river.

The lower White, which has changed its course hundreds of times over thousands of years, is being changed by man. And the life the river nurtures is changing with it.

The White River arises near Pettigrew in the northwest Arkansas Ozarks and flows erratically for 722 miles before joining the Mississippi. In the Ozarks, it's a spirited colt of a stream, kicking cold, whitewater heels through wooded valleys and gaps. In the Delta, it's a sluggish, brutal river, cutting S-curves and near figure-eights through a gigantic area of flatland. There's as much difference between the two portions of the stream as there is between the fast-falling Niagara and the peaceful Suwannee.

Lake Sequoyah, thirty-one miles below the White's headwaters, is a small but poignant reminder that the river is no longer untamed. A water-supply lake for Fayetteville, four-hundred-acre Sequoyah is a gateway of sorts to the "Great Lakes" country beyond, several hundred miles of once-vibrant river in Arkansas and Missouri now plugged with dams and reservoirs.

This part of the story began in the 1930s when Congress authorized the Corps to build dams for flood control and power. In 1944, Norfork Dam on the North Fork River was completed. Bull Shoals Dam followed in 1951, Table Rock and Beaver in 1958 and 1964.

The dams completely changed the river's character. In 1970, Bill Mathis, then chief of the Game and Fish Commission's Fisheries Division, wrote, "The most immediate change was noted when the cold water from both Bull Shoals and Norfork dams completely eliminated the warm-water fishery as far downstream as Lock and Dam No. 3 near Mountain View. Severe damage occurred as far down as Lock and Dam No. 1 at Batesville."

More subtle effects proved equally destructive. ". . . the old-river lakes in the basin no longer flooded as in the old days, resulting in a decline in fishing in the lakes," Mathis wrote. Drainage and channelization programs caused an "increased load of silt" that "smothered bottom organisms and damaged the fish population even further." And as more of the watershed was cleared, "agricultural chemicals began to take their toll."

Man's impacts on the White were becoming increasingly apparent.

By most accounts, the lower White River starts in Batesville, just below the low-level weir called Dam 1. Farther south, the river begins cutting away at its banks. The mountains no longer contain its sweeping turns, and the river snakes back and forth in such a fashion that in many places, you almost meet yourself coming back. Upland pastures and woodlands give way to fertile agricultural country, and oxbow lakes spring up as testimony to the river's vagrant tendencies.

This stretch of river has changed as dramatically as the upper reaches. In the early 1800s, this was wild, forbidding territory. Foot travel, while possible, was not very profitable; huge, almost impenetrable cane thickets were everywhere, with swamps and bayous blocking the way in all directions. The only access to these bottomlands was by boating the rivers and bayous.

This remoteness and wildness, coupled with rich soil and abundant water, made the lower White River country unbelievably rich in wildlife. Deer, turkeys, and bears were abundant, and at night, one could hear the red wolves howl. There were passenger pigeons, too, untold millions of them, and in winter, when the bottomlands flooded, ducks swarmed the backwaters in flocks that literally blotted out the sun.

In 1916, the Game and Fish Commission recognized the White as one of the country's greatest fishing streams. "The amount of fish annually caught on lower White River . . . is something almost unbelievable," the commission asserted in its first annual report. In the twenty months preceding the report, almost four million pounds of fish from the lower White were shipped to markets elsewhere.

It was not to last forever, though, this wild country. Large-scale logging began in the 1870s. Marked expansion in agriculture followed. Cotton was planted on reclaimed land, then later rice, soybeans, and other commodities. By 1920, a third of the Delta was cleared. Unregulated hunting and habitat destruction had nearly wiped out the deer, bears, turkeys, wolves, and other creatures of the bottoms.

In the late 1920s, a period of heightened concern about decreasing numbers of ducks and geese, a committee of nationally prominent conservationists gathered to recommend locations for new federal waterfowl refuges. Their unanimous selection as the most important area to be acquired was a large swath of overflow bottoms along the lower White River. Thus, in 1935, White River National Wildlife Refuge was established, and the wave of destruction began shifting to a tide of preservation and restoration.

Land for the refuge was purchased largely from logging companies, which had high-graded the timber. But the scars of cutting healed quickly, and within the 113,000-acre refuge were 100,000 acres of bottomland hardwoods, the largest remnant of an immense floodplain ecosystem that once encompassed 24 million acres between Cairo, Illinois, and the Gulf of Mexico, an ecosystem William Faulkner called "The Big Woods." Some of North America's most productive fish and wildlife habitat finally was given federal protection.

The Arkansas Game and Fish Commission continued the trend of wetlands preservation in the lower White River basin. In 1952, the agency purchased 5,265 acres of bottomland hardwoods between Cache River and Bayou de View, which later became Dagmar Wildlife Management Area. In 1958 and 1959, Hurricane Lake and Wattensaw WMAs were established along the White River in White and Prairie Counties.

While two agencies rallied to protect the remnants of forested wetlands along the lower White, a third was doing its best to eliminate what remained. In 1969, the Corps of Engineers, under the banner of the Flood Control Act of 1950, started dredging and channelizing a proposed 232 miles of the Cache River and Bayou de View for flood control. The project, if completed, would dump dredge spoil on 10,000 acres of wetlands and encourage the private clearing of another 170,000 acres for agriculture. By this time, however, the tide had fully turned. Preservation of natural resources was considered more important than flood control for agriculture, and the Corps' actions drew national outcry. President Jimmy Carter stopped the dredging in 1977, and Congress cut off funding in 1978 after the Fish and Wildlife Service labeled it "the single most damaging project to waterfowl in the nation." Even so, seven miles of the Cache were dredged before the project was halted.

By the time the Cache project was stopped, only one-eighth—1,015,166 acres—of Arkansas's original wetlands remained. From that point forward, however, the crusade to conserve wetlands and woodlands in the lower White River basin, and elsewhere, proceeded on a broad front.

*1983. 1,694 acres purchased by the Nature Conservancy were deeded to the Game and Fish Commission to expand 3,888-acre Rex Hancock/Black Swamp WMA, established on the Cache River near Augusta in 1971. Additional acreage added in 1990 and 1995 brought the WMA acreage to 6,394.

*1985. The Statewide Comprehensive Outdoor Recreation Plan prepared by the Arkansas Department of Parks and Tourism issued a simple but direct policy statement: "Destruction of Arkansas's wetlands must be stopped." Six plans of action are recommended.

*1986. The U.S. Fish and Wildlife Service established Cache River NWR with the purchase of 35,000 acres along the river.

*1989. The Cache-lower White floodplain joined Everglades National Park, Okeefenokee NWR and five other U.S. sites on the Ramsar Convention's "List of Wetlands of International Importance."

*1992. A land swap between the federal government and Potlatch Corporation added 41,000 acres to White River NWR and linked it to Cache River NWR.

*1994. The 14,900-acre Bald Knob NWR, along the Little Red River near its confluence with the White, became Arkansas's ninth NWR.

What lessons have been learned? More than 280,000 acres of bottomlands in the lower White River basin have been acquired and are now protected, by state and federal wildlife agencies.

The lower White River basin encompasses the finest and last example of the immense floodplain forest ecosystem that once dominated the alluvial plain of the Mississippi River. The importance of this cannot be overstated.

This unique area, which depends on seasonal flooding from the White River and its tributaries, supports interior least terns, pink mucket mussels, and other endangered and threatened species; the largest concentration of wintering mallard ducks in North America; the only remaining population of native black bears in the lower Mississippi Valley; and numerous species of neotropical songbirds and other nongame wildlife. More than one hundred species of fish swim the basin's rivers, bayous, and oxbow lakes. Public lands here are world renowned for their extraordinary hunting, fishing, and wildlife watching opportunities. The hardwood forests are characterized by some of the richest and most diverse plant life in North America. The White River wetlands purify polluted waters and check the destructive power of floods and storms.

It would seem we learned our lesson. For more than two decades now, state and federal agencies, private organizations, and individuals have worked together to protect and restore more than a quarter of a million acres of wetlands in the White River basin. With the knowledge we have now, it seems the only sensible thing to do. And so, we have done it.

But despite the gains we've made, our work is not done. Last year, sitting at Montgomery Point, watching the bottomland hardwoods being pushed into piles and burned, watching the wetlands being pumped dry, and the pillars of concrete going up, I realized that more than ever.

Other projects also threaten the river basin. And if the project proponents have their way, they will turn this magnificent national treasure into nothing more than a barge canal lined with rock dikes and dredge spoil.

And let me repeat myself, folks, just in case you haven't been listening: these people usually have their way. Montgomery Point provides a glaring example.

These tragedies can be prevented, however. That was proven in 1988 when Congress deauthorized a White River dredging project strongly opposed by conservationists and environmental agencies. And it was proven more than a decade before when a Stuttgart dentist named Rex Hancock stood before the Corps of Engineers and said, "Enough's enough."

"I couldn't stand by and watch a bureaucratic federal agency thumb its nose at Arkansas," Hancock said, explaining why he single-handedly organized the Citizens Committee to Save the Cache River in October 1972. The committee eventually included thirty-five national organizations and eight states in the Mississippi Flyway. And through the efforts of Dr. Hancock and these groups, the economically unfeasible and environmentally disastrous Cache River channelization project was stopped.

Success did not come to Hancock and his supporters without great effort, however, and preventing similar disasters today will require no less toil. But before you decide that stopping this trend would be too difficult or too expensive or too contrary to previously conceived opinions, consider the alternative.

Picture the lower White as a clean, deep, barge-friendly river. Rock dikes and wing dams serve their intended purpose, diverting the river's flow and scouring the bottom. The river is slowly strangled down to one nice, neat artificial channel.

The oxbow lakes, sloughs, and bayous connected to the river start silting in at their mouths and are cut off. Fish spawning areas are degraded and lost. Fish suffer. Fishermen suffer.

The surrounding bottoms no longer receive winter and spring overflows that are the ecosystem's lifeblood. Thousands of acres of the world's most important wintering duck habitat disappear. Important habitat for bottomland whitetails, native black bears, migrant songbirds, American alligators, bald eagles, and endangered species of mussels and birds no longer exists. Wildlife suffers. Hunters and wildlife watchers suffer.

Barges can now travel the "better" river, but those who benefit most from them suffer, too. Soil erosion worsens as woodlands are cleared and the bottoms dry. Underground aquifers are not replenished. Levels of soil moisture required to farm certain commodities no longer exist. Drougths and floods worsen.

Imagine the lower White River ecosystem, an international treasure, a setting of incomparable natural beauty and diversity, turned into a barge highway. And you, dear citizens, will pay hundreds of millions of dollars to make it so, unless we stand together before the proponents of these projects and say "Enough's enough."

Montgomery Point should spur us on. It will stand forever as a monument to lessons we did not learn, passions we did not follow, banners we did not wave.

What we do, or fail to do, in the next few months, will determine the future of the lower White River.

Wilderness and Wildlife

JOHN SUNDERLAND

Writing in the Arkansas Game and Fish
Magazine *in 1985, John Sunderland, planning
coordinator of the Arkansas Game and Fish
Commission, reflects on the significance of the
then-newly designated Wilderness Areas.*

To my dad back during the Great Depression, wilderness was an Ozark pasture where no boy was grubbing out persimmon sprouts with a mattock or where the weeds and briars were too rank for a horsedrawn mowing machine or where a fencerow was so neglected that you couldn't see your bird dog for the overgrown vegetation. Wilderness was land that was unmanaged, abandoned, or overgrown. It was not respectable.

The land had started to change in the forties and fifties when he returned to the family farm after searching for a better life in California. He resumed his pursuit of the bobwhite with the same Model 97 Winchester 12 gauge he had purchased second-hand at age nineteen. But the land was different. As I followed him, we looked for places where the Bois d'Arc fencerows hadn't been bulldozed out or where fescue hadn't replaced the native lespedeza. As wildlands became harder to find, they became more valuable to us.

Years later, as I took up my conservation career in Arkansas and my dad retired here, I think this was a symbolic continuation of our search for wilderness. Wilderness had gained a special personal value to us both. And most of our wild places were gone.

In 1964, the Wilderness Act established a preservation system for the "permanent good of the whole people" to assure that the increasing population would not "occupy and modify all areas within the United States." A representative majority of Congress, reluctant to impose constraints on private land, recognized the need for untrammeled areas on public lands. Federal land managers and citizens began the process of identifying candidate areas for wilderness status. Twenty years later, with the passage last October of the Arkansas Wilderness Act, 91,100 acres of National Forest land were added to the Big Lake National Wildlife Refuge Wilderness, the Caney Creek Wilderness, and two areas along the Buffalo River for a total of 154,687 Arkansas acres in the National Wilderness Preservation system. That is nearly 242 square miles of wilderness.

How will wilderness designation affect people? In my involvement during the legislative process, my observation is that wilderness designation has, to this point, produced more human than wildlife impact. I have seen evidence of stress, threat or bluffing behavior, escape behavior, feigned death, and euphoria displayed by participants in the wilderness debate.

Making a prediction for wildlife species can be hazardous because Arkansas wilderness areas are relatively small and subject to influence from management practices on adjacent lands. Too, most predictions assume a continuation of existing human use patterns—and that is unlikely.

An example of an animal which will likely benefit from wilderness designation is the cougar. The question is no longer whether or not the cougar occurs in Arkansas but whether or not Arkansans are willing to tolerate its presence. Females range over five to twenty square miles, and males range over fifteen to thirty square miles. With such large territorial requirements, the cougar is not a species to be introduced in an Arkansas wilderness and expected to remain there as the top predator. The cougar may also be less of a wilderness creature than thought and capable of benefiting from an expanded deer and small mammal food source favored by current forest management practices. Cougars will not, though, be able to survive the combination of road, vehicle, gun, dog, and light that prevails over much of the public and private forest land of the state. Relief from these intrusions is what wilderness can offer the cougar.

Wilderness areas will serve as key sanctuary for some wildlife species, but consideration needs to be given to the management of adjacent lands. While it was the clear intent of Congress to release lands not designated as wilderness to management for other purposes, restricting vehicle use in a buffer area is consistent with preservation of wilderness character and within the administrative authority of federal land managers.

Access roads necessary for timber sales in the buffer areas should be developed to adequate standards and closed after logging. Traditional hunting and other use would not be disrupted significantly. Direct vehicle access to designated points on the wilderness boundary would still be provided.

In the combination referred to above (road, vehicle, gun, dog, and light), it is the misuse of the vehicle that blurs most the distinction between ethical and unethical hunting on public lands and aids abuse of the other elements in the combinations. Are we willing to park sooner, leave the off-road vehicle in the truck, and walk, or will we insist that the federal forestland manager open every logging road to vehicle traffic? Our answer will have much to do with the sanctuary value of designated wilderness areas.

One of the least recognized but very important benefits of wilderness designation is the protection afforded to unique, sensitive animal species for which little information exists. Salamanders are sensitive to forest floor conditions. Darters and madtoms (both small rare fish) are sensitive to increased sediment and water quality changes. Wilderness designation will protect populations of these species, some of which occur nowhere else in the world. These species, which are incapable of moving or greatly extending their range, must either survive under prevailing land management practices or be eliminated. Comparison of their status in wilderness and nonwilderness may yield an early warning of undesirable habitat change, long before it shows up in more tolerant, widely distributed species.

Have we finished designating wilderness areas in Arkansas? I hope not! We need examples of wilderness on Crowley's Ridge, along a major Delta river, and in the Gulf coastal plain.

What are we trying to do, stop progress? No. Wilderness designation won't do that. It won't even halt change—but we will be able to watch the dynamic process of change with fewer man-induced causes.

We've come a long way from the depression to Earth Day to the Wilderness Act. My dad responded to wilderness in his time in his way and I in mine. What pleases me is that my son will be able to have his chance to develop his own ethic.

Pensive on the Parkway

PAM STRICKLAND

Pam Strickland teaches journalism and writing at the Cathedral School in Little Rock. This piece was originally written in 2001 for public radio where Pam does regular commentary.

We were like ants sucking up spilt honey. There were perhaps one hundred of us crammed into a Chenal Parkway office supply store in the midst of a going-out-of-business sale. The store is, or shall I say was, an anchor to one of the numerous strip malls that have sprouted in west Little Rock over the last few years, weeds on what had been beautiful forest land. My guess is that, like myself, none of my fellow shoppers had ever been in this particular store before. It was, after all, closing while two other chain office supply outlets in very close proximity remained open.

Yet, there we were spending part of our Sunday afternoon taking advantage of the retail war booty. Taking advantage of the ever-evident poor planning allowed by the elected officials in Little Rock city government. Dry erase boards at a steal. Deep discounts on business envelopes. Enough off on printer ink cartridges to make having a couple extra on hand worthwhile.

As I placed my purchases in the trunk of my car, I noticed the not-so-new strip mall across the street had five, perhaps six, store fronts that apparently have never been filled. As I drove the three miles from the defunct store to my home, I lost count of all the empty storefronts, but I did manage to note five large empty retail buildings. That doesn't include the silenced singing-waiter restaurant sometimes used as a landmark in directions to my house. It does not include the massive vacant warehouse store that casts a shadow from its hilltop on the other route I could have taken, a symbolic ode to greedy developers who know how to smooth talk landowners and bureaucrats. Not so long ago, the places where these empty stores stand had trees and grass, instead of poorly drained parking lots.

My friend, a small business owner, has been known to leave soliloquies on my voice mail when her work forces a trip west of Shackelford Road. The messages always include the descriptive that she is in "[expletive] Houston," a Texas city that has suffered untold economic, environmental, and social troubles because of the lack of a local zoning code. Little Rock has zoning, but there are so many exceptions that the code itself seems nothing but a paper tiger designed to give lawyers for the developers a chance to bill another few thousand as they wiggle yet another exemption for what they insist, with a straight face nonetheless, is THE solution to all the city's economic problems.

Not long after I moved here in the mid-eighties, I found myself making regular visits to a building just west of Shackelford on what was then Financial Centre Parkway. My business was not always pleasant, usually quite the opposite, but whatever frustration and anger it brought was always smoothed over by the setting. The building was nestled in the woods, surrounded on three sides by trees, flowers, and birds. It was a tiny bit of tranquillity in the midst of a harried life.

Another thing about those meetings was that traffic was no big deal. I could count on getting there and back to my downtown office in a reasonable amount of time. Now, the mere thought of traveling that street means allowing a couple of hours, more if there is the unfortunate timing of a Friday afternoon or certain times on Saturday. The building I used to visit is still there, but there are not trees. Any flowers are part of meticulous landscaping. The birds have nowhere to sing their songs.

Empty buildings everywhere. Trees and grass destroyed. Traffic jams comparable to a city four times the size of Little Rock. West Little Rock is a mess. I don't know much about development, but I do know that more of the same isn't the answer. A co-worker who lives in

Leawood, a stone's throw from the vulnerable University Avenue, worries about the value of his property. I have yet to encounter a person who believes this mall idea is good, who has said to my face, "It's a really good idea to damage the environment, while taking steps that would gut one of the city's main business corridors." But then I don't tend to run in circles occupied by Dillard's executives or out-of-state developers. The people I'm most likely to talk to are working people—teachers, computer programmers, college students, health care workers, small business owners—people who vote and who have long memories.

City officials have been slow to listen to the voices of the people when it comes to the proposed Summit Mall, just down Shackelford from that large collection of empty buildings and traffic jams. The Little Rock Board of Directors apparently haven't learned the lesson that poor planning results in massive waste of both money and natural resources. The numbers reported by the local media that the developers have been hand feeding the board members don't add up, and the only thing that isn't murky about the proposal is the very clear plan of leveling a very large hill, killing more trees and pouring millions of dollars' worth of concrete and asphalt.

The Spirit of Nature

ERIN DALTON

*Erin Dalton of Cabot, a student at Hendrix
College, wrote this final exam essay for her
Literature and the Natural World class in 2001.*

When I picture nature, I always begin in the country. Perhaps this is because that is where my beginnings are. For a number of years I lived in a small gray brick house about five miles outside of the city limits. This was a place full of trees to climb, fields to roam, and streams for catching crawdads. Nature was my playground. Yet, as is the way of things, my life changed. When I was nine years old, my family and I moved out of that little gray house. We left the crayon-decorated walls, Franklin Stove, neighbors we knew, and wide-open spaces for the greater conveniences of the city.

Although living in town was more convenient, it seemed to me that the gain never transcended the loss. I missed my miles of forest and fields to journey through. I missed the privacy and safety that the country afforded. For the first time in my life we had to padlock our shed and bring in our bicycles. As soon as I stepped outside, somebody could watch my every move. My life had definitely changed.

I realize now that our move into town was not the only reason that things were changing. The town itself was also changing, growing at a rapid pace. Almost overnight it seems Cabot had ceased to be a little town just north of Little Rock and had turned into a place in its own right. With the growth came problems and new requirements for keeping safe. Life was changing overall at the same time mine was. Not that Cabot had become a mecca for organized crime or anything;

in fact, one major reason for the population boom is that parents wanted to move to a place where their children would be safe. Still, even though the center of Cabot was not some hot bed for criminal activity, it was different. It was definitely different. In that move to the center of Cabot, I had lost the connection that I had with nature. In fact, it was so far lost that I had all but forgotten that it had even existed until a few months ago.

My parents have decided that they too are tired of the confines of the middle of town; so they are moving to its edges, not quite so far as the home of my childhood, but out nonetheless. They bought a wooded lot on a street, off a street, off a street, and there they are going to build their new house. They had told me about this place for months before I finally got to see it.

After the huge ice storm this winter, my father decided we needed to go survey the damage to the property. So we all piled in the car (my brother had even come up from Little Rock) and went to check the place out. I was in heaven. The forest and fields that I had loved so passionately were here. A small stream ran just along the edge of the property. If things were extremely quiet, I could even hear it babble. And, of course, there was the smell. That smell of earth and life and water that makes you want to breathe in as deeply as you can and try your hardest to never let it go. I could remember some of that joy I had felt as a child.

My mother and father were scanning the lot trying to find the damaged trees and seeing what needed to be done. My brother was in a desperate battle with a vine wrapped around one of the trees. The vine had the upper hand. Left to my own devices, I decided to do a little exploring of my own. I spotted a hill that looked like the perfect (as A. A. Milne said best) "thinking spot." But on my way I was struck by the sight of two stately oak trees. I just had to go over and study them.

Now I tell this as the weirdest experience I have ever had in my life. When I touched those oak trees, I felt the life inside of them. Never before had I felt such a thing, not ever. Nature has always been awe-inspiring for me, and I had always known that it was alive in my head, but, for the first time, felt its life with my heart. I have had such a feeling only once before, and it, at least on the surface, had nothing to do with nature. It had to do with God.

When I was in high school, I began questioning the church of my childhood, truly questioning. For many years, I had had problems with the doctrines, but had always believed in the core of the church's teachings. However, my senior year my questioning just took me too far afield. I felt like nobody could give me any answers and maybe this whole God and Jesus thing was something that humans had contrived to comfort themselves. This was my working theory for several months, and I had no idea what to do about it. Luckily, something was done for me.

My church had just obtained a priest after being without one for several months. He was so excited about leading our congregation that he moved up to Arkansas from New Orleans straight away without even obtaining a place to live. So, my parents, being the good-natured people that they are, and knowing how badly our church needed this man, promptly offered him my brother's former room. This man showed a love and compassion and interest that really sparked something in me—although I was still pretty skeptical about this whole Son of God thing.

The night that our new reverend was installed, something wonderful happened to me. The service was absolutely breathtaking, and my mother said later, "It felt like Christmas." I knew exactly what she meant. At Christmas, there is always a feeling of love and awe that seems to echo through the sanctuary. On that night, that feeling was relived even more intensely. This man was what our church had needed for a very long time. And as I came to the communion rail, I suddenly felt the spirit of God. It touched my heart in a way that I had never felt, not even at my baptism or confirmation. As I knelt there, waiting to receive communion, I knew that something was happening that I would never be able to express. The closest I can come is to say that I knew that something was happening that was incredibly right.

Now before I explain exactly what this had to do with my experience in the woods, I want to clarify a few things. My personal belief is not that the Christian Church is the perfect way, truth, and light, and the only ticket to salvation. I started questioning because of problems I had with the church, and those problems did not go away in some flash of white brilliance. I still have them; I just came to the realization that there may be a reason to work on them. So the story of my experience is by no means meant to be a sermon. I am just trying to convey the feeling that I had that fall evening.

That feeling I was able to relive in that wooded lot that my parents had just recently purchased. Suddenly I realized that what I was feeling was more than natural. It was actually a spiritual experience. Once again, I could feel God, but this time it was not in a church, or perhaps just not in my usual definition of a church.

The Celts believed that nature was their "church" and that they needed no buildings or priests to worship. They felt their spiritualism in the trees, and many historians even believe that they may have had a special spiritual connection with the oak. The Celts are my people. Admittedly, one has to search generations upon generations into the past to know that, but maybe, just maybe, part of their heritage was passed on to me. Nature had been a sanctuary to the Celts, as it had to several other peoples, long before it became one for me.

How long I stood at that tree and pondered these things I do not know. Eventually my parents wandered by, and I was suddenly struck by a horrifying thought. My parents had bought this place to build a house, and that meant chopping down trees. What if it meant chopping down my trees? Tentatively, very tentatively, I asked exactly where they were planning to build their house. I began breathing again when they pointed to a spot fairly far away. I was joyous, and my father noticed my expression and said he would make sure that my oaks never got torn down. He then noticed something that I had not. There were several oak trees around the two to which I had been drawn, and they actually formed a circle, a sort of fairy ring in the forest.

I know I will not forget my experience at the altar rail or at the circle of oaks. Both happenings were very real and very vibrant. I hope I will also never again forget my connection with nature. For with that connection comes a nurturing and understanding that will aid me for the rest of my life.

Experts Save Cave Art— This Time

MARK MINTON

This feature on Petit Jean State Park by Arkansas Democrat-Gazette *writer Mark Minton appeared in January of 2001.*

Centuries after prehistoric American Indians drew the first pictographs in Rock House Cave, conservators are laboring to protect the designs from modern artists whose doodles, carved initials, and declarations of love threaten to blot out the ancient artwork. Removing graffiti from boxcars or telephone booths is one thing. But what to do when the crude images and inscriptions obscure irreplaceable rock art?

For stewards of Rock House Cave, the painstaking cleanup was a chore that spanned thirteen years and cost nearly $50,000. After all of that, frustrated caretakers discovered fresh graffiti scratched in the sandstone just three months after one of the country's only rock art graffiti experts had applied the last touches to the cave and pronounced the job complete.

"Man, it's really reappearing—that's horrible," former Petit Jean State Park interpreter Ben Swadley said last week as he surveyed recent inscriptions such as one memorializing "Patty + Clint 10-25-00," carved in the bluff shelter's back wall.

"This Clint guy, I think he's been here before," Swadley said. Countless others have left lasting marks in the shelter over the years. Although Rock House Cave is one of 136 Indian rock art sites discovered in Arkansas, most of the others are kept secret to protect them.

Rock House Cave is vulnerable because it's so visible and is beside one of Petit Jean's main trails.

Visitors armed with everything from sharp-edged rocks to nail polish and crayons have used the cave as a sandstone ledger since as long ago as 1888, the year inscribed by "BJ McCoy, Idaho LT." Bobbie Wells evidently visited in 1925, and Mark Wells in 1929. "KeiTH-N ROnda" followed in 1983.

The most grotesque of the lot was the large "Melissa Sneezer" epigraph that appeared on the back wall last spring, said Swadley, who left Petit Jean several years ago for a job as director of the state-operated Plantation Agriculture Museum in Scott but who remains at the center of the graffiti-containment efforts. In stylized green and black letters two feet tall, the spray-painted nickname covered some five hundred square feet, counting the accompanying cartoon turtles and marijuana leaf. Fortunately, Swadley said, the design somehow missed all eighty of the original rock art designs—mostly paintings in red pigments—thought to have been created during the Mississippian and Woodland eras, as long ago as 500 B.C.

No one can be certain what tribe produced the art or precisely when, much less what the cryptic designs represent. One of the most distinct is an "obvious" paddlefish, Swadley said, and nearby is a presumptive deer head and at least two masks. But examining the marks is like taking a Rorschach personality analysis test, Swadley conceded; one man's scorpion is another's figure in a headdress.

Easier to decipher is the intent of the graffiti artists, whose motives seem more rooted in ignorance than malice, according to researchers familiar with the cave. Many of the visitors probably never even realized the rock art was there, said George Sabo, an archeologist for the Arkansas Archeological Survey who has led excavations in the cave. After all, the fading Indian paintings are mostly above eye level and can be difficult to spot, depending on the light. Visitors who see only the graffiti take it as an invitation to leave their own, Sabo said.

"It's kind of an innocent mistake people make," he said. "They see 'Kilroy Was Here' and feel compelled to do the same, with no clear indication that it's rock art they're obscuring."

While graffiti takes only a few solitary moments to produce, cave restoration is an arduous task. In Rock House Cave, it began in 1986 when Sabo, fellow survey archeologist Jerry Hilliard, and a crew of volunteers dug eleven test plots in the cave floor to check for artifacts that could be damaged if chemical solutions were applied to remove graffiti on the cave walls. The team uncovered fire pits, tapered points, and other artifacts, halting any notion of applying chemicals to the cave walls. With no clear direction or funding, the project languished until a recent flurry of grants from preservation agencies, totaling $46,000, brought in a consultant from North Dakota and a rock art conservationist from Oregon to work with Arkansas volunteers to restore the cave.

After spending a week listening to lectures and practicing with Linda Olsen, an assistant art professor and rock art documentation consultant at North Dakota's Minot State University, volunteers began the painstaking process of documenting the art in the cave. Not just the ancient art but the modern graffiti had to be documented, first with field sketches and later on acid-free paper handled only with gloves. Each mark on the wall had to be plotted with compasses and tape measures, using cracks as reference points, and then drawn to scale and described in detail. Even the painted-on marijuana leaf had to be recorded in detail, recalled Robin Giles of Little Rock, a volunteer who found investing such time and effort in a marijuana leaf to be more than a little frustrating, especially in the heat of July.

"It made you mad," Giles said.

But only after documentation was complete could Clair Dean of Portland, Oregon, the principal conservator on contract for the Petroglyph National Monument in Albuquerque, among other rock art sites, go to work on the graffiti. A leader in the new field of rock art conservation, Dean uses a variety of techniques, from chemicals to "micro-abrasion"—an extremely light sanding. When all else fails, as it mostly did in the badly damaged Rock House Cave, Dean covers over the graffiti with paints mixed on site to match shades of rock, even carefully matching algae growing in the cracks.

Once vandalized, no rock art site can be returned to pristine condition, according to Dean, who worked on Rock House Cave for two and a half weeks, finishing in late September. But only the faintest traces of the graffiti were visible on a recent visit, and now the work is done, state park officials hope a change in strategy will keep major problems from reappearing.

Though Petit Jean is not moving as aggressively as other parks that have tried iron bars, fencing, and Plexiglas shields to protect rock art sites, the park does intend to step up patrols and post signs warning visitors that they will be monitored. Though no one has ever been arrested for vandalizing the cave, the high costs of restoration would make any violation a felony, park ranger Mike Decker said.

Swadley said the park will also post signs to ensure visitors know ancient art is inside, to report the penalties for vandalism, and to outline rules of etiquette to be observed in the cave, such as not touching the rock art.

"Hopefully, this will lead to a little respect," Swadley said. "I think a lot of people who do this have no clue they're harming something important."

Preface to *The High Ozarks: A Vision of Eden*

NEIL COMPTON

Although Dr. Neil Compton was awarded many national and state conservation awards as founder of the Ozark Society, credited with the designation of the Buffalo River as a national river, in this statement from a book he wrote in 1982, he reveals an even larger passion.

Whether or not some of us arrive on this earth with an innate awareness of its miraculous attributes I do not know. Perhaps to have been born into that Arcadian world on Falling Springs Flats long ago was enough to imprint this writer, as a little boy, with an abiding fascination and concern for it all.

Down in Crumby Hollow, Falling Springs gushed from a hillside to form one of the tributaries of Spavinaw. Many years later we would learn to sing that lovely Irish air that told of "the pure crystal fountain that flows from the vale of Tralee." It took almost too long to arrive at the realization that such waters were not just those across the ocean. They were our own Falling Springs and Spavinaw and the thousands of others that flowed through the Ozark hills.

But there was so much more to it all than crystal waters.

In those days there were patches of the original woodland on the Spavinaw hills, colonnades of oak, hickory, walnut, and other hardwoods. On misty summer mornings the sun's rays penetrating their high canopy revealed the understory of dogwood and redbud, and nearer the ground, that carpet of fragrant and delectable Ozark blue-berry or huckleberry. The hills themselves stretched away endlessly to where we knew not, with their limestone bluffs and caverns and val-leys in between. Separating the stream systems were wide stretches of flatland; Falling Springs Flats and Mount Zion Flats, or if larger, Round Prairie and Beatie's Prairie with their sunny multicolored summer vegetation. Out on the prairie and in the flatwoods there were natural ponds and wet spots from whence on spring nights there was carried on the south wind the joyous chorus of frogs of every kind welcoming the new season as they had for all of those millions of years since their beginning. Not to be outdone, the more sophisticated melody of the birds echoed in the land on into the summer.

In those days we were avid readers of the *Youth's Companion*, which carried a small advertisement for the Old Town canoe. This stirred in me a boyish yearning to somehow come by enough money to purchase one and to paddle it down Spavinaw through the Cherokee country to where it ran into the Grand River. But it was never to be. Spavinaw became, after the White River at Powersite, the second in that multitude of drowned valleys that dot the Ozarks today.

To have witnessed this transformation along with the loss of the forests and prairies to the bulldozers, chain saws, brush hogs, and 2-4-5-T begot in this writer an increasing agony. Was there no limit to man's destructive use of his newfound technology? Was there no one to mount an effort to salvage the dwindling natural charm and beauty of our Ozark land? The answer was no. In spite of their good inten-tions, not the Nature Conservancy, the Isaac Walton League, the Sierra Club, or the Audubon Society, whose interests did not include our forgotten bit of America.

By 1960 the day of judgment had arrived for that best of our Ozark rivers, the Buffalo. As fate would have it I knew something about it, had some photographs of it, and had presented a few programs for service and conservation clubs. Since there were no prominent or dis-tinguished personalities available, Harold Alexander, hoping for the best, asked that I take the ball and run with it. There was nothing else to do, however dim the prospect of victory over the Corps of Engineers.

The first step was to organize a sensible, determined regional group to devise and bring to the attention of any who would listen a better plan for the Buffalo. Without the Ozark Society nothing could have been accomplished. The next step was to pay close heed to the political arena from whence emanate all decisions of this nature and to take advantage of whatever breaks might fall. There were several, and we did not fail. The Buffalo became our first national river under the National Park Service, protected from developers and by virtue of its unique grandeur a joy to all who know it.

For those who feel in their hearts a compassion, whether inborn or acquired, for the beauty of our land there remain a multitude of places, some hidden and some well known, in need of the attention of anyone willing to strive to preserve them. It is hoped that this volume [*The High Ozarks*] will serve as a modest inspiration toward that end.

Bayou Bartholomew

CATHY FRYE

Cathy Frye is a reporter for the Arkansas
Democrat-Gazette, *which published this feature
article in 2001.*

Long before the railroad thundered into southern
Arkansas, the Bayou Bartholomew was the lifeblood that fed hundreds of tiny, thriving communities perched along its banks. Known
for its unusual length and snakelike curves, the waterway was a
steamboat channel, the scene of almost every social occasion, from
Fourth of July picnics to baptisms, and the source of dozens of legends and ghost stories.

Today, it is a restoration project.

The stream that was once lined regularly with steamboats is in a
dismal state. Its banks are eroding, and its waters have been slowed by
logjams. Industry, agriculture, and the clear-cutting of timberland
have polluted the water that people used to drink without question.

As a result, community swimming holes lost their popularity long
ago. Few people would be willing to dip even one bare toe into
the bayou these days. But exactly how the now-murky, sluggish
Bartholomew should be "fixed" is an issue for debate.

One local organization proposes making the bayou "like it used to
be" and preserving it in that fashion. A second group would like to see
water from the Arkansas River diverted into the bayou, making it
more beneficial to farmland in need of irrigation. Those with the most
stake in Bartholomew's fate, however, are the descendants of the
people who settled along the bayou generations ago. Most of the land
involved in both proposals is private.

And landowners feel strongly about Bartholomew, says Rebecca DeArmond-Huskey, who recently finished a book about the bayou, its history, and the stories of those who grew up on its banks.

"They love it. It is in their blood," the author says.

"Even though the old swimming holes are gone and there are no longer baptisms in it, they still love that stream and hate what has happened to it."

The Bartholomew watershed is made up of 997,000 acres and encompasses portions of six counties in southeast Arkansas. The bayou begins in Jefferson County about ten miles northwest of Pine Bluff and follows a leisurely, winding route through Lincoln, Desha, Drew, Ashley and Chicot Counties. It then heads into Louisiana, where it eventually rendezvous with the Ouachita River.

It's touted by those who study it as "the longest bayou in the world," and given its meandering yet tenacious flow along a 359-mile bed, few are tempted to argue. People will, however, bicker over how Bayou Bartholomew got its name and just how long ago that happened.

"Some people in Jefferson County like to think it was named after some Bartholomew who settled there," DeArmond-Huskey says. "Not true."

"Some like to think it was after St. Bartholomew, one of the disciples. My theory is that it was named after Bartholomew, the little Parisian who left the LaSalle expedition in Texas after LaSalle was murdered."

In researching for her book, *Bartholomew's Song,* DeArmond-Huskey found a letter from a Spanish commander in which the bayou is mentioned by name. It is dated "Jan. 12, 1781," she says.

A historical marker in Pine Bluff's Byrd Park says the bayou was named Bartholomew as early as 1786, and Baron De Carondelet refers to it by name in a 1795 letter. The sign also reads: "A man named Barthelemy is known to have been in the area as early as the 1680s."

Early settlements depended on the bayou until the railroad came to town. Then, most moved a few blocks over, abandoning the once-bustling ports for depots. Before trains, however, Bartholomew was the focal point of many southeastern Arkansas communities. Things always seemed to happen down on the bayou, be it hauntings or hangings.

"Every community had a hanging tree down on the bayou," DeArmond-Huskey says. She found lots of accounts of lynchings— including one of a murderer who bloodied the bayou near Portland before he finally died—as well as trips made by the famous and infamous down the waterway.

"I found an account of women lynching a man in Parkdale," the author says. Apparently, the man had been abusing women, and the ladies of the town decided to form a league and get revenge, DeArmond-Huskey says.

"I've got Jesse James on the bayou, going to Portland. And it seems ghosts prefer hanging out in houses along the bayou."

What fascinates most people, including DeArmond-Huskey, are the steamboats, whose submerged remains have been found in the lower-bayou area, in the southernmost part of the state. Steamboats brought goods from New Orleans, as well as news and gossip. DeArmond-Huskey says she was able to document ninety-four boats that once used the bayou. There may be more, she adds. Many captains didn't always fill out their logs.

In Portland, an early settler named John Fisher furnished his two-story home with chandeliers and furniture from France. These luxurious items arrived at Fisher's plantation via steamboat, DeArmond-Huskey says, adding, "The old Portland is a mile west of town and was on the bayou. And Parkdale was definitely a steamboat town. It was originally called Poplar Bluff. There's not much left of it at all, but there are some pretty homes and you just get a feeling of being back in the past."

Even scientists are intrigued by the remnants of the past and other people's lives found along Bartholomew. Bill Layher, a biologist who does field research and consulting for area agencies, works for the nonprofit agency trying to restore the bayou. He and his assistant have stumbled across everything from an old cypress tree estimated to be 800–1,200 years old (it takes four to six people to encircle its massive trunk) to a federal-issue safe from which the back appears to have been removed with a blowtorch.

Bartholomew is described by those who love it as a mystic place. Its banks are fringed with tupelo swamps and ancient trees adorned with Spanish moss. At least 111 species of fish reside in the bayou's muddy waters.

The Bayou Bartholomew Alliance was formed in 1995 as a nonprofit organization designed to clean up and improve the waterway, helping it to once again run cleanly into Louisiana. It began after Curtis Merrill decided that his daily commute from Monticello to Pine Bluff was depressing because he had been forced to watch the bayou's deterioration for fourteen years, each time he crossed a bridge on his way to work.

Since its creation, the alliance has planted hardwoods along the banks and helped educate farmers about irrigation, pesticides, and erosion. Alliance members also have picked up trash that once threatened to consume many segments of the stream.

In the next several years, the group hopes to restore the bayou's beauty, and by doing so, take care of a few other problems. Improving the water quality, for example. The alliance also hopes to open the bayou up for recreation by persuading counties to open boat ramps for fishers and hunters. Once again, the bayou could become a place where people gather, Merrill says.

But farther south, where vast farm acreage surrounds Bartholomew, farmers are talking about not just restoring and preserving the bayou, but finding better ways to use it.

"What you're looking at is the biggest depressed area in Arkansas," says John Currie Jr., a member of the Boeuf-Tensas Water Management District. He and other farmers would like to see the bayou cleared of its logjams and regularly filled with water diverted from the Arkansas River.

The U.S. Army Corps of Engineers is doing a feasibility study, he says, but it will be several years before any proposals will be presented.

"That's not what anybody wants, to channelize the bayou," Currie says. "We want it the way it was when steamboats used it. But right now all that water is just running into the Gulf of Mexico. And we could use that water."

William DeYampert used to have a rope from a steamboat that wrecked near Wilmot. His daddy bought it when items from the boat were salvaged and sold.

"When he died, I got ahold of it," he says. "I pulled tractors around with it. I wish I had it now."

DeYampert doesn't really remember steamboats. But he does have fond recollections of the bayou. The old swimming hole doesn't look anything like it used to. But DeYampert, now eighty-four, has no trouble finding it when asked. He points to a bend in the bayou and sighs. "It sure was a nice place."

Around Portland, folks call George Pugh, "Mr. George." His family's been here a long time. The Pughs were plantation owners. They still farm, but also run the town's cotton gins and sell farm equipment. There's a piece of land he bought that is bordered by Bartholomew, and one day, Mr. George hopes to create a fishing area where people can gather for picnics and social occasions.

"This town flourished here for a while because of the bayou," he says. But when the railroad came, the city moved, and things changed.

"When I was young, I would float the bayou in an old cypress boat," he says. These days, Pugh takes his grandson to the piece of land he bought and tries to make him see what he once did. He points his truck in the direction of the bayou and heads down a barely discernible path.

He smiles. "I tell my little grandson this is the secret road. And this is my field of dreams."

Using a Hammer on *David*

MIKE MASTERSON

Mike Masterson is a columnist for the Arkansas
Democrat-Gazette. *This article appeared in 2001
at the height of public and legal controversy over
gravel mining on Crooked Creek in north-central
Arkansas.*

Creeks are like people. They age and change their
appearance over time.

So it is no surprise that the stream of my childhood has added
wrinkles and lumps over the four decades since my father introduced
me to Crooked Creek.

This pristine stream that winds through the Ozarks in Boone and
Marion Counties is fed by scores of fresh water springs that surge
from the surrounding bluffs and outcroppings. Until the past few
years, its crystal-clear flow has sustained and nurtured all manner of
plants and animals.

Any young boy or girl fortunate enough to discover the magic of
this creek found an enchanting world. Where else could you find turtles
and minnows and crawdads and sunfish and bass and birds and
plants and such seemingly infinite forms of life congregated in such a
scenic and tranquil sanctuary?

When my son Brandon became old enough, I brought him to this
place. Over time, his reverence for it soon rivaled my own. He came to
appreciate, as would my daughter, Anna, the spiritual implications of

the stream. Now that he is grown, Brandon and I still make time from the daily demands to spend at least a couple of summer days wading Crooked Creek in a silence broken only by the rush of surrounding rapids, chirping birds, and the occasional screech of a red-tailed hawk circling overhead.

There is no place else like this in Arkansas, and few elsewhere in the world. When I was away from my state, Crooked Creek was always at the forefront of my daydreams. We in Arkansas were given Crooked Creek to cherish, as surely as we received the magnificent Buffalo River.

I set this scene so you might better understand my pride last week in the Arkansas Department of Environmental Quality after its members rejected Len Halliday Hauling Inc.'s attempts to extend its gravel mining into undamaged stretches of the creek near Pyatt between Yellville and Harrison.

Allowing gravel miners to further damage this state treasure for personal gain would be like allowing marble salesmen to take ball-peen hammers to Michelangelo's *David* or dog food manufacturers to poison the zebras at the Little Rock Zoo.

Gravel miners already have damaged this creek sufficiently in the region between Yellville and Flippin. I believe the havoc they have wreaked can never be repaired in our lifetimes, or even in another generation. Many others feel that way as well. You may have seen the postcard sent out three years ago—an aerial photograph of the God-awful mess these people have made of Crooked Creek. I wonder how much of the gravel plundered from this unique resource has been sold out of state to help build their roads.

Crooked Creek, you see, is about much more than tons of pea gravel to provide a few gravel miners' personal incomes. This extensive gravel helps filter impurities, foster tiny life forms, and sustain the remarkable smallmouth bass population, as well as all the other life I mentioned earlier. Most states would give anything to have such a creek to preserve and protect for all.

During our father-son trip together last week, I also noticed how the water, while still clear, carries the endless trails of telltale foam from fertilizers and animal excrement. This runoff seems to have increased the blanket of moss over the stones along the creek bottom, making them dangerously slick to traverse. I can't help but wonder how much longer she can sustain her health under such a constant onslaught of bacteria and chemical runoff.

My concerns for the welfare of Crooked Creek at this point stretch beyond any one person's personal desire to profit from years of continually ripping out and peddling her vital organs. I feel moved, as I have in the past, by something larger than myself, to join the voices that speak for her welfare. Who knows? Perhaps those echoes of conscience come from my father, or his, as well as from others who so deeply valued this place in their lifetimes.

Now I realize most of you have never stood waist-deep in these cool waters on a summer's day and slowly closed your eyes to absorb everything the creek offers to the human senses. I also understand that most of you haven't even seen Crooked Creek, much less cast a line into her shadowy holes and swirling eddies. Yet I believe most of you care as much as I do about how we treat the natural gifts we have been given to preserve and to appreciate.

It is reassuring to see that the Arkansas Department of Environmental Quality apparently does, too.

Environmental Ethics:
A Lawyer's Plea

DON HAMILTON

*A former board member of the National Wildlife
Federation and a leading advocate for Arkansas
preservation, Don F. Hamilton is general counsel
for the Little Rock Wastewater Utility. This article
is based on his remarks made at the
Business/Environmental Ethics Campus
Symposium, sponsored by the Philosophy
Department, held at the University of Central
Arkansas in 1992.*

My studies in philosophy approximately thirty-five
years ago can be summarized by two observations. The first is con-
tained in a quotation from Alfred North Whitehead that "all philosophy is but a footnote to Plato," which I found to be true in studying
the writings of the philosophers of western civilization. The second is,
that while I learned much from the writings of philosophers and theo-
logians about (1) our ethical relationship to each other, (2) logic,
(3) the theory of knowledge, and (4) aesthetics, I learned absolutely
nothing of our ethical relationship to the land. Any concern in that
regard seemed to be lost in the history of the native Americans whom
our forebears referred to as "savages." Finally, the notion that human
beings had an ethical relationship to land was not even mentioned, let
alone discussed in any of my economics or business courses in col-

lege; and in law school, the only concern was title and "highest and best use" in terms of economic return.

In a similar vein, my religious training was typical of the Judaeo-Christian teachings about the Abrahamic concept of land, that is, having dominion over the land and all of its creatures. After all, land in the eyes of generations of Americans for centuries was viewed as merely a commodity to be bought or used to obtain its highest economic return or sold for a profit, or even thrown away if the land could not produce economic gain of some sort. My teachers from the first grade through high school emphasized that our natural resources were unlimited, which was the reason why America was so great.

When I grew up in Little Rock in the 1940s and 1950s, the city was merely an overgrown country town with a rural atmosphere. There were nearby forests, creeks, and wetlands within a few minutes walking distance. Like many of my friends, I grew up with the beauty of nature as an everyday part of life which I took for granted.

I never knew how important the natural world had become to me until I came back home after being away for approximately nine years in college, military service in Korea, and then law school. When I returned home, I found that most of the natural world I knew as a boy was gone.

Later, I realized that no other person would ever again know the beautiful areas as I once knew them. Where once were located upland forests and creeks in the western edge of Little Rock, there are now residential subdivisions, drainage ditches, shopping centers, and acres of paved parking lots to accommodate the seemingly unending flow of cars and trucks. Where once were wetland and a bottomland forest on the south bank of the Arkansas River, we now have a developed park and a golf course, sometimes empty and sometimes full of people and cars.

When I began the private practice of law and was working long hours in the 1960s and 1970s, it did not take too long for me to realize that there were at least as many answers in the beauty of nature as in all of the books ever written or words ever spoken. So it was that I developed an attachment for such beautiful natural areas in Arkansas as the Buffalo River, Hurricane Creek, Lost Valley, Twin Falls of Big Devils Fork and Long Devils Fork which unite and flow into Richland

Creek, and so many other parts of the Ozark Mountains, as well as our bayous and bottomland hardwood forests in the Delta.

Henry David Thoreau had Walden Pond, Aldo Leopold had his shack near the banks of the Wisconsin River, Sig Olson had his Listening Point in the boundary waters of Minnesota, and Ed Abbey had his desert solitaire and rim rock canyons in Arizona and Utah. These were all places of natural beauty and solitude to them. Such places are necessary for the human spirit in all of us, whether these places are located in our backyard or a few minutes or miles away. These places help us to put life in perspective and they help us to appreciate the need for a land ethic.

Thanks to the writings of Thoreau, Emerson, John Muir, Theodore Roosevelt, Aldo Leopold, Sig Olson, Ed Abbey, Wallace Stegner, and Michael Frome (among others), countless Americans (including myself) have developed, or are attempting to develop, a land ethic which recognizes that, just as we have an ethical obligation to each other as human beings, we also have an ethical obligation to the land as a living organism. This ethic is based upon love, respect, and admiration for land and a high regard for its value. I mean "value in the philosophic sense," to quote Aldo Leopold. In my opinion, the development of this ethic on this beautiful planet we call "Earth" is our greatest challenge today.

We are the trustees of our environment, and we all are responsible for the health of the land. We must be good stewards. By health, I mean the capacity of the land for self-renewal so as to adequately provide for the existence of all communities of life irrespective of their commercial value. One thing appears certain: all parts of the biotic community are essential for the healthy functioning of our environment which we do not now fully understand and perhaps never will. We should never forget the first rule of intelligent tinkering. That rule is to save all the pieces.

There are important national and local environmental issues which are facing us and which must be resolved. These national issues include global warming, threats to the ozone layer, rainforest destruction, loss of the old-growth forests in the Pacific Northwest, ocean pollution, vanishing species, human population growth, and pollution of our land, water, and air by toxic substances. The local issues in Arkansas are many. Animal waste, solid waste, loss of wetlands, and protection of air and water quality in our state seem to me to rank among the most important. These issues are real, and the problems related to them will not go away if we ignore them. The politicians do not have the answers, and we do not even know all of the questions to ask. But each of us should do his or her part in some way to help solve these problems. Without a land ethic to help find the answers, we will fail. We can not allow that to happen for the sake of our children and future generations who will someday have that wonderful gift of life on this planet and the rare privilege of living in this beautiful place we call Arkansas.

Former senator Gaylord Nelson, founder of Earth Day, suggested an agenda for action in his book, *America's Last Chance*. In doing so, he argued that there is a great need for the introduction of new values in our society—where bigger is not necessarily better, where slower can be faster, and where less can be more. This attitude must be at the heart of a nationwide effort whereby this country puts gross national quality above gross national product. Each business and private citizen not only need a periodic financial audit, but also an environmental audit in order to minimize, if not eliminate, the adverse environmental impacts of doing business or simply living so that we can exist in harmony with the other diverse communities of life with which we share the land, the water, and the air. We must all practice good stewardship and wisely use the gifts of nature.

Lawyers are more able and better qualified than any other professionals in society to promote the land ethic which we all need in order to deal with the environmental issues of today and tomorrow. Such a land ethic for our clients, as well as for us, can accomplish more in protecting our environment than all the environmental laws ever enacted, court decisions ever rendered, or the political promises ever made. Whether in our voluntary civic activities or the day-to-day practice of law, members of the legal profession have an opportunity to make a lasting benefit to society in promoting the land ethic. We should not fail the public in this regard any more than we should ever stray from the pursuit of justice.

Life as a Dumping Ground

JOHN BRUMMETT

This article by well-known Donrey Media Group columnist John Brummett appeared in the Arkansas Times *in May 2001, shortly after an explosion at a south Arkansas industrial park.*

It's 7:30 on a Saturday evening, and all seems quiet enough in south Arkansas. A few pickups dot the highway. Some kids are surely drinking, drugging, and enjoying the recorded thumps and reverberations of that popular urban music, since south Arkansas is no different in that regard from the rest of America.

Folks relax on their porches or their decks, drinking iced tea and admiring the look and smell of the freshly mowed yard, not so fancy as to be a lawn. Mom tells Dad the hydrangeas will bloom soon, all purply and blue, but that the ice really did a number on the gardenias.

All of a sudden Mom is knocked nearly out of her chair and squeals. There is a blast even louder than the recorded reverberations of that popular urban music. It beats anything you've ever heard. The house rocks, and the sheetrock splits.

For a few seconds you don't know what to think. Maybe it's Jesus. It might be Saddam Hussein. Then you wonder whether a plane crashed.

In a few minutes you gather yourself and notice the black smoke rising down the way. You figure that something must have just blown up at the industrial park at East Camden, about ten miles away, where they have all those military stockpiles. You wonder if you're safe. What might be in that dark cloud moving toward you, anyhow?

It crosses your mind to keep an eye on that cloud lest it take a mushroom shape. You tell Mom to get inside. You dial the sheriff's office, where a man says they know that the explosion happened at the industrial park, but that the feds will have to investigate and that the only thing the officials out there want the sheriff's office to do is keep people out. You ask if you're safe. Probably, the man says.

You spend Saturday night measuring the cracks in the sheetrock and waiting for Channel 7 to give you the real story. But at 10 o'clock it turns out Channel 7 doesn't know much more than you. They show the deputy, old what's-his-name, grinning and saying he doesn't know anything.

But they do have that aerial shot of that massive crater where the explosion happened. Not until late Monday afternoon, nearly forty-eight hours after the explosion, do the authorities tell anyone the first thing about what happened—and not much then.

It turns out there's a firm from out of state with a defense contract to manufacture unspecified propellant material. Then this firm ships the stuff to south Arkansas, where it leases land for the privilege of burying it. The company and government won't say what's in the propellant or whether it might prove harmful. They say they don't know what caused the explosion.

In other words: A firm in another state has a federal contract to make mysteriously explosive stuff, then foists the stuff off on our poor, unsophisticated, ever-willing state—one of the nation's poorest, and most poorly educated, one consistently bringing up the rear of national rankings in government contracts and qualities of life and health. Then when the stuff blows, the company and the government stonewall the locals.

There's something to be said for rural simplicity, for the good life of drinking iced tea and watching hydrangeas grow, perhaps even for the mantra of poor, but proud. But only if it's a quiet and safe life.

When you get blown out of your chair and the government can't or won't tell you what's in that black cloud going over your house, then it might be time to think about how Arkansas might augment rural simplicity with a pride that's not necessarily poor.

Maybe it's time to ponder how Arkansas might better educate itself to reach for that level where it makes stuff instead of stores stuff. Maybe it's time to aspire vigorously to industrial parks that are actually parks, and actually feature industry, instead of so-called industrial parks that actually are nothing more than warehouses, dumps, and monuments to a poor state's surrender.

Development Is Eroding Arkansas's Soul

MICHAEL HADDIGAN

Michael Haddigan, a writer for the Arkansas Times, *frequently covers issues related to the environment in Arkansas. This article appeared in March 2001.*

The Ozarks, the Ouachitas, Crowley's Ridge, and the countless hills and hillocks that dot the Delta define Arkansas as much as the coastlines of Maine or California define them. But little by little, piece by piece, we are tearing away the hills. Sometimes we tear down the hills for good reason. Road cuts make way for interstates and country roads that carry Arkansans to work, to market, and to school.

Sometimes we tear off the side of a mountain simply to build another motel or convenience store. There's always a reason. But as Arkansas moves mountains to clear the way for the march of progress, huge pieces of the state's identity are disappearing.

"We are children of our landscape," wrote novelist Lawrence Durrell. "It dictates behavior and even thought in the measure to which we are responsive to it." The Arkansas hills inspired the paintings of Thomas Hart Benton, the poetry of C. D. Wright, and the fiction of Donald Harington. They influence our music, our language, and our politics.

Within the state's boundaries are the highest mountains between the Appalachians and the Rockies. To be sure, Arkansas will never be flat. But as the digging continues, hills big and small are going away probably at the fastest rate in Arkansas's history.

Development, sprawl, and roads have taken big bites out of the hills. Look at western Little Rock, where construction of big-box stores moved thousands of tons of dirt and rock and transformed the landscape over just a few years.

In Conway, look at the commercial strip at the U.S. Highway 65 exit on Interstate 40. Developers carved out a whole mountainside to build a motel, a gas station, and other businesses. A few years back, John David McFarland of the state Geological Commission was alarmed at the way engineers cut into the hill and stopped one day during construction to talk to excavation supervisors.

"I said, 'Excuse me. Do you realize the landslide problem you have here?'" he recalled recently. "They *still* have a landslide problem."

Farther west along I-40, look off to the south just outside the Conway city limits, and you'll see the massive Hogan Road cut recently completed to provide access to a new housing development. At the westbound parking area outside Russellville, look across the lake at the huge gash being dug into the hillside. Along Interstate 540, look at the titanic efforts to move the mountains to make way for the timesaving route from Fort Smith to Fayetteville and the lifesaving alternative to precipitous old Highway 71.

Look at Fayetteville's Northwest Arkansas Mall.

"I remember when the place where the mall sits now was a mountaintop," said Cyrus Sutherland, 81, of Fayetteville. "I couldn't believe the hundreds of tons of rock and soil that was moved to create that site. I was appalled."

Sutherland, a University of Arkansas emeritus professor of architecture, said he was no happier with the site preparation for the new development near the mall, which included the destruction last summer of a stand of venerable oak trees.

"I'm sure there are some people who say, 'Thank God for bulldozers and dynamite,'" Sutherland said, "but most people, I think, would oppose this."

Even in the Mississippi Delta and south Arkansas you'll see similar changes in the few hillocks that rise up out of the land. Look around most anywhere in the state, and you'll see hillsides and mountainsides under assault.

Yes, business plans, profit-and-loss statements, and jobs that people really need are usually at stake. That's important. We all know that. And there are plenty of advocates for all those things. But no one speaks for the hills. And if you have noticed, no one is building *new* hills to replace them. No one can.

Scientists roll their eyes when writers ask them to describe complex concepts in twenty-five words or less. But when asked recently for a short course on Arkansas geology, John David McFarland took a shot at it.

Geologists, he said, recognize five Arkansas physiographic provinces. The Ozark province resulted from sediment deposited when northern Arkansas was the floor of shallow sea. The sediment hardened. And after the sea receded, weathering shaped the Ozark Mountains.

"The erosion has essentially carved out the topography we see now," McFarland said.

The Arkansas River Valley province was formed by the namesake river and its ancestors at the edge of the ancient continental shelf. Here the layers of rock are thicker.

"In the Ozark province they are a few hundred feet thick, and the sequences in the Arkansas River Valley are thousands of feet thick," he said.

Erosion formed the river valley we now know. Mount Magazine, Mount Nebo, and Petit Jean Mountain resisted the erosion. If you stood at the top of any of those mountains 250 million years ago, McFarland said, the surrounding land would be level with the mountaintops.

Moving southward, you enter the Ouachita Mountain province.

"The sediments we find in the Ouachita province were deposited farther off shore, probably in ten thousand feet of water," he said.

Three hundred million years ago, a colossal continental collision began distorting the Arkansas earth. Erosion later formed the hills of the Arkansas River Valley and the Ouachita Mountain provinces.

"Take a flat piece of paper. That represents the sediment," McFarland said. "Push the ends of the paper toward the middle. That's the Arkansas River Valley. Crumple that paper, and that is the Ouachita Mountains."

Pinnacle Mountain outside Little Rock and the so-called zigzag mountains near Hot Springs resulted from this process.

"Rock has been folded up just like an accordion," McFarland said.

South of the Ouachitas is the Western Gulf Coastal Plain province. Erosion put on the finishing touches.

Northbound drivers passing the Maumelle exit on Interstate 430 will notice a hill literally cut in half (and available for sale or lease, by the way).

"You could argue that it took three hundred million years to create that hillside that it took people probably a few weeks to carve up," McFarland said.

Some sixty-five million years ago, Little Rock would have been a coastal city on the Gulf of Mexico. The prehistoric ocean of that time covered much of south Arkansas. What was once the sea floor is now known as the Western Gulf Coastal Plain province. The hills that remain there resulted from sediments piled up with the sea's evaporation over time.

The fifth of Arkansas's physiographic provinces, the Mississippi embayment, lies east and north of Bayou Bartholomew, from modern-day Jefferson County down to the Louisiana border in Ashley County. Crowley's Ridge rises from the floor of the embayment to form a ribbon of highlands from Piggott to near Helena.

"Crowley's Ridge is basically a pile of dirt between two river valleys that hasn't washed away yet," McFarland said.

So that's where the hills came from. Where are we taking them?

Arkansas's hills are more than simple bumps on the plain or jagged outcrops against the sky. The mountains, hills, ridges, and bluffs are part of our lives.

We've named our communities after them, sometimes lovingly. We have Mountain Home, Mountain View, Mountain Pine, Blue Mountain, Mountain Valley, Rich Mountain, Alpine, and Mounts Ida, George, Holly, Judea, Olive, Pleasant, Sherman, Vernon, and Zion.

There's Chapel Hill, Canehill, Cherry Hill, Violet Hill, Walnut Hill,

Silver Hill, Coal Hill, Fountain Hill, South Lead Hill, Shannon Hills, Social Hill, Springhill, and Spring Hill.

We've got Pine Bluff, Bluff City, Crocketts Bluff, DeValls Bluff, Bluffton, Pencil Bluff, Center Ridge, Gravel Ridge, Hickory Ridge, Milligan Ridge, Mounds, Pine Ridge, Vimy Ridge, Walnut Ridge, West Ridge, Caddo Gap, Calico Rock, Sulphur Rock, Rocky, Rocky Mound, Highland, and Hillcrest.

Then, of course, there's Little Rock. The "little rock" on the Arkansas River made its own contribution to civilization when railroad engineers blasted a good bit of it to smithereens to build the railroad bridge that crosses the river there in what is now Riverfront Park. The Big Rock upstream was another early landmark and the geologic feature that, by comparison, gave the capital city its name. Big Rock, too, gave some of itself to mining.

Many of the European-Americans who settled in Arkansas before statehood came from the hills of Appalachia and their people before them came from the highlands of Scotland or the headlands of Ireland. The inhospitable quality of those places is well known, and many of the immigrants brought with them to Arkansas the dogged endurance, physical stamina, love of nature, and cussed independence of their ancestors. Many of our newest neighbors come from the hills of Laos and the rugged mountains of southern Mexico and Guatemala.

Some of us see Arkansans as—whatever else we might be—a proud and noble people. And maybe the hills have something to do with these qualities.

"It is a country lending itself readily to romantic interpretation. It has rolling hills, deep valleys, jagged bluffs, rich foliage and clear streams," Thomas Hart Benton wrote of the Ozarks in 1934. "The future is and must continue to be heavily conditioned by the past and in this land flavored by the pioneer spirit, the nature of our fundamental American psychology can best be understood."

For at least the last few hundred years, Arkansas's hills and hollows have been a refuge for smallholders, hermits, outlaws, and nonconformists of one kind or another. The story of the Lost Bands of the Quapaw, though likely apocryphal, best illustrates the phenomenon. During the removal of Arkansas's native Quapaw tribe to Oklahoma, the story goes, the Indians slipped away from the columns as they snaked through the Arkansas River Valley. Once free, the Quapaw headed for the hills, eventually settling in the Ozarks as farmers and blending in with the white farmers already there in the hills. Although scholars scoff at the tale, Arkansans believing themselves to be descendants of the Lost Bands insist their Quapaw heritage is genuine.

In any case, as poet Miller Williams used to tell his University of Arkansas students, a good story isn't necessarily what happened but what *should* have happened.

It is no accident that people the world over site churches, monasteries, and holy places of all kinds on the hilltops. The trek to the top often takes the form of a pilgrimage. From the heights, you see it all. You rise above the petty squabbles of the crowded towns, achieving a certain clarity. The air seems fresher and more invigorating.

No one seems sure exactly why they built them, but I think Arkansas's mound-building Indians had something like this in mind when they constructed the mounds near Parkin in St. Francis County and near Scott in Pulaski County. Both are now the sites of state parks. Scholars think the Parkin site may be the site of the village of Casqui visited by Hernando de Soto in 1541. Archeologists believe the Toltec Mounds site near Scott was occupied from about A.D. 700–950. The two sites were likely part of a system of such mounds in the Midwest that served as ceremonial centers, trading posts, or residences for political and religious leaders.

Yes, the Indians had reasons too. And building the mounds likely disrupted the landscape around them. And like Arkansas's present-day hills, many of the mounds disappeared under the assault of agriculture, looting, and general carelessness. We'll never know what the mounds might have told us about our past.

In the present, there's no easy way to tell how much or how many hillsides are being carted off or at what rate. But casual observation over the years indicates the bulldozers are working overtime.

But hold on. The hills aren't taking this lying down.

When engineers dammed rivers to form Arkansas's many lakes, the highest hills resisted. While their neighbors sank below the waters, some—like Sugarloaf Mountain on Greers Ferry Lake—survived as islands.

Much of downtown Hot Springs lies in the shadow of a mountain. Some of the city's most historic buildings and popular haunts are built into mountainsides. Sometimes the hills object to human intervention. In 1984, the hillside next to the Arlington Hotel in Hot Springs roared down onto a parking area beside the hotel. No one was hurt. But occasionally the mountains take a life. In 1995, a thirty-foot slab of rock slid off West Mountain and crashed into a Central Avenue novelty shop, killing a clerk.

"Every place that people cut into a hillside, you destabilize the hillside to some degree," McFarland said. "In many cases, it doesn't cause a problem because you haven't changed the dynamics enough to cause a problem. On some, the hillside will fail sooner or later."

Slides are frequently a headache for Arkansas highway engineers, he said. Slides often block mountainous roads in north Arkansas and along Crowley's Ridge. Numerous slides delayed construction of I-540, he said.

Landslides resulting from earthquakes, heavy rain, and human activity are the world's "most destructive natural process," McFarland said.

And in Arkansas, geologists are often frustrated in efforts to predict slides.

"I can say what is going to happen, why it is going to happen, and how it is going to happen, but I can't say when," he said. The hillside above U.S. Highway 65 near I-40 at Conway, he said, may take decades to come down. But sooner or later, some of it will come down.

Eureka Springs has also seen its share of slides. But Sutherland says Eureka has done a good many things right. Many of the town's most prominent structures were built *onto* the side of the hills, rather than *into* them, he said. Serious architects, notably Frank Lloyd Wright and Arkansas's Fay Jones, try to "marry the building to the site on which it is built," Sutherland said.

Buildings require a level surface—there's just no way around that. And in Arkansas that can be a problem, he said. But terracing, using support columns and employing other techniques often do the job better without wounding the landscape, Sutherland said.

"Don't put the building *on* the hill, but make it *of* the hill," Sutherland said. "Make it feel like it was born there."

Practical people often shrug off such suggestions as too complicated and expensive. A kinds of lust is at work, too. I used to cut firewood each fall with two friends in the woods of an agreeable landowner. Cranky chain saws usually got us off to a late start. We started out cutting the deadfall of the previous year, and if it were up to me I would have left it at that, out of laziness if nothing else.

But on each of our annual outings, sometime after lunch I'd begin to notice a kind of fury building in my friends. Before long they'd be slicing through everything in sight, cutting live trees along with the dead ones. By dusk, the woodcutters were wild-eyed and frantic, under the spell of their chain saws. Unsatisfied with a full load of firewood, they seemed overtaken by some deep need to tame the woods altogether.

Taming the hills seems to some as important as simply making temporary use of them.

Henry David Thoreau, the least practical of men, saw as arrogance such attempts to dominate the natural world.

"I should not like to think that some demigod had come before me and picked out some of the best of the stars," he wrote. "I wish to know an entire heaven and an entire earth."

If Gravity Should Fail

LOUISE BARDEN

*"If Gravity Should Fail" was awarded the
Charlotte Writer's Club Poetry Prize in 2000.
Louise Barden is a freelance writer in Charlotte,
North Carolina, who attended Hendrix College and
the University of Arkansas.*

On this mountain ridge, we camp at the lip
of the world, lean back in grass to feel
how a tilt of earth could make us slip
from our solid peak and spill
into the dome of starry dark.
It would be an easy way to leave
this land, rising like a spark
above our rock-ringed blaze, retrieved
by God straight into his heaven.
We have already half forgotten life
in those narrow valleys almost hidden
by spreading fog below. The grief
of ordinary days fades, expires,
and we are pulled by night's cold fires.

Epilogue

We Arkansans have a saying: "It's not that our mountains are so high, but that our valleys are so deep."

—SUSAN MORRISON

Congressional Wilderness Hearing Testimony 1984

Dreams of Bear

DANA STEWARD

Dana Steward received the Memphis Magazine *annual short-story prize for a fictionalized version of this piece, published in 1999. This is the true story.*

Bear came to me in my dreams. I have for almost forty years had a recurrent dream of bear. I consider it their gift to me. Bear have embraced me in my dreams.

—Mark Spragg

Unlike essayist Mark Spragg, for a half century I had no bear dreams. But in the summer of my fiftieth year, the same year that my mother died and my blood no longer flowed, I began to dream of bear.

Night after night, the dreams became progressively more terrifying: a pair of bears attacked a deer, a rogue bear stalked a family, then angry bears invading my bed huffed and charged me. I would be mere inches from being slashed by their ferocious teeth or claws when I bolted into wakefulness, pulse racing, breathing ravaged. Often I did not sleep again that night.

Over time, the dreams of bear changed. The bears which appeared presented a less frightening demeanor. For several months, when these bears visited my bedroom, they were no longer angry bears; they simply watched me, distant but not disinterested. I would be sleeping, and the bear in my dream—always heavy and black—would rise on its hind legs and study my body, then my face closely. Usually I would wake gently from these dreams, left wondering, as flashes of them returned to me, what the bear had seen or was looking for.

These dreams of the ineffable "watcher" bear also became infrequent. As time went on, I scarcely dreamed of bears at all. Almost five years passed before I had "The Dream" and met the bear the others seem to have foreshadowed. This time I was waked in the gray dawn by my own tears; actual tears, not dreamed ones, streamed down my cheeks and soaked my pillow. I had been embraced by a bear.

Coming out of the dream, it took me an instant to recognize the tears were mine and to recapture the emotion of the dream. Then I realized that I had been in the arms of a bear, a great hulking sow, who held me cradled to her body and tenderly rocked me. Her soft luminous eyes reflected how much she loved me, that bear, and I could smell her raspberry breath as she hummed to me. I saw myself reaching up a chubby childish fist to touch her face (bizarre since I was an adult even in the dream), and at that point the dream vanished. I was left weeping in the dark both for the joy of the bear's absolute unconditional love and for the inconsolable pain of being separated from her.

Unlike my earlier dreams, this one would not release me in the light of day. I doubt it ever will. I knew though that it was no longer possible to ignore the dreams of bear. For two years, their memory sent me thumbing through musty Game and Fish records, visiting university Native American Archives, deep in conversation with mainstream theology professors and oddball astrologists. I sketched bears at the zoo, even joined a wildlife biologist tagging black bears as part of a repopulation project. Although my research informed me that every culture on earth has told stories in an effort to come to terms with bear, I still did not understand that this story was mine.

My research began with data on the physical nature of bears in general and the black bear of my native Arkansas in particular. I learned that the animals are elusive, secretive, and solitary omnivores, primarily eating natural foods such as nuts and berries and insects, but meat eaters given the opportunity. Adult male black bears frequently weigh four hundred pounds or more; they can run thirty miles an hour through heavy underbrush, and they can easily kill a person with one paw swipe. Moreover, they are wild, unlikely to be moved by our fear or our intentions or our tears. Their only known enemy is man.

According to an article by Jim Low of the Arkansas Game and Fish Commission, bear hunting was "the stuff that makes Arkansas legends. Of all the state's game species, the black bear is, and always has been, a kind of wilderness touchstone for testing a sportsman's mettle." Low tells the legend of one such bear that gave more than full measure, quoting the self-written epitaph found on the frozen body of an unfortunate mountain man, his fingers still tightly gripping his gun: "this is the gun that kilt the bar that kilt me."

Hunters almost took the black bear to extinction in numerous southeastern states in the early part of the century as they stalked them for food, for oil, for clothing and bedding, and in sport. However, in recent years concerted conservation efforts have returned the black bear to viable populations. In Arkansas, for example, the population has grown from as few as fifty bears in 1958 to more than three thousand recorded at the end of the century with the help of wildlife biologists and enthusiastic volunteers, who regard them as a symbol of wilderness. When I managed to join one of the bear-research expeditions which monitor the bears' progress, I learned that bears left in their habitat in the wild are not considered dangerous; in fact, only three incidents of bear biting humans in Arkansas have been recorded in the modern day.

Although all this factual knowledge about bears was quite fascinating, it did little to satisfy my yearning to comprehend my dreams. Then I encountered an old friend. In a yellowed anthology of American literature, William Faulkner's classic story, "The Bear," unfolded and I found my first meaningful clue to the bear's mythology in the author's description of the relationship between an enormous, venerated black bear, and the young hunter. "The bear had run in his [the boy's] listening and loomed in his dreams since before he could remember." Faulkner continues, "He would not even be afraid, not even in the moment when the fear would take him completely: blood, skin, bowels, bone, memory from the long time before it even became his memory." I was intrigued by the line "memory from the long time before it even became his memory" because it resonated with my dream; I had always known this bear.

Further reading acquainted me with more stories: peoples of varied, widespread cultures told of visitations by bear, battles with a bear, a marriage to a bear, a loving bear. I was astonished to learn that these dreams were not "my" dreams alone. Suddenly words like "archetypal" which had previously had only academic, intellectual purchase sprang alive as I read in *Mark of the Bear* natural historian Paul Scullery's quote from mythologist Joseph Campbell: "Neanderthal bear-skull sanctuaries in Old World Caves are our earliest evidence anywhere on earth of the veneration of a divine king." Indeed, man once worshiped bear.

For the Neanderthal 100,000 years ago bear was God. The modern bear's earliest ancestor of the Pleistocene Epoch, the bear of the cave whose sign is found in the caves of Europe, provided for the spiritual as well as the physical well-being of our lowbrowed forefathers. On the one hand, the bear was life-sustaining food and shelter. Even as they ate of its flesh and drank of its blood after a successful hunt, in this communion they revered the enormous cave bear as a god, arranging its bones in sacred rites, offering its skull lifted up on the lodge pole the first flesh from the sacrificial feast of its own body. On the other hand, when, as more often than not, the massive bear bested the man, they praised the bear for so honoring one of their own by death at the bear god's hands. It is this story of the ritual death of the sacred bear that human ecologist Paul Shepard in *The Sacred Paw* calls the "cornerstone of a [cosmogenic] scheme, a tale of the secret of perennial success, and therefore renewal."

This is the sacramental feast of flesh of the divine animal combined with the sacrifice of the hunter that may have given rise in early cultures to the idea of a "mystic union between a human and divinity producing offspring who became intermediaries between man and a powerful god." According to Shephard, possibly two attributes of the bear help to foster this idea: first, the bear's hibernation and subsequent return express the man's longing for rebirth; and second, the mother bear's licking of the cubs at birth, seemingly taking "shapeless lumps of flesh and molding them into shape." Shakespeare even borrows that idea when he compares a man's lack of character to "a unlick'd bear-whelp that carries no impression of the dam."

A day spent in the extensive Native American Archives at the University of Arkansas at Little Rock drew me even closer to my

quarry, this numinous bear. Although the Native Americans most frequently speak of bear as warrior and healer, they identify their spiritual well-being with its own. A most frequently told tale is that of the
bear who lures the berry-picking young woman away from home to
become his mate and mother of his children, only to lay down his own
life when he is hunted by her brothers. Clearly celebrating the sacrificial role of the bear, medicine men, or shamans, wore proudly the fur
of the bear as vestment.

The myth of the nurturing but mystical bear remains in Native
American culture today. Images in the Native American journal, the
Blue Cloud Quarterly, include drawings of the earth as the muzzle of
an almost invisible black bear, whose glittering claw tips have a sure
grip on everything, and another of a man in a bear skin, with the bear
superimposed. Most compelling to me in light of my dream was the
image of a mother bear pictured seated, holding a cub nursing at her
human breasts.

Although all my reading resonated with my own encounter with
the embraceable bear, it was a manner of theosophy that contradicted
my own religious heritage. Such speculation about a relationship
between God, human, and other creatures, such as bears, would
require holographic shifts in thinking. After all, had not the early
Christian church attempted to domesticate the bear, unable to ignore
such a pervasive pagan symbol? The prophet Elisha cursed bears
(forty-two of them); the bear became a symbol of God's vengeance,
with Jeremiah comparing God in his anger to a bear lying in vail. We
are given the anecdote of St. Augustine to whom a bear comes, head
bowed, to serve the man of God. For one to entertain the idea that
God indwelt the bear, and that our knowledge of God came partially
from creatures, not *apart* from them, is no less than heresy. The idea
of the man occupying the earth and ordained by God for dominion is
fully ingrained in the western mind.

So what does a twentieth-century Methodist, fairly well-versed in
Old and New Testament scripture and steeped in the concept of the
caretaker tradition, do with the experience of the Loving Bear? Moses
had heard God in the burning bush. Paul the apostle was convicted by
a blinding light. Mother Teresa saw Jesus in the face of the leper. Now,
in my fifty-fifth year, I had been cradled by Bear. Where had the

dreams come from? Who was this loving mother, who had rocked me like an infant at the same time she was fierce and terrible in her power? I was shortly to find out; the time had arrived for the bear to come out of my subconscious into my waking life.

At about the same period the bear dreams had begun, I had taken up walking for exercise. Most of the walks were five miles or so at most, but one day each year I set aside for a long walk—a solitary retreat on trails in the Ozark Mountains.

The first weekend in May each year my husband and I camped at Turner Bend Campground on the Mulberry River because he volunteered at the annual Arkansas Canoe School. It was an ideal time for me to be break away from the group and take my long walk alone. Each year I had walked farther, covering sixteen miles or so in 1998. The following year I hoped to walk more than twenty miles, putting onto the Ozark Highland Trail above Cass, and walking out of the wilderness area near White Rock Mountain.

The OHT is well-marked, but as usual I carried compass and water shoes and whistle and fire starter just in case because the area is among the remotest in Arkansas. I am never truly afraid on these walks but wary. Walking the woods alone, one hears bird sounds and wind sighing and tree limbs chafing, but it is what you don't hear that is so haunting—no voices, no telephone ringing, no car engine's whine, only the infrequent surreal hum of a jet far up in the heavens.

I had left Turner's Bend just at eight o'clock, and the morning had gone well. I had not even needed the water shoes to cross Fane Creek, which last year ran almost waist high in raging brown water but now chattered amicably over sunny stones. By the time I reached the clearing overlooking Fane Creek Valley I had already seen two deer, an armadillo, a dozen squirrels, and prolific wildflowers. (Also the footprints of a walker, perhaps a day old, and his very, very large dog.) After a half-hour break at the pond doing plant identification, I moved on, and by noon I had walked almost twelve miles without meeting a soul.

Lunchtime was taken on a pedestal rock just off the trail, my hiking boots airing in the sunshine while I tapped my toes in velvety moss. As I savored my peanut butter sandwich and drank the cool water, I could literally hear myself chew and swallow in the silence.

Finally, licking the filling off my Oreo, totally at peace with myself, I slid down from the rock with authority, took up my walking stick, and set off. But in the first step, I faltered. Standing fifteen feet in front of me was an enormous black bear, grubbing on the trail. Even as I froze, the bear lifted his head, saw me, and shot away—about ten feet away. Then he slowed, shuffled another twenty feet, turned toward me, and sat down directly in my path. For several minutes the bear and I were locked in contemplation, me standing, him sitting, with our faces almost on the level.

How can I describe going face to be face with this bear? My eyes took in his foolishly tiny ears on the massive head, the black, glossy richness of his outer coat rippling down layer after layer of flesh. The comical way he shifted his shaggy body to the left and cocked his head as he studied me. Since bears are nearsighted, I wondered how well he could see me. I knew (from my bear research) that he could see colors. Did he like or dislike my bright red pack? What was he thinking?

All the advice I had read about surprise encounters with bears ran through my mind. "Shout and make noise to frighten him away." I almost laughed aloud at the ludicrous idea that I might frighten this huge beast, and so I remained quiet, accepting the fatality of my situation. My sense of the numinous was acute: I had returned to the religion of prehistory: as it had been for the ancient ones, my position must be that if that tree-climbing, marathon-running black bear, three times my size, wanted me, my only pleasure would be in the honor of my death.

However, the bear never threatened me at all, never huffed or looked aggressive. He simply sat and silently watched, and watched me watch, for a few precious moments. Then (to quote Faulkner) he "faded back into the wilderness" and disappeared down a ravine, and I was left standing naked and alone in the bright spring air. Once again, I had been embraced by a bear.

After my personal encounter with the bear, my mind literally rejected eons of intellectual "development." I came face-to-face not only with the bear but with a vitalism I had not known I possessed. The Cave People and I were one, we had both seen God in the form of a bear; our lives in the Bear's hands, and secure in the knowledge that not even death could sever the relationship.

Struggling to find words to signify my bear experience, I was gratified to find writer Winifred Gallagher's response to her own encounter with a bear. She writes, "Jolted out of automatic pilot, my perception sharpened and focused on the unexpected truth. There are real bears in the woods. Things are not necessarily what they seem. There's more to reality than meets the eye. A so-called transformative experience, this ursine epiphany not only filled me with a need to dance, to kneel, but changed my perception of the world and my place in it."

What meaning was I to take from my encounter? I read the comments of Doug Flaherty in *Blue Cloud:* "I went to the Indian legends as a way to be led back, under their priestly guidance, to a reaffirmation of life—simple, mystic, spiritual and physical. I believe in the mythic narrative; I believe in the outward and inward sign between man and nature. I look at physical symbols as a direct extension of man's vision of himself."

Each of us takes our notions of Truth from our own experiences. No doubt my willingness to embrace this philosophy so readily is influenced by my prior deep conviction that we must preserve the environment, not just for ourselves but for the sake of wild places and wild creatures themselves. But now my former anthropomorphic caretaker ideology seems woefully shallow. The idea of preserving wilderness for man's use is the height of arrogance. Or even to endorse preservation of some "lesser" species because there might be some serum or toxin humans need from that species. Ultimately, we must set aside, we must preserve, because it is not ours to destroy. When we destroy the habitat of the bear, we destroy that which is us and that which is of God.

As a writer on issues of ecology, I write about the return of the bald eagle, the reseeding of the prairie, the redefinition of wilderness. And on the bear, who, in all its solitary mysterious power, remains the spiritual symbol of that wilderness and indeed the wilderness in each of us. For every hundred hunters who go into the woods to harvest bear during season, one will encounter the animal. Hikers, usually in pairs or groups, banging down a trail, almost never do. We do not need to see the bear in wilderness; it is enough to know that it is there.

Acknowledgments

Jim Allen: "If Turkeys Were Monogamous." From *The Ozarks Mountaineer* April/May 2001: 15–16. Reprinted with permission of Jim Allen.

Jim Allen: "The Urban Paul Bunyan." First Publication.

Richard Allin: "Should've Built the Wall." ©*Arkansas Democrat-Gazette* 22 February 2001: 4E. Reprinted with permission of Richard Allin and the *Arkansas Democrat-Gazette*.

Louise Barden: "If Gravity Should Fail." First Publication.

Louise Barden: "River Travel." From the *Chattahoochee Review*, 1993. Reprinted with permission of Louise Barden.

Vicki Bennett: "Ice Storm." First Publication.

Ann Bittick: "Southwest Arkansas Images." First Publication.

Dee Brazil: "Magic of Nature." First Publication.

John Brummett: "Life as a Dumping Ground." *Arkansas Times* 4 May 2001: 20. Reprinted with the permission of John Brummett of the Donrey Media Group Little Rock Bureau.

John Churchill: "Bayou Bluff: The Beauty and Darkness of Nature." From *Somewhere Apart*. Ed. Staff of the *Arkansas Times* and of the University of Arkansas Press. Fayetteville: University of Arkansas Press, 1997. 13–18. Reprinted with permission of *Arkansas Times*.

Maxine Clark: "Botany Notes." From *Ozark Society Bulletin*, Vol. 11, No. 2: 1977: 7. Reprinted with the permission of Joe Clark.

William Coleman: "Hurricane Creek Wilderness." From *The Arkansas Wilderness*. Eureka Springs: Morrison*Woodward Gallery, 1983. Reprinted with the permission of William Coleman and Morrison*Woodward Gallery.

William Coleman: "Leatherwood Wilderness." *The Arkansas Wilderness*. Eureka Springs: Morrison*Woodward Gallery, 1983. Reprinted with the permission of Morrison*Woodward Gallery.

Neil Compton: "Preface." From *The High Ozarks: A Vision of Eden*. Little Rock: Ozark Society Foundation, 1982. Reprinted with permission of Ellen Compton.

Erin Dalton: "The Spirit of Nature." First Publication.

John Day: "Returning." From *Arkansas Wildlife*, Spring 1997: 16–17. Reprinted with permission of John Day.

Tom W. Dillard: "Between a Rock and a Hard Place: Gardening in the Ouachitas." From *Mountain Signal*, April 2000, Vol. 5, No. 6: 18–19. Reprinted with the permission of Tom W. Dillard.

Valerie Dunn: "Wild Wisteria." First Publication.

Matt Forester: "Disturbance." First Publication.

Larry Don Frost: "The Mystery of the Horsehair Worm." First Publication.

Cathy Frye: "Bayou Bartholomew." ©*Arkansas Democrat-Gazette*, 4 February 2001: 1B State. Reprinted with permission of *Arkansas Democrat-Gazette*.

Watkins Fulk-Gray: "Backpacking with Bill." First Publication.

Ryan Grace: "Nature's Draw." First Publication.

Michael Haddigan: "Development Is Eroding Arkansas's Soul." ©*Arkansas Times*, 9 March 2001: 12–14. Reprinted with permission of *Arkansas Times*.

Don Hamilton: "Environmental Ethics: A Lawyer's Plea." ©*The Arkansas Lawyer*, Fall 1992: 20–21. Reprinted with permission of Don Hamilton and The Arkansas Bar Association. All Rights Reserved.

Glynn Harris: "Birds: Humanity's Barometer." *Arkansas Wildlife*, Summer 1998: Inside Last Page. Reprinted with permission of Glynn Harris.

John Heuston: "The Boy on the Memorial." From *Ozark Society Bulletin*, Summer 2001. Reprinted with permission of John Heuston.

Francie Jeffery: "Kentucky Wonders." First Publication.

Lil Junas: "Prologue: The Cadron." From *Cadron Creek: A Photographic Narrative*. Little Rock: Ozark Society Foundation, 1979. Reprinted with permission of Lil Junas.

Gina Kokes: "Mad Scientist." First Publication.

Bob Lancaster: "Terror Hangs in the Trees." ©*Arkansas Times*, 10 November 2000: 62. Reprinted with permission of *Arkansas Times*.

Jon Looney: "My Father's Dream." From *Headwaters*. Little Rock: August House, 1979. Reprinted with permission of Jon Looney.

Mike Masterson: "Using a Hammer on *David*." ©*Arkansas Democrat-Gazette*, 5 July 2001: 5B. Reprinted with permission of Mike Masterson.

Elaine McKinney: "Groundhog Lying Dead." First Publication.

George Oxford Miller: "An Ozark Crusader Leads On." From *The Ozarks: The People, the Mountains . . . the Magic*. Stillwater, Minn.: Voyageur Press, 1996. 79–82. Reprinted with the permission of George Oxford Miller.

Mark Minton: "Experts Save Cave Art—This Time." ©*Arkansas Democrat-Gazette*, 14 January 2001: 1–2B. Reprinted with permission of *Arkansas Democrat-Gazette*.

Lisa Mongno: "Gates and Fences." First publication.

Susan Morrison: "The Buffalo." From *The Arkansas Wilderness*. Eureka Springs: Morrison*Woodward Gallery, 1983. Reprinted with permission of Morrison*Woodward Gallery.

Laura Neale: "Bamboo Grove." First Publication.

Howard Nobles: "Sea of Grass." First publication.

Stewart Noland: "New Water: Baker Creek." From *Ozark Society Bulletin*, Autumn 1980. Reprinted with permission of Stewart Noland.

Cindy Perlinger: "You Find It, You Keep It." First Publication.

Barbara Pryor: "Boston Mountains: My Roots Are in Cass." From *Somewhere Apart*. Ed. Staff of the *Arkansas Times* and of the University of Arkansas Press. Fayetteville: University of Arkansas Press, 1997. 87–94. Reprinted with permission of *Arkansas Times*.

Diane Taylor Reeves: "Coming Home." From *A Scoundrel Breeze*. Little Rock: August House, 1983. 52. Reprinted with permission of Diane Taylor Reeves.

Joe David Rice: "Arkansas Waterfalls Pour Refreshment for Spring Adventurers." From *Front Porch*, March/April 2000: 5–6. Reprinted with permission of Joe David Rice and *Front Porch* magazine, a publication of the Arkansas Farm Bureau Federation.

Jim Spencer: "Blackwater Reflections." *Arkansas Wildlife*, Summer 1997: 2–5. Reprinted with permission of Arkansas Game and Fish Commission.

Jim Spencer: "Land of the Big Sky: Grand Prairie." From *Arkansas Wildlife*, November/December 2000: 2–5. Reprinted with permission of Arkansas Game and Fish Commission.

Jim Spencer: "Why We Hunt." *Arkansas Wildlife*, Fall 1998: 33. Reprinted with permission of Arkansas Game and Fish Commission.

Milton John Stephens: "Catch and Release Smallmouth Therapy." From

PYX. Little Rock: Department of Rhetoric and Writing at University of Arkansas at Little Rock, 1996. 27–29. Reprinted with permission of Mrs. Marie Stephens.

Dana Steward: "Plugging Turtles." First Publication.

Melissa Stover: "Return of the Peacock." First Publication.

Melissa Stover: "The Taste of Dust." From *Quills & Pixels*. Little Rock: Writers' Network, University of Arkansas at Little Rock, 1998: 138–42. Reprinted with permission of Melissa Stover.

Pam Strickland: "Pensive on the Parkway." First Publication.

John Sunderland: "Wilderness and Wildlife." From *Arkansas Game and Fish Magazine,* September/October 1985: 6–7. Reprinted with permission of Arkansas Game and Fish Commission.

Keith Sutton: "Downriver: Reflections on the Lower White." From *Arkansas Wildlife,* Fall 1999: 3–7. Reprinted with permission of Arkansas Game and Fish Commission.

GibAnn Tam: "Letting Go." From *Quills & Pixels*. Little Rock: Writers' Network, University of Arkansas at Little Rock, 1999: 91–98. Reprinted with permission of GibAnn Tam.

Steve Taylor: "Catching More Than Fish." From *Arkansas Wildlife,* Spring 1997: Inside Back Cover. Reprinted with permission of Steve Taylor.

Lindsey Thomsen: "The Fancy of the Ouachita Trail." First Publication.

Kirk Wasson: "Buffalo River Friends." First Publication.

Kirk Wasson: "Of Luck and Stupidity." First Publication.

Kane Webb: "At the River with an Old Friend." ©*Arkansas Democrat-Gazette,* 25 March 2001: 8B. Reprinted with permission of Kane Webb and *Arkansas Democrat-Gazette.*

Shari Williams: "If Only Life Could Be a Float down a River." First Publication.

Amylou Wilson: "Communing with Black Bears." ©*Environmental News,* March/April 1996: 9–10. Reprinted with permission of Amy Wilson and Arkansas Envirnomental Federation.

Crystal Wilson: "The Plantation." From *Hearts and Bones*. Little Rock: University of Arkansas at Little Rock Expository Writing Anthology, 1996. 1–4. Reprinted with permission of Crystal Wilson.

Wes Zeigler: "Seasoned." First Publication.

Sources

Book and Chapter Epigraphs and Photos

Llewellyn, Richard. *How Green Was My Valley*. New York: Macmillan
     Company, 1964.
Steward, Bill. Cover and chapter photographs. First Publication.
United States. House. Subcommittee on Forests, Family Farms and
     Energy of the Committee on Agriculture, House of Representatives,
     98th Congress, 1st sess., H.R. 2452 and H.R. 2917, the proposed
     Arkansas and Oklahoma Wilderness Act of 1983, May 26, 1983.
     Washington: GPO, 1983. John Leflar, 70.
————. Senate. Subcommitte on Public Lands and Reserved Water of
     the Committee on Energy and Natural Resources, 98th Congress,
     2nd Sess., S. 2125, a Bill entitled the "Arkansas Wilderness Act of
     1983." Little Rock, February 15, 1984. Washington: GPO, 1984. Alice
     Andrews, 394; Katie Guion, 380; Bob James, 265; Barbara Meyer,
     400; Tom McCormick, 405; Susan Morrison, 331.

Sources for the Introduction

Bass, Sharon M. W. *For the Trees*. Blanchard Springs Caverns
     Interpretative Association in cooperation with the Forest Service,
     U.S.D.A., 1981. Revised 1986.
de Linde, Henry. "Minerals and Hot Springs in Arkansas." *The Record*.
     Hot Springs: Garland County Historical Society, 1999.
Dougan, Michael B. *Arkansas Odyssey*. Little Rock: Rose Publishing
     Company, Inc., 1994.
Finch, Robert. "Landscape, People, and Place." *Writing Natural History:
     Dialogues with Authors*. Ed. Edward Lueders. Salt Lake City:
     University of Utah Press, 1989. 39–65.
Foti, Thomas, and Gerald Hanson. *Arkansas and the Land*. Fayetteville:
     University of Arkansas Press, 1992.

Johnson, Ben F., III. *Arkansas in Modern America.* Fayetteville: University of Arkansas Press, 2000.

Howard, J. Michael, George W. Colton, and William L. Prior. *Mineral, Fossil Fuel, and Water Resources of Arkansas.* Little Rock: Arkansas Geological Commission, Bulletin 24, 1997.

Poinsett County, Arkansas. Poinsett County Historical Society. Paducah, Ky.: Turner Publishing Company, 1998.

Sabin, A. N. "Minerals and Hot Springs." *Arkansas Gazette,* 25 December 1827. William E. Woodruff. No. 52; Whole No. 416; Arkansas Territory.

Smith, Kenneth L. *Sawmill.* Fayetteville: University of Arkansas Press, 1986.

Williams, C. Fred, S. Charles Bolton, Carl H. Moneyhon, LeRoy T. Williams, eds. *A Documentary History of Arkansas.* Fayetteville: University of Arkansas Press, 1984.

Sources for the Epilogue

Faulkner, William. *Big Woods.* New York: Random House, 1955.

Flaherty, Doug. "Man Inside the Bear Skin." *Blue Cloud Quarterly* 28 (1983): 1.

Gallagher, Winifred. *The Power of Place: How Our Surroundings Shape Our Thoughts, Emotions, and Actions.* New York: Poseidon Press, 1993.

Low, Jim. "Bear Hunting: Living the Legend." *Arkansas Wildlife* (November/December 1987), np.

Salisbury, Ralph. "Spirit Beast Chant." *Blue Cloud Quarterly* 28 (1982): 2.

Scullery, Paul, ed. *Mark of the Bear.* San Francisco: Sierra Club Books, 1996.

Shephard, Paul, and Barry Sanders. *The Sacred Paw.* New York: Viking, 1985.

Spragg, Mark. "Adopting Bear." *Scullery* (1996): 111–15.

Index